THE WRITER'S GRAMMAR

THE WRITER'S GRAMMAR

Patricia Silber
Marymount College of
Fordham University

PEARSON
Longman

New York   San Francisco   Boston
London   Toronto   Sydney   Tokyo   Singapore   Madrid
Mexico City   Munich   Paris   Cape Town   Hong Kong   Montreal

Vice President and Editor-in-Chief: Joseph Terry
Senior Acquisitions Editor: Steven Rigolosi
Senior Marketing Manager: Melanie Craig
Senior Supplements Editor: Donna Campion
Production Manager: Donna DeBenedictis
Project Coordination, Text Design, and Electronic Page Makeup: Elm Street
    Publishing Services, Inc.
Cover Design Manager: Wendy Ann Fredericks
Cover Designer: Maria Ilardi
Manufacturing Manager: Dennis J. Para
Printer and Binder: Courier Corporation/Stoughton
Cover Printer: Phoenix Color Corporation

Library of Congress Cataloging-in-Publication Data

Silber, Patricia
    The writer's grammar/ by Patricia Silber
        p. cm.
    Includes bibliographical references and index
    ISBN 0-321-09570-7
        1. English language--Grammar--Problems, exercises, etc. 2. English
    language--Rhetoric--Problems, exercises, etc. 3. Report writing--Problems,
    exercises, etc.
    I. Title.
    PE1112.S5417 2004
    428.2--dc21   2002043850

Please visit our website at http://www.ablongman.com

ISBN 0-321-09570-7

1 2 3 4 5 6 7 8 9 10—CRS—06 05 04 03

For all the students
who showed me the way

Contents

. . . .

Preface   xi

The Oh-So-Correct Writer
    Introduction to Students: You *Do* Know Grammar   1

◈ Unit I

In the Beginning Is the Sentence   5

Lesson 1   Subjects and Verbs   7
Lesson 2   The Sentence Again   11
Lesson 3   Clauses and Conjunctions: Two Sentences in One   15
Lesson 4   Dependent and Independent Clauses   19
Lesson 5   Infinitives and Participles: Verbs Without Tense   23
    YOUR WRITING: *Finding a Thesis*   27

◈ Unit II

With a Little Help...   29

Lesson 6   Verbs Combined with *Have*   31
Lesson 7   Verbs Combined with the Past Tense of *Have*   35
Lesson 8   Verb Combinations with *Be* and Its Forms as Helpers   39
Lesson 9   Helpers Without Tense   43
Lesson 10   A Special Kind of Helper   47
Lesson 11   The Many Forms of *Do*   51
    YOUR WRITING: *Developing the Thesis*   55

◈ Unit III

Endings and Their Meaning   57

Lesson 12   The *-s* Ending and Its Uses: Singular and Plural Nouns   59
Lesson 13   The *-s* Ending and Its Uses: The Third-Person Exception   63
Lesson 14   The *-s* Ending and Its Uses: Possessives   67
Lesson 15   The *-s* Ending and Its Uses: Spelling   71
    YOUR WRITING: *Filling in the Details*   75

Lesson 16   The Meanings of the -*d* Ending   77
Lesson 17   The Past Participle   81
Lesson 18   Past Participles as Adjectives   85
Lesson 19   Word Roots Ending in -*d*   89
            YOUR WRITING: *Details for Clarity   92*
Lesson 20   The -*ing* Ending and Its Uses   94
Lesson 21   The Present Participle as a Noun   98
Lesson 22   The Present Participle as an Adjective   101
Lesson 23   The -*ing* Ending as Spelling   105
            YOUR WRITING: *Using Anecdotes   108*
Lesson 24   Endings That Form Nouns   110
Lesson 25   Endings That Show Who or What Performs an Action   114
Lesson 26   Endings That Form Adjectives   118
Lesson 27   Endings That Show More or Most   122
            YOUR WRITING: *Being Specific   126*

Unit **IV**

What We *Really* Say: Idiomatic Uses   129

Lesson 28   Prepositions That Indicate *Where* and *When*   131
Lesson 29   Prepositions That Indicate *How* and *Why*   135
Lesson 30   Prepositions That Show Possession   139
Lesson 31   Two-Word Verbs   143
Lesson 32   Articles   147
            YOUR WRITING: *Making Connections   151*

Unit **V**

Making Connections   153

Lesson 33   Coordinating Conjunctions   155
Lesson 34   Subordinating Conjunctions   159
Lesson 35   Dependent Clauses with Relative Pronouns   163
Lesson 36   Transitions That Connect   167
            YOUR WRITING: *Combining Sentences   171*

Unit VI

How to Tell One Look-Alike Word From the Other 173

Lesson 37 Words That Look Alike 175
Lesson 38 Look-Alikes That Have Different Meanings 179
Lesson 39 Words That Sound Alike: Homophones 183
Lesson 40 Irregular Verbs 187
Lesson 41 Plural Nouns, Irregular Plurals 193
           YOUR WRITING: *Putting it Together* 196

Unit VII

Nuts and Bolts 197

Lesson 42 The Period 199
Lesson 43 The Question Mark 203
Lesson 44 The Exclamation Point 207
Lesson 45 Capitalization 211
Lesson 46 The Semicolon 215
Lesson 47 The Comma 219
Lesson 48 Commas That Set Off Subordinate Clauses 223
Lesson 49 Commas That Set Off Connecting Words and Phrases 227
Lesson 50 The Apostrophe 231
Lesson 51 Quotation Marks 235
           YOUR WRITING: *Making a Point* 238

Review Exercises 241
Glossary 281
Bibliography 285
Index 289

Preface

. . . .

One day at a committee meeting I heard a college administrator debate with an English department chair whether confusion in student papers about where to use *their* and *there* reflected an error in spelling or grammar. The grand irrelevance of this exchange led me to wonder, not for the first time, what such niceties, a momentary diversion for the super-literate, might signify to the basic writer who knows only that any paper submitted will be returned with marks indicating dozens of errors. Most of these marks—*sp, s-v agr, ref,* and the rest—are all too familiar to students, who have, often enough, little comprehension of what they refer to beyond "a run-on is a long sentence," or "a paper must have commas." In reality, little is achieved in terms of improved writing by this intense concentration on error, yet a widely used pedagogy is to *teach* error as a guide to correctness. For a generation, compositionists have emphasized the writing process; this emphasis suggests that we would do better to address the *process* of correctness rather than the *product* of an error-free paper.

It is relatively easy to direct students to whatever section in a handbook provides a grammatical explanation of an error—that is, if we can agree on whether *there/their* and the like fall under the category of spelling or grammar—but it is considerably more difficult to determine what students think they are doing. After all, people seldom make errors deliberately, so there must be a reason for continued mistakes. All of us, basic writers and holders of advanced degrees alike, use and write grammatical forms long before we know what to call them. And we use them no more effectively after we know their names. We have, in short, developed an intuition about how words combine to make sense. Thus, it is not a lack of knowledge of rules that leads students to persist in error. In fact, the rules often get in their way and further their confusion, causing them to overcorrect or misinterpret.

What, then, accounts for their alarming divergence from "correctness"? It may be dialect interference, unfamiliarity with preferred usage, or misinterpretation of instruction, a frequent occurrence. Most often it is because students communicate orally and are unaccustomed to written forms. Hardly ever are their errors attributable to an inability to recite rules of grammar.

The Writer's Grammar is based on the belief that writing is essentially a positive act and that concentrating on errors can have only a negative effect, intensifying student problems, problems that must—and can—be dealt with. To this end the lessons in this book are grounded in the way children learn language: in context, prompted by hearing the language used by those around them or by reading the language of standard usage. The lessons follow the pattern of many foreign language texts: a brief excerpt from a published work containing the preferred form the lesson demonstrates, a brief explanation of the form, an opportunity for the student to identify, copy, and use the form. The rationale of this book is that it is more beneficial to lead students to recognize correct forms in the context of real and correct writing rather than to teach them to identify error and to help them distinguish between forms that cause confusion. No incorrect forms are shown in the book. This positive approach takes into account three ways students get into difficulty by trying to follow rules:

1. Students are so paralyzed by fear of error that they overcorrect. For example, many will cross out a correct *looks* or *does* to substitute *look* or *do* not because they don't know singular from plural but because endings in general baffle them.
2. Students misunderstand the rules, sometimes because they interpret helpful hints from teachers as rigid, unchanging strictures. One student persisted in using *in which* as a connective in unlikely places as a result of being told that *because* signals a fragment.
3. Sometimes the rules make little sense. To tell students, especially those whose native language or dialect is not standard English, that subjects and verbs must agree is not only overstating the matter—only third person singular present tense verbs agree with their subjects in English—but opening the way to agreement errors never before dreamed of.

Similarly, we accuse students of run-ons, the usual code for a comma splice, and of fragments, without noting how frequently professional writers employ these constructions. Is it because our students are encountering these forms in their recreational reading that we must work so hard to teach their incorrectness?

The Writer's Grammar, therefore, keeps rules and technical terms to a minimum while addressing the actual confusion of words and endings that are found in student papers. The seven units are arranged to some extent in order of frequency of error, but they also take into account the most appropriate order for introducing concepts. Recognizing sentence boundaries is essential to producing even the simplest composition and thus is the subject of Unit 1. Mechanics, however, are left for last, not so much because the topic is a difficult one but because only a student who has produced a certain amount of writing and has some confidence about it can be expected to attend to matters of punctuation and capitalization. The units cover seven areas in which students have difficulty without attempting to address every possible aspect of English grammar; instead only those topics to which the most common student errors are attributable are included.

1. **Sentences:** The sentence is the basic unit of communication—a structure that has an infinite number of forms, all of which must contain a subject and a verb. This is not a difficult concept for students; it underlies all of the instruction in this book. Although a large part of the traditional composition curriculum is spent on teaching students sentence errors, in this book the emphasis from the beginning is on what a sentence is and how to write one. Every exercise requires students to write at least two sentences. One of these is often a sentence-combining exercise that provides valuable practice in methods of relating ideas.

2. **Compound verbs:** Students face two possibilities for confusion when they encounter verbs with auxiliaries: first, they must deal with the inflected forms of the auxiliary, and second, they will find in the participles that complete the compound more unfamiliar forms, particularly of irregular verbs. This book provides practice in recognizing compound verbs and their auxiliaries in context rather than isolated in paradigms unconnected to sentences.

3. **Inflections and suffixes indicating parts of speech:** Students tend to omit or affix indiscriminately when they are unsure of preferred usage. Thus the *-s* indicating third person singular present tense is confused with the plural *-s* of the noun and the *-'s* of the possessive. A similar mix-up occurs with the participle endings and with those for adjectives, nouns, and adverbs. One that crops up frequently is failure to recognize the distinction between "I am excit*ed*" and "I am excit*ing*." Because a word's root is more readily registered than the affix that also carries meaning, the ending is often either confused or omitted.

4. **Common idioms:** Although not often treated as such in handbooks, prepositions are extremely idiomatic, whether used as part of a prepositional phrase or semi-adverbially with two-word verbs. The entry in *Webster's New World Dictionary* for the preposition *for* contains twenty-one separate definitions for its idiomatic use. Articles are even more elusive—witness the difficulty of explaining why we say "to *the* school" but "to *the* hospital" (or why the British say "in hospital"). Only by repeated recognition of these forms in context will students develop the necessary familiarity with their use.

5. **Transitional devices:** Whether conjunctions or adverbials, these are not often used by students in speech, although they are essential in writing to establish relationships. When attempting to make such connections in writing, basic writers often resort to something like the all-purpose *which* or give up and settle for a comma splice. Yet, students are eager to learn these words and phrases, and while their initial efforts produce some awkward sentences, they are quick to master the use of conjunctive devices. This is especially true of writers who have some command of the matter of earlier units and are beginning to be conscious of style.

6. **Homonyms, homophones, and polysemous pairs:** *Their/there* and *to/two/too* are only the tip of this iceberg as student papers demonstrate vividly. Whether the problem is labeled spelling or grammar is far less important than that students begin to see the differences and likenesses in these words in their reading and to develop an intuition about where to use them. And because students need to be made aware of the complications of exceptions, a selection of irregular verbs and of plural nouns is included in Unit 6.

7. **Mechanics:** Many students would like to begin the writing course with instruction on where to put commas, not realizing that these and other marks of punctuation and capitalization can be used only after the process of writing has been understood. There is little reason, with students below the level of freshman composition, to go into every subtlety of sophisticated punctuation; their greatest need is to gain a secure sense of how to mark clause boundaries and when to capitalize.

All of the above topics are treated in traditional handbooks in a variety of unrelated sections on tense, agreement, plurals, verb parts, and kinds of pronouns—abstract grammar rules rather than concrete letters or words, rules that are often interchangeable as students perceive them. *The Writer's Grammar* introduces these matters to students as part of the organic whole that writing is rather than as an unchanging set of laws of usage exemplified by isolated sentences framed to demonstrate the rule. By concentrating on one ending, or group of endings, at a time while preserving the context of a piece of writing of intrinsic interest, this book helps students generalize about the environments in which certain forms occur. It encourages students to operate on several cognitive levels simultaneously which, as writers, they must do: reading comprehension, morpheme perception, writing practice, and composition. The aim here is to provide students with an ease and familiarity regarding the forms that give them most trouble, so that they can engage themselves fully in the writing process uninhibited by fear of the red pencil. The format of *The Writer's Grammar* is simple:

1. A brief reading passage chosen from published fiction or nonfiction dealing with material they may recognize from other courses. The reading selections are connected thematically and provide a continuity to the writing assignment with which the unit ends.

2. A brief exercise asking students to write a sentence commenting on the passage, or to combine sentences to produce a commentary.

3. An introduction to the student explaining the form in question and using terms from the brief glossary included at the end of the book.

4. An exercise asking students to identify the form in the passage—for example, words that end in -s—and space to copy those words.

5. An exercise asking students to write a sentence using the form being discussed.

After each lesson, at the teacher's discretion, students may be directed to turn to an appendix of review exercises for further practice. Each unit ends with writing instruction and a suggestion for a writing assignment based on the readings in the lessons. These are phrased to elicit the kind of expository writing in which students most need practice rather than the personal experience or opinion papers they frequently produce.

Initially the writing assignments are restricted to sentences and later expanded to paragraphs. Some students may wish to attempt more ambitious work; they should be reminded that in writing, as in perfecting a tennis game or learning a musical instrument, intensive practice in the basic moves is essential to perfecting performance.

The Teaching and Learning Package

A complete Instructor's Manual/Test Bank accompanies *The Writer's Grammar*. The Instructor's Manual emphasizes approaches to motivating students. It, in addition, provides a guide to organizing the writing class as a workshop centered on student writing. Group activities, writing exercises, and suggested ways of dealing with persistent problems are included, along with samples of syllabi and composition topics. The use of portfolios as assessment tools and examples of assignments the portfolio might contain are dealt with in detail. Ask your Longman sales representative for ISBN 0-321-09572-3.

In addition to this book-specific supplement, many other skills-based supplements are available to both instructors and students. All of these supplements are either free or offered at greatly reduced prices.

For Additional Reading and Reference

The Dictionary Deal.   Two dictionaries can be shrinkwrapped with *The Writer's Grammar* at a nominal fee. *The New American Webster Handy College Dictionary* is a paperback reference text with more than 100,000 entries. *Merriam Webster's Collegiate Dictionary*, tenth edition, is a hardback reference with a citation file of more than 14.5 million examples of English words drawn from actual use. For more information on how to shrinkwrap a dictionary with your text, contact your Longman sales representative.

Penguin Quality Paperback Titles.   A series of Penguin paperbacks is available at a significant discount when shrinkwrapped with any Longman Basic Skills title. Some titles available are Toni Morrison's *Beloved*, Julia Alvarez's *How the Garcia Girls Lost Their Accents*, Mark Twain's *Huckleberry Finn, Narrative of the Life of Frederick Douglass*, Harriet Beecher Stowe's *Uncle Tom's Cabin*, Dr. Martin Luther King, Jr.'s *Why We Can't Wait*, and plays by Shakespeare, Miller, and Albee. For a complete list of titles or more information, contact your Longman sales consultant.

100 Things to Write About.   This 100-page book contains 100 individual assignments for writing on a variety of topics and in a wide range of formats, from expressive to analytical. Ask your Longman sales representative for a sample copy. ISBN 0-673-98239-4

Newsweek **Alliance.**   Instructors may choose to shrinkwrap a 12-week subscription to *Newsweek* with any Longman text. The price of the subscription is 59 cents per issue (a total of $7.08 for the subscription). Available with the subscription is a free "Interactive Guide to *Newsweek*"—a workbook for students who are using the text. In addition, *Newsweek* provides a wide variety of instructor supplements free to teachers, including maps, Skills Builders, and weekly quizzes. For more information on the *Newsweek* program, contact your Longman sales representative.

Electronic and Online Offerings

The Longman Writer's Warehouse.   This innovative and exciting online supplement is the perfect accompaniment to any developmental writing course. Developed by developmental English instructors specially for developing writers, The Writer's Warehouse covers every part of the writing process. Also included are journaling capabilities, multimedia activities, diagnostic tests, an interactive handbook, and a complete instructor's manual. The Writer's Warehouse requires no space on your school's server; rather, students complete and store their work on the Longman server, and are able to access it, revise it, and continue working at any time. For more details about how to shrinkwrap a free subscription to The Writer's Warehouse with this text, your Longman sales representative. For a free guided tour of the site, visit **http://longmanwriterswarehouse.com.**

The Writer's ToolKit Plus.   This CD-ROM offers a wealth of tutorial, exercise, and reference material for writers. It is compatible with either a PC or Macintosh platform, and is flexible enough to be used either occasionally for practice or regularly in class lab sessions. For information on how to bundle this CD-ROM free with your text, contact your Longman sales representative.

GrammarCoach Software.   This interactive tutorial helps students practice the basics of grammar and punctuation through 600 self-grading exercises in such problem areas as fragments, run-ons, and agreement. IBM only. ISBN 0-205-26509-X

The Longman Electronic Newsletter.   Twice a month during the spring and fall, instructors who have subscribed receive a free copy of the Longman Developmental English Newsletter in their e-mailbox. Written by experienced classroom instructors, the newsletter offers teaching tips, classroom activities, book reviews, and more. To subscribe, visit the Longman Basic Skills website at **http://www.ablongman.com/basicskills,** or send an e-mail to **BasicSkills@ablongman.com.**

For Instructors

Electronic Test Bank for Writing. This electronic test bank features more than 5,000 questions in all areas of writing, from grammar to paragraphing, through essay writing, research, and documentation. With this easy-to-use CD-ROM, instructors simply choose questions from the electronic test bank, then print out the completed test for distribution. CD-ROM: ISBN 0-321-08117-X Print version: ISBN 0-321-08486-1

Competency Profile Test Bank, Second Edition. This series of 60 objective tests covers ten general areas of English competency, including fragments; comma splices and run-ons; pronouns; commas; and capitalization. Each test is available in remedial, standard, and advanced versions. Available as reproducible sheets or in computerized versions. Free to instructors. Paper version: ISBN 0-321-02224-6 Computerized IBM: ISBN 0-321-02633-0 Computerized Mac: ISBN 0-321-02632-2

Diagnostic and Editing Tests and Exercises, Sixth Edition. This collection of diagnostic tests helps instructors assess students' competence in Standard Written English for placement purposes or to gauge progress. Available as reproducible sheets or in computerized versions, and free to instructors. Paper: ISBN 0-321-19647-3 CD-ROM: ISBN 0-321-19645-7

ESL Worksheets, Third Edition. These reproducible worksheets provide ESL students with extra practice in areas they find the most troublesome. A diagnostic test and posttest are provided, along with answer keys and suggested topics for writing. Free to adopters. ISBN 0-321-07765-2

Longman Editing Exercises. Fifty-four pages of paragraph editing exercises give students extra practice using grammar skills in the context of longer passages. Free when packaged with any Longman title. ISBN 0-205-31792-8 Answer key: ISBN 0-205-31797-9

80 Practices. A collection of reproducible, ten-item exercises that provide additional practices for specific grammatical usage problems, such as comma splices, capitalization, and pronouns; includes an answer key. Free to adopters. ISBN 0-673-53422-7

CLAST Test Package, Fourth Edition. These two 40-item objective tests evaluate students' readiness for the CLAST exams. Strategies for teaching CLAST preparedness are included. Free with any Longman English title. Reproducible sheets: ISBN 0-321-01950-4 Computerized IBM version: ISBN 0-321-01982-2 Computerized Mac version: ISBN 0-321-01983-0

TASP Test Package, Third Edition. These 12 practice pretests and posttests assess the same reading and writing skills covered in the TASP examination. Free with any Longman English title. Reproducible sheets: ISBN 0-321-01959-8 Computerized IBM version: ISBN 0-321-01985-7 Computerized Mac version: ISBN 0-321-01984-9

Teaching Online: Internet Research, Conversation, and Composition, Second Edition.   Ideal for instructors who have never surfed the Net, this easy-to-follow guide offers basic definitions, numerous examples, and step-by-step information about finding and using Internet sources. Free to adopters. ISBN 0-321-01957-1

Teaching Writing to the Non-Native Speaker.   This booklet examines the issues that arise when non-native speakers enter the developmental classroom. Free to instructors, it includes profiles of international and permanent ESL students, factors influencing second-language acquisition, and tips on managing a multicultural classroom. ISBN 0-673-97452-9

Using Portfolios.   This supplement offers teachers a brief introduction to teaching with portfolios in composition courses. This essential guide addresses the pedagogical and evaluative use of portfolios, and offers practical suggestions for implementing a portfolio evaluation system in a writing class. ISBN 0-321-08412-8

The Longman Guide to Classroom Management.   Written by Joannis Flatley of St. Philip's College, the first in Longman's new series of monographs for developmental English instructors focuses on issues of classroom etiquette, providing guidance on dealing with unruly, unengaged, disruptive, or uncooperative students. Ask your Longman sales representative for a free copy. ISBN 0-321-09246-5

The Longman Instructor Planner.   This all-in-one resource for instructors includes monthly and weekly planning sheets, to-do lists, student contact forms, attendance rosters, a gradebook, an address/phone book, and a mini almanac. Ask your Longman sales representative for a free copy. ISBN 0-321-09247-3

For Students

Researching Online, **Fifth Edition.**   A perfect companion for a new age, this indispensable new supplement helps students navigate the Internet. Adapted from *Teaching Online,* the instructor's Internet guide, *Researching Online* speaks directly to students, giving them detailed, step-by-step instructions for performing electronic searches. Available free when shrinkwrapped with this text. ISBN 0-321-09277-5

Learning Together: An Introduction to Collaborative Theory.   This brief guide to the fundamentals of collaborative learning teaches students how to work effectively in groups, how to revise with peer response, and how to co-author a paper or report. Shrinkwrapped free with *The Writer's Grammar.* ISBN 0-673-46848-8

A Guide for Peer Response, **Second Edition.**   This guide offers students forms for peer critiques, including general guidelines and specific forms for different stages in the writing process. Also appropriate for a freshman-level course. Free to adopters. ISBN 0-321-01948-2

Ten Practices of Highly Successful Students.   This popular supplement helps students learn crucial study skills, offering concise tips for a successful career in college. Topics include time management, test-taking, reading critically, stress, and motivation. ISBN 0-205-30769-8

Thinking Through the Test, **by D. J. Henry.**   This special workbook, prepared specially for students in Florida, offers ample skill and practice exercises to help students prep for the Florida State Exit Exam. To shrinkwrap this workbook free with your textbook, contact your Longman sales representative. Available in two versions: with answers and without answers. Also available: Two laminated grids (one for reading, one for writing) that can serve as handy references for students preparing for the Florida State Exit Exam.

The Longman Planner.   This daily planner for students includes daily, weekly, and monthly calendars, as well as class schedules and a mini-almanac of useful information. It is the perfect accompaniment to a Longman reading or study skills textbook, and is available free to students when shrinkwrapped with this text. ISBN 0-321-04573-4

The Longman Writer's Journal.   This journal for writers, free with any Longman English text, offers students a place to think, write, and react. For an examination copy, contact your Longman sales consultant. ISBN 0-321-08639-2

[NEW] The Longman Writer's Portfolio.   This unique supplement provides students with a space to plan, think about, and present their work. The portfolio includes an assessing/organizing area (including a grammar diagnostic test, a spelling quiz, and project planning worksheets), a before and during writing area (including peer review sheets, editing checklists, writing self-evaluations, and a personal editing profile), and an after-writing area (including a progress chart, a final table of contents, and a final assessment). ISBN 0-321-10765-9

Acknowledgments

I am grateful to all of those students whose encounters with the written word have taught me much about what goes on during the writing process. I must acknowledge my indebtedness as well to William Kerrigan's *Writing to the Point* and its approach to composition, a method that leads students to value their written work as something more than an exercise in correction for the teacher. My thanks also to all those whose thoughtful reading and perceptive comments helped me revise and strengthen this book: Linda A. Austin of Glendale Community College, Marta O. Dmtrenko-Ahrabian of Wayne State University, Stevina Evuleocha of California State Univeristy at Hayward, Caren Kessler of Blue Ridge Community College, Drema Stringer of Marshall Community and Technical College, Kendra Vaglienti of Brookhaven College, and Jayne L. Williams of Texarkana College. Thanks to Steven Rigolosi for his guidance and encouragement and to Brandi Nelson for tactful suggestions on what works. Not least, a very large and special thank you to Sheila Kovacs and Lita Porter who, with unfailing good cheer, did so much to make it happen.

Patricia Silber

THE WRITER'S GRAMMAR

The Oh-So-Correct Writer

Introduction to Students: You *Do* Know Grammar

The French playwright Molière wrote about a rather foolish man who, having made a good deal of money, decided to buy for himself all the accomplishments he imagined fashionable people to have. He hired dance teachers to show him the latest steps, topflight designers to make him the trendiest clothes, and writing teachers to help him write love letters. When he demanded of the last to be taught prose, he was astonished to learn that he had been speaking prose all his life.

Many writing students today—especially those who say, "I don't know anything about grammar"—are like that character in Molière's play; they don't realize they have understood grammar all their lives. Think about the sentence "I don't know anything about grammar." It follows a variety of grammatical rules that determine word order, pronoun case, negation of verbs, contraction, idiomatic prepositions, and perhaps a few others. You can look any of them up in a grammar book and find detailed explanations about their usage.

Whether you need these detailed explanations is another question. The point is that you do understand grammar, easily and naturally, without reciting the rules. Some language authorities say that we are programmed to speak our native language before we even learn to speak. Like most of us, you probably began talking somewhere around the age of two. Almost immediately you put your words into the grammatical forms of the language spoken around you. What's more, you produced sentences, even if they came out as "Me catch the ball," or "Mommy taked it away from me." Silly baby talk? Not at all. These two examples follow some of the same rules of grammar mentioned in the previous paragraph: word order, use of pronouns, and prepositions. They also demonstrate that the foundation of any human language is the sentence, a very short story in which someone or something is or does something. Does that happen in our examples? Of course! It is clear that the speaker of the first sentence has made a great catch. . .and that the child knows the following about grammar:

1

1. That it has pronouns—*I, we, she, it, they, ours*—that stand for names like Tanya or Joey, or ball, or coat, or parents. (Don't worry about the child's use of *me* as the subject; she will soon find that *I* is the way most people say it. How many adults do you hear say "Me go to class"?)
2. That a sentence usually begins with a subject, followed by a verb and, often, an object.

The baby who invented the second sentence knows these two things about grammar and more besides, most importantly that verbs have *tenses* that tell us whether an action is taking place now, took place in the past, or will take place in the future. (Again, don't worry about *taked* instead of *took*; Baby will learn the preferred form very soon.) Why did I say "invented" rather than "imitated"? First, it is clear that no one but a very young child would say "Mommy *taked* it away from me." Second, the sentence shows that even a baby knows, without having learned any rules, about tense, and is able to make up a past tense verb.

Now, neither this child we're talking about nor you sat down with a grammar book before producing sentences, hundreds and thousands of them, all of them grammatical, even if they sometimes contain an "incorrect" form. Well, fine, you've been speaking under the influence of grammar for years. Why, then, have teachers been telling you, and—worse—you agreeing with them, that you "don't know anything about grammar"? The answer is related to the *me* and *taked* in our sample baby talk and to the difference between the language we speak and the language we write. Many of the forms that we use in our writing are forms that we neither use nor hear when we speak. "I shoulda talk to im" is what we say. When we write it, it comes out, "I should have talked to him." This difference between the way we talk and the way we write, by the way, is true of everybody, including teachers; listen to yours and see if you don't agree.

There is still another reason beginning writers get into trouble with teachers because of their "grammar": the preferred forms in formal written English often differ from those in informal speech. Think about it. Do you use the same words and expressions when you speak to your parents and to your friends? How about when you're in a job interview? Or when you're introduced to your girlfriend's parents? Of course, your language changes depending on who you're talking to. And the same is true of writing. When we write, we don't have the advantage of seeing the person addressed and observing reactions, or being able to answer questions. We have to make clear what we mean in the words we choose and in the form we put them in. That is why we use standard forms understandable and acceptable to anyone.

Still, it is not necessary to memorize pages of grammar rules in order to find out where spoken forms creep into our writing and to change them to the appropriate written forms; in fact, too much worry about the rules can keep us from concentrating on something much more important: clear writing that makes a point.

To sum up, while everyone knows quite a lot about grammar and follows the rules all the time, many people do not know all the acceptable forms for writing, forms that college students, and graduates, are expected to use routinely. That is the point of this book. We do need to know these forms, but before we can use them easily, we need to see how writers use them.

This book will *show* you these preferred forms, not tell you the rules that govern them, and will show them used by writers whose work is read and enjoyed by millions of people. No one worries much about whether these writers "know grammar"; what they have written gives us too much pleasure. But their writing *does* follow the standard usage we have been talking about, and shows us how we can do the same.

In each unit you will be asked to read excerpts from a published work by an author whose books are read, not because they are "correct" but because their stories are exciting or because they show us another time or place or help us understand our own lives better. In their writing you will have a chance to pick out the ways they use formal written language to get their meaning across and to arouse the reader's emotions. Best of all, you will begin to use the forms these writers use in your own writing.

But before you go on, you should keep in mind a few terms we use when we talk about writing.

Sentence: The group of words that tells what something or someone is or does. It must have a subject and a verb.

Subject: The something or someone that is or does something in a sentence. Usually it is a noun or pronoun that answers the question "who" or "what."

Who drives that old Beetle?

Millicent drives the Beetle and *it* burns a lot of gas.

Verb: One or more words that answer the question "what's happening?" The car *burns* oil, too.

In most sentences, the verb will consist of more than one word. Together, all of the words that go with the verb are called the *predicate.*

Tense: The verb form that tells *when* something happened. Often this is shown by adding an ending to the root word. It stall*ed* on a hill yesterday. Sometimes it is another word. Millicent *will sell* it next week.

Clause: A group of words containing a subject and verb and connected to another sentence. For example: When the *car was* new, *it drove* like a dream. The first clause is *dependent,* the second *independent.* Many sentences consist of more than one clause. The exercises in this book will give you practice in combining short sentences into more meaningful ones.

Adjective: A word that answers the question "what kind?"

The *ugly* Beetle is a clunker.

Adverb: A word that answers the questions "When?" "Where?" "How?" or Why?

It breaks down *often.* [when]

It stalled *here.* [where]

It drives *noisily.* [how]

Therefore, it isn't safe to drive. [why]

Participle: A form of a verb that can be used as an adjective or noun. The *present participle* ends in *-ing.*

Driving that car is a headache.

The *past participle* either ends in *-ed* or is a different word.

Our trip ended with a *heated* argument.

The *broken* transmission was the last straw.

Infinitive: A form of a verb that is written with *to.* It can be used as a noun, but not as the verb of a sentence.

She had hoped *to drive* it to the junk yard.

Root Word: The part of a word that carries the main meaning.

girl, a young female;

girl*s,* more than one young female;

girl*ish,* like a young female.

UNIT I

In the Beginning Is the Sentence

Without sentences nothing we say or write would ever make any sense. Did you ever think about that? In a sentence someone or something *is* or *does* something. The first someone or something is the subject, and a subject all by itself doesn't have any meaning. "The mouse." Well, what about the mouse? "The *mouse tells* the cursor where to go." *Mouse* is the subject, *tells* is the verb, and without both subject and verb there is no sentence; something is missing.

Most sentences, like the one above, have more than just a one-word subject and a one-word verb, of course. Pick out the subjects and verbs in these sentences:

> The retreat began at seven that night. They made their way back about a quarter mile to a fairly solid floe, and pitched camp. All hands were called early the next morning. Most of the men were sent out to hunt seals.
>
> —Alfred Lansing, *Endurance*

In the first sentence *the retreat* is the subject and *began* is the verb. In the next sentence *they* is the subject of two verbs: *made* and *pitched. All hands* is the next subject, with *were called* as its verb. Finally, *most of the men* is the subject of *were sent out*. You probably noticed that both subjects and verbs sometimes consist of more than one word. We'll be talking further about that.

All of this sentence making is something you've been doing without even thinking about it since you were about two years old. Why does it become such a chore when you have to write sentences for your composition assignments? It's certainly not because you can't make up a sentence. Perhaps it is because writing a sentence needs information that you may give with your facial expression or tone of voice when you speak. Imagine the simple sentence "Duane, come here!" Will it sound the same when a mother sees her

5

toddler heading for a busy street and when a teacher addresses a mischievous sixth-grader? Of course not. So we have to add the extra words and the punctuation that make the difference clear.

Different languages have different ways of saying things, but all of them—more than 4,000 of them throughout the world—arrange their words in sentences.

	English	**Spanish**	**Tagalog**
Present	I go	voy	punta ako

Notice how different these mini-sentences are, not just in the words they use but in the *way* they use them: English places the subject first, followed by the verb; Tagalog (the main language of the Philippines) places the verb first, then the subject; in Spanish the subject *I* is understood. Some languages, like Swahili and Turkish, put the entire sentence into a single word.

Another notable point about these forms is that all of them change in order to show *when* the action is happening—now, or a week ago, or tomorrow. So we can add to our definition of a sentence that the verb must have *tense*. Notice that sometimes a verb consists of two words, one of them a helper, or auxiliary, usually a form of the verbs *to be, to have,* or *to do*. What's more, the word itself can change, as it does in the English past tense and in the past and future tenses in Spanish.

	English	**Spanish**	**Tagalog**
Past	I went	fui	puntana ako
Future	I will go	iré	pupunta ako

L E S S O N 1
Subjects and Verbs

· · · · · · · · ·

Every sentence must have a subject and a verb (with tense). Most sentences have more than a one-word subject and a one-word verb. Here's an example: *Her blue <u>sweater</u> <u>kept</u> Marina warm in the chilly room.* *Sweater* is the subject and *kept* is the verb, but *blue, Marina, warm,* and *in the chilly room* tell us more about the subject and the verb.

In the lessons that follow, we'll look at some sentences from real writers. Charles Lindbergh wrote *The Spirit of St. Louis* about his historic flight from New York to Paris in 1927, the first ever to cross the Atlantic Ocean. In it he uses a variety of sentences. Read the following description about what Lindbergh sees as his plane begins the flight.

On the Way

¹The great landscaped estates of Long Island pass rapidly below: mansion, hedgerow, and horse-jump giving way to farms and woodlands farther east. ²I hold my plane just high enough to clear treetops and buildings on the hills. ³By flying close to the ground, I can see farther through the haze. ⁴That finger of water on my left is part of the bay-broken shore line of the Sound. ⁵It must be at least five miles away. ⁶Then visibility to the north is improving. ⁷The clouds look a little higher too.

—Charles Lindbergh, *The Spirit of St. Louis*

■ Write a sentence explaining why Lindbergh is flying close to the ground.

_____

_____

■ Even though there are additional words and phrases in the story, each sentence has one subject and one verb, sometimes a verb made up of two words. Write the subjects and verbs below. The first one has been done for you.

Subject	Verb
1. _____ *estates* _____	_____ *pass* _____
2. _____	_____
3. _____	_____
4. _____	_____
5. _____	_____
6. _____	_____
7. _____	_____

■ If you had a choice, where would you like to fly to? Write a sentence about the place you chose. _____

_____

LESSON 1a
More About Subjects and Verbs

No matter how many words a sentence has, it must always have at least one subject and one verb. Both subject and verb will usually consist of more than one word. In the passage below, the subject is *Miss Crawford's entrance hall,* and the verb is *opened,* although the entire predicate is *opened onto a magnificent room with a huge white Christmas tree at the end and many brilliantly wrapped presents.*

Hollywood Christmas

[1]Miss Crawford's entrance hall opened onto a magnificent room with a huge white Christmas tree at the end and many brilliantly wrapped presents. [2]Crawford came to the door in person. [3]And she was drawing all the limelight of the afternoon to herself, very much lady of the manor in a white satin dressing gown and white mules with pom-poms. [4]I didn't know why the star was in a dressing gown in the afternoon. [5]She and her white satin gown were the stuff of dreams. [6]Well, I already loved Joan Crawford. [7]And I had, since seeing her as a child in the Tivoli Theater. [8]Indeed she was larger than life. [9]Glamorous, cagey, smart, ambitious, ruthless, tough, always acting, pretending to be sick in bed the night she feared they wouldn't give her the Oscar.

—Liz Smith, *Natural Blonde*

■ Combine these sentences:

When she was a child, Liz Smith saw Joan Crawford movies. She loved Joan

Crawford. _____

_____

■ Find the subjects and verbs in *Hollywood Christmas* and list them below. The first one has been done for you.

Subject	Verb
1. *entrance hall*	*opened*
2. _____	_____

Subject	Verb
3. _____	_____
4. _____	_____
5. _____	_____
6. _____	_____
7. _____	_____
8. _____	_____
9. _____	_____

■ Have you ever been close to a celebrity on the street or in a store or other public building? Write a sentence about how it happened. _____

_____

LESSON 1b
Another Look at Sentences
· · · · · · · · · ·

Many sentences have more than one subject and verb, but some have only one of each. *The <u>class</u> <u>begins</u> at nine A.M.* is an example. Look at the sentences in the following excerpt.

A Lonely Airport

[1]I <u>sat</u>, once more in the late hours of darkness, in the airport of a foreign city. [2]I had missed a plane and had almost a whole night's wait before me. [3]I could not sleep. [4]The long corridor was deserted. [5]Even the cleaning woman had passed by. [6]In that white efficient glare I grew ever more depressed and weary. [7]I was tired of customs officers and police. [8]I was lonely for home. [9]My eyes hurt. [10]I had an ocean to cross; the effort seemed unbearable. [11]I rested my aching head upon my hand.

—Loren Eiseley, *One Night's Dying*

■ Why is an airport depressing late at night? Write your answer in a sentence.

_____

■ For each subject on the lines below, write the verb that goes with it in *A Lonely Airport.*

	Subject	**Verb**
1.	I	sat
2.	The long corridor	
3.	the cleaning woman	
4.	the effort	

■ What is the loneliest place you can think of? Write a sentence about why you find it lonely. ―――――――――――――――――

―――――――――――――――――――

For more subject-verb identification, see Review Exercises 1, 3, 4, 6.

L E S S O N   2
The Sentence Again

Sometimes a sentence will have more than one subject or one verb: *Angela and Lewis found the lost book.* Sometimes a sentence will have more than one verb for one subject: *The angels sang and danced.* And sometimes there will be several subjects and verbs in one sentence. We can see examples in this paragraph.

Staying Awake

[1]The brilliant light and the strangeness of the sea awaken me. [2]Any change stimulates the senses. [3]Changing altitude, changing thought, even the changing contours of the ice cakes help to stay awake. [4]I can fly high for a while and then fly low. [5]I can fly first with my right hand and then with my left. [6]I can shift my position a little in the seat, sitting stiff and straight, slouching down, twisting sidewise. [7]I can create imaginary emergencies in my mind. I can check and recheck my navigation. [8]All these tricks I must use and think of others.

—Charles Lindbergh, *The Spirit of St. Louis*

■ What does Lindbergh do to keep awake? Write a sentence to explain. _____

_____

■ For all of the verbs listed below, show the subject or subjects from *Staying Awake.* The first has been done as an example. Note that some of these verbs have a helper, *can,* which becomes part of the verb.

Subject	Verb
1. *light, strangeness*	*awaken*
2.	*stimulates*
3.	*help*
4.	*can fly*
5.	*can shift*
6.	*can create*
7.	*can check*

■ What people or happenings distract you from concentrating on studying for an exam? Write a sentence naming two things that take your mind off what you should be doing. _____

_____

LESSON 2a
Sentences with More Than One Subject and Verb

. . . .

Depending on the complexity of the idea being expressed, a writer can choose to use two or more subjects and verbs in one sentence. *Mrs. Purlman* *handed out* the papers and then *wrote* the questions on the board. The subject is *Mrs. Purlman* and the two verbs are *handed out* and *wrote*.

The Slingshot

¹Jody took his slingshot from the porch and walked up toward the brush line to try to kill a bird. ²It was a good slingshot, with store-bought rubbers, but while Jody had often shot at birds, he had never hit one. ³He walked up through the vegetable patch, kicking his bare toes into the dust. ⁴And on the way he found the perfect slingshot stone, round and slightly flattened and heavy enough to carry through the air. ⁵He fitted it into the leather pouch of his weapon and proceeded to the brush line. ⁶In the shade of the sagebrush the little birds were working, scratching in the leaves, flying restlessly a few feet and scratching again. ⁷Jody pulled back the rubbers of the sling and advanced cautiously. ⁸When he was twenty feet away, he carefully raised the sling and aimed. ⁹The stone whizzed; the thrush started up and flew right into it. ¹⁰And down the little bird went with a broken head.

—John Steinbeck, *The Red Pony*

■ Combine these sentences:

Jody had a good slingshot and the perfect stone. The stone hit the thrush. _____

_____

■ Note that some subjects in *The Slingshot* have two verbs. For each of the subjects listed below, write the verbs that go with it.

	Subject	Verb or Verbs
1.	*Jody*	*took, walked*
2.	*He*	
3.	*Jody*	
4.	*the thrush*	

■ Have you ever hiked in the woods? Write a sentence about what you might expect to see on such a hike. _____

_____

LESSON 2b
Sentences with Two Subjects and One Verb

Very often a sentence will have two or more subjects. Note that this will make the subject plural, which means it must be followed by the *plural* form of the verb in the present tense. So, while we write, *Nanci likes to watch basketball,* we change the verb when we write, *Nanci and her friends like to watch basketball.* There is no *-s* on the plural form of *like.* (See Lesson 13 for more about this topic.) Some sentences will have more than one subject, and some will have more than one verb: *Mike and Joe jumped in the car and drove to Seven-Eleven. Mike* and *Joe* are subjects and *jumped* and *drove* are verbs.

Goodbye Before Sailing

[1]By midafternoon the *Andrea Gail* is ready. [2]The food and bait have been stowed away, the fuel and water tanks have been topped off, spare drums of both have been lashed onto the whaleback, the gear's in good order, and the engine's running well. [3]Bobby climbs off the boat without saying anything to Bugsy and walks across the parking lot to Chris's Volvo. [4]They drive back across town to Thea's and trot up her front steps in a soft warm rain. [5]Thea hears their feet on the stoop and invites them in. [6]"I've got some errands to do," she says. [7]"Make yourselves at home." [8]Outside the rain taps on. [9]Chris and Bobby can't see the ocean but they can smell it, a dank taste of salt and seaweed that permeates the entire peninsula and lays claim to it as part of the sea.

—Sebastian Junger, *The Perfect Storm*

■ Why does the rain make this scene seem sad? Write your answer in a sentence. _____

_____

■ Find the subjects and verbs in *Goodbye Before Sailing* and write them below. Be sure to include *all* the subjects when there are more than one. Sentence 2 has examples of more than one subject.

Subject or Subjects	Verb
1. _____	_____
2. _____ food, bait _____	_____ have been stowed _____
3. _____	_____
4. _____	_____
5. _____	_____
6. _____	_____
7. _____	_____
8. _____	_____
9. _____	_____

■ Has the weather ever affected your mood? Write a sentence about a time when it made you happy, excited, or sad. _____

_____

For more work on subjects and verbs, see Review Exercises 1, 3, 4, 6.

LESSON 3
Clauses and Conjunctions: Two Sentences in One

Very often a sentence with its subject and verb will be connected with another sentence with its own subject and verb. When this happens, each of the sentences is called a *clause*, and the two must be connected by (1) a *coordinating conjunction*—words like *and, but, for*, (2) a *subordinating conjunction* like *although, because, as*, or (3) a *relative pronoun*—*who, which, that*. The entire sentence is classified as either *compound* or *complex*. For example, two independent clauses like, *It's a rainy day* and *The class canceled the trip to the beach* can be combined with a coordinating conjunction to become a compound sentence: *It's a rainy day, and the class canceled the trip to the beach.* We'll have more about this in Lessons 33 and 34. For now, let's continue to look for subjects and verbs.

Iceberg Alert

[1]Soon there are icebergs everywhere—white patches on a blackened sea, sentries of the Arctic. [2]The wisps of fog lengthen and increase in number until they merge to form a solid layer on ahead. [3]But, separating as I pass above them, they leave long channels of open water in between—stripes of gray fog and black water across my course. [4]With every minute I fly, these channels narrow. [5]Finally all the ocean is covered with a thin, undulating veil of mist. [6]At first it doesn't hide the denser whiteness of the icebergs, but makes their forms more ghostlike down below. [7]Then the top of the veil slopes upward toward the east—real fog, thick, hiding the ocean, hiding the icebergs, hiding even the lights of ships if there are any there to shine. [8]I ease the stick back slightly, take five miles from my speed, and turn it into a slow and steady climb.

—Charles Lindbergh, *The Spirit of St. Louis*

■ Combine these two sentences into one that describes how the icebergs look from the air:

The icebergs are ghostlike. Fog covers their tops. _____

_____

■ Underline the subjects and verbs in *Iceberg Alert*. For each of the subjects listed below, write the verb that belongs with it. If the sentence has more than one clause, write the connecting word as well.

15

Subject	Verb	Connective	Subject	Verb
1. icebergs	*are*			
2. wisps			*they*	
3. I			*they*	
4. channels				
5. all				
6. it				
7. top			*any*	
8. I				

■ Write a sentence about some sign of danger from the weather that you have experienced. _____

_____

LESSON 3a
Coordinating Conjunctions

. . . .

The common coordinating conjunctions are *and, but, for, or, nor, so,* and *yet.* They join independent clauses—clauses that can stand alone as sentences. For example: *Mona likes to watch daytime serials. She doesn't like talk shows.* These two sentences can be combined into one: *Mona likes to watch daytime serials, but she doesn't like talk shows.*

The Seven Coordinating Conjunctions

and	but	for	nor	or	so	yet

Gandhi and His People

[1]Mahatma Gandhi loved not mankind in the abstract but men, women, and children, and he hoped to help them as specific individuals and groups of individuals. [2]He belonged to them and they knew it and therefore they belonged to him. [3]By harboring the disloyal, he dispelled their disloyalty. [4]His loyalty begot theirs. [5]In this wise, during the worst years of defeat and depression from 1924 to 1929, he prepared for later triumphs. [6]India now called him "Bapu," Father.

—Louis Fischer, *Gandhi: His Life and Message for the World*

■ Combine these sentences:

Gandhi saw people as individuals. People regarded him as a father. _____

_____

■ Find the subjects and verbs in the excerpt on the previous page. If the sentence has more than one clause, write the conjunction as well.

Subject/Verb	Conjunction	Subject/Verb
1. *Mahatma Gandhi loved*	*and*	*he hoped*
2.		
3.		
4.		
5.		
6.		
7.		

■ Think of a person who is admired by everyone you know. Write a sentence about that person. _____

_____

LESSON 3b
Subordinating Conjunctions, Relative Pronouns

• • • • • • • • •

Subordinating conjunctions are the words used to join clauses. They include *though, while, before, because, if, when, where,* and *although*. Relative pronouns like *which, that,* and *who* also serve to join clauses. *Sasha, who likes fast cars, could only afford an old Chevy.* The two clauses are *Sasha could only afford an old Chevy* and *who likes fast cars.*

Subordinating Conjunctions

after	although	as	because
before	if	though	when
where	whereas	while	

After the Hurricane

[1]About two hours after the windows first broke in young Ryan Ochmanski's bedroom in Whispering Pines, the winds start to ease up a little. [2]As dawn breaks and the winds begin to let up, the Ochmanskis find a haven at a nearby house, which has plywood covers over the windows and seems to be in good shape. [3]A neighbor who is a registered nurse treats Tom's cuts and bruises, and the bruises the others have suffered. [4]Miraculously, none of the family is severely injured. [5]Later that morning, as the rain ends and the winds decrease, Tom and some neighbors return to their houses to see what's left of them—in several cases, not much, almost nothing at all. [6]It turns out that the object that has destroyed the front of the Ochmanski house is a very large chunk of a concrete tie beam. [7]It had sailed with part of the roof still attached over the tops of the houses across the street from the Ochmanski home before crashing into their living room wall.

—Dr. Bob Sheets and Jack Williams, *Hurricane Watch*

■ Combine these sentences:

The storm destroyed houses. The people were not seriously injured. _____

_____

■ For each of the clauses below, indicate whether it is dependent or independent.

Clause	Dependent/Independent
1. *after the windows first broke*	*dependent*
2. *as dawn breaks*	
3. *the Ochmanskis find a haven*	
4. *who is a registered nurse*	
5. *none of the family is severely injured*	
6. *as the rain ends*	
7. *It turns out*	
8. *the object that has destroyed the front*	
9. *It had sailed*	

■ Think of a time when a neighborhood got together to help someone in need. Write a sentence about what everyone did to help. _____

_____

For more work on clauses, see Review Exercises 2, 5, 9, 12, 21, 46.

LESSON 4
Dependent and Independent Clauses

Clauses that can stand by themselves as sentences are called *independent* clauses. *I slept late this morning* is an example. Clauses that *must* be connected to an independent clause to form a sentence are called *dependent* clauses. An example of this is *Because the alarm didn't go off.* Even though it has a subject and verb, to make sense it has to be joined to *I slept late this morning.*

The Future of Flying

[1]What limitless possibilities aviation holds when planes can fly nonstop between New York and Paris! [2]The year will surely come when passengers and mail fly every day from America to Europe. [3]Of course flying will cost much more than transportation by surface ship, but letters can be written on lightweight paper, and there'll be people with such pressing business that they can afford the higher price of passage. [4]With multiengined flying boats the safety of operation should be high. [5]Weather will be the greatest problem. [6]We'd have to find some way to fly through sleet and land in fog.

—Charles Lindbergh, *The Spirit of St. Louis*

- How accurate was Lindbergh's prediction about flying? Write a sentence explaining your answer. _____

_____

- Underline all of the subjects and verbs in the above paragraph. You will see that some of the clauses are independent and some are dependent. For every sentence that has more than one clause, rewrite each of the clauses as a separate sentence as in the example below.

Clause 1	Clause 2
1. *What limitless possibilities aviation holds*	*Planes can fly nonstop between New York and Paris.*
2. _____	_____
3. _____	_____

- Write a sentence describing either what you like or do not like about flying.

_____

19

LESSON 4a
More Clauses

Most writers use a combination of dependent and independent clauses to make clear the relationships between their ideas. For example: *The spaghetti got cold while we played Scrabble.* In this sentence *the spaghetti got cold* is an independent clause, and *while we played Scrabble* is dependent on what happened to the spaghetti. Look for both independent and dependent clauses in the following passage.

Saved!

[1]At that moment the boss noticed that a fly had fallen into his broad inkpot, and was trying feebly but desperately to clamber out again. [2]Help! Help! Said those struggling legs. [3]But the sides of the inkpot were wet and slippery; it fell back again and began to swim. [4]The boss took up a pen, picked the fly out of the ink, and shook it on to a piece of blotting-paper. [5]For a fraction of a second it lay still on the dark patch that oozed round it. [6]Then the front legs waved, took hold, and, pulling its small sodden body up, it began the immense task of cleaning the ink from its wings. [7]Over and under, over and under, went a leg along a wing, as the stone goes over and under the scythe. [8]Then there was a pause, while the fly, seeming to stand on the tips of its toes, tried to expand first one wing and then the other. [9]It succeeded at last, and sitting down, it began, like a minute cat, to clean its face. [10]Now one could imagine that the little front legs rubbed against each other lightly, joyfully. [11]The horrible danger was over; it had escaped; it was ready for life again.

—Katherine Mansfield, *The Fly*

■ Combine these sentences:

The fly was drowning in the ink. It recovered when it was lifted out. _____

_____

■ Identify the clauses in *Saved!* If a clause is *dependent*, change its wording so that it becomes *independent*. The first has been done as an example.

1. *A fly had fallen into his broad inkpot, and it was trying feebly but*
   desperately to clamber out again.

2. _____

3. _____

4. _____

5. _____

- Do you remember seeing or reading about an animal being rescued? Write a sentence describing what happened. _____

_____

LESSON 4b
Dependent Clauses with
Relative Pronouns

. . . .

One of the most common ways of connecting clauses is with the relative pronoun *which*, but *who* and *that* are also frequently used. For example: *My car, which needs an oil change, stalled on Main Street*. The independent clause is *my car stalled on Main Street*, and the dependent clause is *which needs an oil change*. Note how relative pronouns that connect clauses can sometimes be the subject of the clause, as *that* is in this sentence.

A Record Tying Pitch

[1]On the afternoon of October 2nd, 1968—a warm, sunshiny day in St. Louis—Mickey Stanley, the Detroit Tiger shortstop, singled to center field to lead off the top of the ninth inning of the opening game of the 1968 World Series. [2]It was only the fifth hit of the game for the Tigers, who by this time were trailing the National League Champion St. Louis Cardinals by a score of 4–0. [3]The next batter, the dangerous Al Kaline, worked the count to two and two and then fanned, swinging away at a fastball, to an accompanying roar from the crowd. [4]A moment later, there was a second enormous cheer, louder and more sustained than the first. [5]The Cardinal catcher, Tim McCarver, who had straightened up to throw the ball back to his pitcher, now hesitated. [6]The pitcher, Bob Gibson, a notoriously swift worker on the mound, motioned to his battery mate to return the ball. [7]Instead, McCarver pointed with his gloved hand at something behind Gibson's head. [8]Gibson, staring uncomprehendingly at his catcher, yelled, "C'mon, c'mon, let's *go!*" [9]Still holding the ball, McCarver pointed again, and Gibson, turning around, read the illuminated message on the centerfield scoreboard, which perhaps only he in the ballpark had not seen until that moment: "Gibson's fifteenth strikeout in one game ties the all-time World Series record held by Sandy Koufax."

—Roger Angell, *Late Innings*

- Why did Gibson want McCarver to return the ball? Write your answer in a sentence. _____

_____

■ Underline all the relative clauses in *A Record Tying Pitch*. Rewrite them as *independent* clauses, following the example given below.

1. *The Tigers by this time were trailing the National League Champion St. Louis Cardinals by a score of 4–0.*

2. _____

3. _____

■ Write a sentence about an exciting moment in sports that you have experienced. _____

For more work on relative clauses, see Review Exercises 2.21.

LESSON 5
Infinitives and Participles:
Verbs Without Tense

. . . .

Infinitives are verb forms that do not have tense and cannot serve as the verb of a sentence. They are always combined with *to*: *to walk, to go, to see.* *Participles* are verb forms that can have tense only when combined with helping verbs. The *present participle* ends in *-ing* (see Lessons 20–23): *Maria is writing, Jo is reading.* The *past participle* sometimes ends in *-d*, sometimes in another form (see Lessons 17 and 18): *Evan had studied. Randi has spoken.*

Fighting Sleep

[1]The *Spirit of St. Louis* is climbing slowly. [2]I push the stick forward—and left to lift the wing, left rudder to stop the turn. [3]I keep my head in the slipstream, breathing deeply. [4]Now I see clearly. [5]Now, my mind and my senses join. [6]The seriousness of the crisis has startled me to awareness. [7]I've finally broken the spell of sleep. [8]I feel as though I were recuperating from a severe illness. [9]When you're suffering from a disease, the time comes when you know the crisis has passed. [10]The fever leaves; a sense of health returns, and you're increasingly able to use your normal mind and body.

—Charles Lindbergh, *The Spirit of St. Louis*

■ Combine these sentences:

Lindbergh was startled awake. The plane did not crash. _____

_____

■ Find the past and present participles, and the infinitives in *Fighting Sleep*. Write them in the columns below, following the examples.

	Present Participle	Past Participle	Infinitive
1.	*is climbing*		
2.			*to lift, to stop*
3.		*has startled*	
4.			
5.			
6.			
7.			

■ Have you ever fallen asleep in class or on some other occasion when you were supposed to be alert? Write a sentence about it. _____

For more work on infinitives and participles, see Review Exercises 7, 16, 30, 39.

LESSON 5a
More Verbs Without Tense

· · · · · · · · · ·

Remember that verbs without tense—infinitives and present and past participles—cannot serve as the verb of a sentence *unless* they are joined with an auxiliary or helping verb. Look for these forms in the next passage:

The Tribe's Values

¹Chee put down the ledger. ²He was being racist. ³He had been thinking like a racist ever since he'd met Janet Pete and fallen in love with her. ⁴He had been thinking that because her name was Pete, because her father was Navajo, her blood somehow would have taught her the ways of the *Diné* and made her one of them. ⁵But only your culture taught you values, and the culture that had formed Janet was blue-blooded, white, Ivy League, chic, irreligious, old-rich Maryland. ⁶And that made it just about as opposite as it could get from the traditional values of his people, which made wealth a symbol for selfishness, and had caused a friend of his to deliberately stop winning rodeo competitions because he was getting unhealthily famous and therefore out of harmony.

—Tony Hillerman, *The Fallen Man*

■ Write a sentence explaining the belief of Chee's people about values.

_____

_____

■ Find the past and present participles and the infinitives in *The Tribe's Values*. Write them in the columns below, including any auxiliary verbs that go with them.

Infinitive	Present Participle	Past Participle
1. _____	*was being*	_____
2. _____	_____	*had been thinking*

	Infinitive	Present Participle	Past Participle
3.	*to stop*		
4.			
5.			

■ Think of a custom or belief that belongs to your family's culture. Write a sentence about it. _____

_____

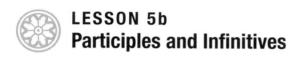

LESSON 5b
Participles and Infinitives

· · · · · · · · ·

   Although infinitives never serve as the verb of a sentence, both past and present participles can do this if they have the help of an auxiliary or helping verb, a part of the verb *to be* or of the verb *to have*. See Lessons 17–18 and 20–22 for more on this topic.

Remember that the forms of *to be* and *to have* are irregular.

The present tense of *to be* is		The present tense of *to have* is	
I am	*we are*	*I have*	*we have*
you are	*you are*	*you have*	*you have*
he, she, it is	*they are*	*he, she, it has*	*they have*

The Story of Hastings

[1]The Battle of Hastings has been fought on paper innumerable times, but strictly military accounts of it have always had to leave some mysteries unsolved. [2]One source of the mysteries is that the early accounts are entirely one-sided. [3]Within the lifetime of the men who fought, nothing was recorded on the English side. [4]So one can only see the English army from the point of view of the men who attacked it: one cannot know what happened inside its ranks. [5]Moreover, the historians on William's side were not writing dry and factual narratives, they were telling exciting stories, each for a receptive audience of his own: Guy for the French, the chaplain for

the Norman admirers of William, and the tapestry designer for the illiterate majority who preferred a strip-cartoon to a written page.

—David Howarth, *1066: The Year of the Conquest*

■ Combine these sentences:

Our knowledge of the Battle of Hastings is one-sided. There are no records from

the English. _____

_____

■ Identify the infinitives and the past and present participles in the above excerpt. Write them below, including the helpers if they are part of the verb.

Past Participle	Present Participle	Infinitive
1. _has been fought_	_____	_____
2. _____	_____	_to leave_
3. _____	_were telling_	_____
4. _____	_____	_____
5. _____	_____	_____

■ Think of an exciting story that you know from history. Write a sentence

about it. _____

_____

For more work on participles, see Review Exercises 7, 16, 30, 39.

YOUR WRITING
Finding a Thesis

Why does virtually every college and university require one or more composition courses of its students? It is quite simply because no matter what we do in life in whatever profession, occupation, or undertaking, we will be called on to write, and to do it in a clear, concise way that will convey significant information to others. A student once challenged me on this, insisting that she knew of a job—dance teacher—that involved no writing. When I asked her what such a teacher does, she replied, "She writes down the steps of the dance. . . ."

Recording dance steps may seem far removed from the kind of composition you are asked to submit in your writing class, but it does confirm the need for writing in your daily life and work. What we do in a writing class can be compared to what we do when learning to play an instrument or mastering a sport like tennis or swimming: we practice, practice, practice.

No one can play a sonata or hit a line drive without many hours of practice. The same is true of writing; behind a first-rate term paper, an impressive annual report, or a persuasive application letter are thoughtful revisions and rewritings.

Where then do we begin if we want to practice the art of writing?

The sentence is the bottom line! It is the basis of all human language. Animals, as you probably know, have ways of communicating: some birds have a call warning of danger, some monkeys can signal with a sound indicating that food is available. But no matter how sophisticated an animal's means of communication may be, we know of none that can produce sentences. We humans are thus unique in being able to communicate in sentences. And we can go on indefinitely producing sentences that have never been spoken before.

It's no wonder, then, with a tool as powerful as the sentence, that all writing should begin with that familiar combination of subject and verb. Of course, not just any old sentence will do. Sometimes you need a sentence that must express in just a few words the entire contents of a composition you are about to write. How can you do that? You do it by saying that someone or something is or does something, and then going on to write a good deal more about *both* the subject and the predicate. For example: *Internet cafes can bring people together.*

Now, a statement like this may seem at first like a contradiction, since we often hear about people being isolated by spending so much time at their computers. But the student who wrote about this managed to find many things to say about people socializing at cybercafes, from sharing meals to playing games.

The point is that she made a statement about something that then called for a good deal more explanation, and that is what you are being asked to do when you're assigned to write a paper.

Whether we call this statement an assertion or, most often, a thesis sentence, without it our papers run the risk of having no structure; we may find ourselves going off in a dozen different directions and, finally, not making a point. And, after all, isn't the reason for writing anything to make a point? Think about that. If your writing doesn't make a point, isn't all the work you put into it in danger of being a waste of time?

What kind of sentence is a thesis statement? First of all, it must be simple. Its purpose is not to tell a story, paint a picture, or show how to do something. But it must say something that you can demonstrate by writing a great deal more about it. Consider, for example, *The computer simplified writing.* You may think immediately of the ease of correcting your work, of the ways it can be saved, and of how professional-looking the printed-out result is.

Write five sentences that could be the thesis statement for a composition. Some of them could be about an invention that has changed peoples' lives.

1. _____

2. _____

3. _____

4. _____

5. _____

Now choose one of these sentences, the one you think you can write much more about. Is it a simple declarative sentence? Does it make one point? Then it can serve as your thesis when we begin the next lesson.

UNIT 11

With a Little Help . . .

Many years ago schools didn't teach English to English-speaking students. After all, the teachers figured, students know their own language; why should they have to be taught it? So instead the students were taught Latin! Now, even though many of our words originally came from Latin, the language itself is almost as different from English in other ways as it can get. For example, every noun, pronoun, and adjective has a different ending, depending on how it is used in a sentence, and they all have to agree with one another. And that's not all! Every verb, in every person, every number, and every tense has a different ending, for a total of 135 verb forms.

Compare all of those with the regular verb endings we have in English: -*s* for the third person singular present tense, -*ed* for the past tense and most past participles, and -*ing* for the present participle. Well, does that mean we can't say as many things in English as we can say in Latin? Far from it. It just means that we have *different* ways of saying them. Helping verbs are one way we do this.

Look at the verbs in the following excerpt:

All afternoon the plane **had soared** through the thin mists of the upper atmosphere, far too high to give clear sight of what lay beneath. Sometimes, at longish intervals, the veil **was torn** for a moment, to display the jagged outline of a peak, or the glint of some unknown stream. The direction **could be determined** roughly from the sun; it was still east, with occasional twists to the north; but where it **had led** depended on the speed of travel, which Conway **could not judge** with any accuracy.

—James Hilton, *Lost Horizon*

More than half of them have a helper, or *auxiliary* to give them a shade of meaning they would not otherwise have. Verbs that are combined with such helpers are called *compound verbs*.

29

LESSON 6
Verbs Combined with *Have*

We use the past tense to indicate that something happened in the past: *Joe saw the light.* Another way of showing that something happened in the past but continues to be true is to write *Joe has seen the light.* This is usually called the present perfect tense. Still another way to indicate a past action is to say that something happened once in the past, but is unlikely to happen again under the same circumstances: *Joe had seen the light.* We call this the past perfect tense.

The present perfect uses these forms of the verb *to have*

I have   *We have*

You have   *You have*

She, he, it has   *They have*

Remember that only the *she, he, it* form has an *-s* at the end.

The past perfect uses these forms of to have

I had   *we had*

you had   *you had*

he, she, it had   *they had*

The Inheritance

[1]The High Lama, after waiting awhile, resumed: "You know, perhaps, that the frequency of these talks has been unusual here. [2]I have waited for you, my son, for quite a long time. [3]I have sat in this room and seen the faces of new-comers, I have looked into their eyes and heard their voices, and always in hope that some day I might find you. [4]My colleagues have grown old and wise, but you who are still young in years are as wise already. [5]My friend, it is not an arduous task that I bequeath, for our order knows only silken bonds. [6]To be gentle and patient, to care for the riches of the mind, to preside in wisdom and secrecy while the storm rages without—it will all be very pleasantly simple for you, and you will doubtless find great happiness."

—James Hilton, *Lost Horizon*

■ Combine these sentences:

The High Lama has chosen his successor. The successor is young but wise.

_____

_____

■ Find the present perfect verbs in *The Inheritance*. Write them below followed by the simple past tense form of the verb, as demonstrated in the example below:

<table>
<tr><th>Present Perfect Tense</th><th>Simple Past Tense</th></tr>
<tr><td align="center">has been</td><td align="center">was</td></tr>
</table>

1. _____   _____

2. _____   _____

3. _____   _____

4. _____   _____

5. _____   _____

■ Identify a character trait that you think indicates wisdom and write a sentence about it. _____

_____

LESSON 6a
Compound Verbs with *Have*

• • • • • • • • •

Present perfect verbs usually indicate something that happens more than once—a continuing action. *I have gone to the beach every weekend this summer. Jake has become a serious student this semester.*

Flying into the Storm

¹Headwinds along the leading edge of the rain band are so strong that it feels as if the helicopter has been blown to a stop. ²Ruvola has no idea what he has run into; all he knows is that he can barely control the aircraft. ³Flying has become as much a question of physical strength as of finesse; he grips the collective with one hand, the joystick with the other, and leans forward to peer through the rain rattling off the windscreen. ⁴Flight manuals bounce around the cockpit and his copilot starts throwing up in the seat next to him. ⁵The pilot starts in on the shutdown procedure, and suddenly the left-hand fuel hose retracts; shutting off the engine has disrupted the air

flow around the wing, and the reel-in mechanism has mistaken that for too much slack. [6]The line has been destroyed by forty-five minutes of desperate refueling attempts.

—Sebastian Junger, *The Perfect Storm*

■ What is the most important quality for a helicopter pilot to have when flying in a storm? Write your answer in a sentence. _____

_____

■ For each of the subjects below, write the compound verb that completes it.

Subject	Compound verb
1. _____ *the helicopter* _____	*has been blown*
2. _____ *he* _____	
3. _____ *flying* _____	
4. _____ *the line* _____	

■ What do you consider an extremely hazardous job—flying a helicopter, washing the windows of a skyscraper, doing police work? Write a sentence about someone you have seen working on a dangerous job. _____

_____

LESSON 6b
More Compound Verbs with *Have*

• • • • • • • • •

The present perfect—*have* plus the *past participle*—is a useful way to talk about an activity that continues over some time, like the study of the universe discussed in the following passage. Often writers will place an adverb between the helping verb and the past participle: *Milo had often called Jenna for help with his homework.*

The Expanding Universe

[1]In the decades that astronomers have debated the fate of the expanding universe—whether it will all end one day in a big crunch, or whether the galaxies will sail apart forever—aficionados of eternal expansion have always been braced by its seemingly endless possibilities for development

and evolution. [2]In the last four years astronomers have reported evidence that the expansion of the universe is not just continuing but is speeding up, under the influence of a mysterious "dark energy," an antigravity that seems to be embedded in space itself. [3]If that is true and the universe goes on accelerating, astronomers say, rather than coasting gently into the night, distant galaxies will eventually be moving apart so quickly that they cannot communicate with one another. [4]In effect, it would be like living in the middle of a black hole that kept getting emptier and colder.

—Dennis Overbye, *The End of Everything*

■ Combine these sentences:

The expansion of the universe may be speeding up. Galaxies will be moving

apart quickly. _____

_____

■ Underline all the compound verbs with *to have* from the excerpt above and write them below, including any adverbs that may divide the verb and the auxiliary.

Helping Verb	**Adverb**	**Verb**
1. _____*have*_____	_____*always*_____	_____*been*_____
2. _____	_____	_____
3. _____	_____	_____

■ Write a sentence about a scientific discovery that you find exciting. It might

be one that took place centuries ago or one that happened recently. _____

_____

For more about helping verbs, see Review Exercises 8, 10, 16, 44.

LESSON 7
Verbs Combined with the Past Tense of *Have*

· · · · · · · · · ·

The past tense of *have*, in all its forms, is *had*. Combined with a verb it becomes the past perfect tense, a tense that shows something happened for the first and only time in the past. For example: *The ship had sailed at dawn.*

Settling in to Shangri-La

[1]By that time the party had settled themselves into something like a daily routine, and with Chang's assistance the boredom was no more acute than on many a planned holiday. [2]They had all become acclimatized to the atmosphere, finding it quite invigorating so long as heavy exertion was avoided. [3]They had learned that the days were warm and the nights cold, that the lamasery was amost completely sheltered from winds, that avalanches on Karakal were most frequent about midday, that the valley grew a good brand of tobacco, that some foods and drinks were more pleasant than others, and that each one of themselves had personal tastes and peculiarities. [4]They had, in fact, discovered as much about each other as four new pupils of a school from which every one else was mysteriously absent.

—James Hilton, *Lost Horizon*

■ What did the travelers find pleasant about Shangri-La? Write your answer in a sentence. _____

_____

■ Find the verbs in the excerpt above that combine the past participle with a form of the auxiliary *have*. Write them below.

Auxiliary	Past Participle
1. _____*had*_____	_____*settled*_____
2. _____	_____
3. _____	_____
4. _____	_____

■ Think about a time you met a new group of friends—the first day of school or at camp. Write a sentence about the experience. _____

_____

LESSON 7a
The Verb *Have* Combined
with the Past Participle

· · · · · · · · · ·

When a story—or *anecdote*—is already being told in the past tense, things that happened even earlier can be told by using a compound verb with a form of the verb *to have*. *The class had a quiz that week. They had had a test every Friday of the semester.*

Adventures of the Round Table

[1]At the feast of Pentecost it was customary for the knights who had been on Table quests to gather again so as to relate their adventures. [2]Arthur had found that this made people keener on fighting in the new way of Right, if they had to tell about it afterwards. [3]Most of them preferred to bring their prisoners with them, as witnesses of their stories. [4]Sir Bedivere came and admitted how he had swapped off his adulterous wife's head. [5]He had brought it with him, and was told to take it to the Pope as a penance. [6]Gawaine came gruffly and told how he had been rescued from Sir Carados. [7]Besides these, there were many people from adventures which we have left out—mainly knights who had yielded to Sir Lancelot when he was disguised as Sir Kay. [8]Kay was inclined to throw his tongue a bit too much, and he had got himself unpopular on account of this. [9]Lancelot had been compelled during the quest to rescue him from three knights who were pursuing him. [10]All these people gave themselves up.

—T. H. White, *The Once and Future King*

- Combine these sentences:

King Arthur held a feast at Pentecost. The knights related their adventures.

_____

- Find the compound verbs formed with a part of *to have* in the passage above and write them below; then write the simple past tense of the verb, as the example shows.

	Compound Verb	**Simple Past Tense**
1.	*had found*	*found*
2.		
3.		

Compound Verb	Simple Past Tense
4. _____	_____
5. _____	_____

■ What is your favorite kind of adventure story: espionage, or police thriller, or science fiction or something else? Write a sentence explaining why you enjoy this type of writing. _____

_____

LESSON 7b
More Verbs with *Have*

A compound verb and its helper are often separated by one or more adverbs, as in this example: *Sonya has definitely decided to major in biology.*

Fred's Failures

[1]His failure in passing his examination had made his accumulation of college debts the more unpardonable by his father, and there had been an unprecedented storm at home. [2]Mr. Vincy had sworn that if he had anything more of that sort to put up with, Fred should turn out and get his living how he could; and he had never yet quite recovered his good-humoured tone to his son, who had especially enraged him by saying at this stage of things that he did not want to be a clergyman, and would rather not "go on with that." [3]Fred was conscious that he would have been yet more severely dealt with if his family as well as himself had not secretly regarded him as Mr. Featherstone's heir; that old gentleman's pride in him, and apparent fondness for him, serving in the stead of more exemplary conduct.

—George Eliot, *Middlemarch*

■ Combine these sentences:

Fred's failures were not very severely dealt with. His family expected him to be

Mr. Featherstone's heir. _____

_____

■ Identify the compound verbs with *have* in this excerpt. If there are any adverbs between the auxiliary and the verb, write them in the appropriate space, as shown in the example.

Verb	**Adverb(s)**
had recovered	*never yet quite*
1. _____	_____
2. _____	_____
3. _____	_____
4. _____	_____
5. _____	_____
6. _____	_____

■ Think of an examination you were particularly worried about passing. Write a sentence explaining why it was so important to you. _____

_____

For more about compound verbs, see Review Exercises 8, 10, 16, 44.

LESSON 8
Verb Combinations with *Be* and Its Forms as Helpers

· · · · · · · · ·

The verb *to be* is very irregular. In the present tense its forms are as follows

I am	*we are*
you are	*you are*
he, she, it is	*they are*

In the past tense the forms of *to be* are as follows

I was	*we were*
you were	*you were*
she, he, it was	*they were*

The Departure

[1]All the time, though he hardly heard him, Mallinson was chattering about the journey. [2]How strange that their long argument should have ended thus in action, that this secret sanctuary should be forsaken by one who had found in it such happiness! [3]Now, at that moment, it was farewell. [4]Mallinson, whom the steep ascent had kept silent for a time, gasped out: "Good man, we are doing fine—carry on!" [5]Conway smiled, but did not reply; he was already preparing the rope for the knife-edge traverse. [6]Towards dawn they crossed the divide, unchallenged by sentinels, even if there were any; though it occurred to Conway that the route, in the true spirit, might only be moderately well watched. [7]Then all was as Mallinson had foretold; they found the men ready for them, sturdy fellows in furs and sheepskins, crouching under the gale and eager to begin the journey to Tatsien-Fu—eleven hundred miles eastward on the China border.

—James Hilton, *Lost Horizon*

■ Combine these sentences:

The two men must cross the precipice. They want to reach the guides for their

journey. _____

_____

■ Find the verbs in the excerpt above that combine an auxiliary, or helper, part of the verb *to be*, with a present participle and write them below, as shown in the example.

Auxiliary	**Verb**
was	*chattering*
1. _____	_____
2. _____	_____
3. _____	_____

■ Write a sentence about a trip you have taken that involved some danger.

_____

LESSON 8a
The Present Participle with *Be*

. . . .

This is a useful way to show that an action goes on for a period of time rather than just happening and stopping. For example, *Lucia looks out the window* does not provide as much information as *Lucia is looking out the window all day instead of studying.*

Birds in Flight

¹It was a late hour on a cold, wind-bitten autumn day when I climbed a great hill spined like a dinosaur's back and tried to take my bearings. ²The tumbled waste fell away in waves in all directions. ³Blue air was darkening into purple along the bases of the hills. ⁴I shifted my knapsack, heavy with the petrified bones of long-vanished creatures, and studied my compass. ⁵I wanted to be out of there by nightfall, and already the sun was going sullenly down in the west. ⁶It was then that I saw the flight coming on. ⁷It was moving like a little close-knit body of black specks that danced and darted and closed again. ⁸It was pouring from the north and heading toward me with the undeviating relent-lessness of a compass needle. ⁹It streamed through the shadows rising out of

monstrous gorges. ¹⁰It rushed over towering pinnacles in the red light of the sun, or momentarily sank from sight within their shade. ¹¹Across that desert of eroding clay and wind-worn stone they came with a faint wild twittering that filled all the air about me as those tiny living bullets hurtled past into the night.

—Loren Eiseley, *The Judgment of the Birds*

■ Why does the writer use *bullets* as an analogy for flying birds in this passage? Write your answer in a sentence. _____

_____

■ Write below the compound verbs in this excerpt formed with the auxiliary *to be* and the present participle. <u>Note that not all words ending in *-ing* are verbs in this excerpt</u>. Then write a sentence using the simple past tense of the verb, as shown in the example.

<table>
<tr><td align="center">**Verb**</td><td align="center">**Sentence**</td></tr>
<tr><td>1. _____ *was darkening* _____</td><td>*The sky darkened in the evening.*</td></tr>
<tr><td>2. _____</td><td>_____</td></tr>
<tr><td>3. _____</td><td>_____</td></tr>
<tr><td>4. _____</td><td>_____</td></tr>
</table>

■ Have you ever watched a flight of birds heading south for the winter? Write a sentence explaining what they reminded you of. _____

_____

LESSON 8b
More Verbs with Present Participles

• • • • • • • •

As with past participles, compound verbs with present participles can be divided by an adverb. For example, *Greg was intently studying his Sociology notes.*

Never Alone

¹It was a bright cold day in April, and the clocks were striking thirteen. ²Winston Smith, his chin nuzzled into his breast in an effort to escape the vile wind, slipped quickly through the glass doors of Victory Mansions

though not quickly enough to prevent a swirl of gritty dust from entering along with him. ³Outside, even through the shut windowpane, the world looked cold. ⁴Down in the street little eddies of wind were whirling dust and torn paper into spirals, and though the sun was shining and the sky a harsh blue, there seemed to be no color in anything except the posters that were plastered everywhere. ⁵The black-mustachio'd face gazed down from every commanding corner. ⁶There was one on the house front immediately opposite. ⁷BIG BROTHER IS WATCHING YOU the caption said, while the dark eyes looked deep into Winston's own. ⁸Behind Winston's back the voice from the telescreen was still babbling away about pig iron and the overfulfillment of the Ninth Three-Year Plan.

—George Orwell, *Nineteen Eighty-Four*

■ Combine these sentences:

There was a telescreen in every room. All of a person's movements were

watched. _____

_____

■ Underline the compound verbs in the passage above, then write them on the lines below. Be sure to choose only verbs formed with *to be* and *-ing*. For each verb write a sentence using the simple present tense of that verb.

	Verb	**Sentence**
1.	*were striking*	*The clock strikes the hour.*
2.		
3.		
4.		
5.		

■ Think about a poster you have seen that surprised or frightened you. Write a sentence explaining why it had this effect. _____

_____

For more about present participles, see Review Exercises 7, 16, 30, 39.

LESSON 9
Helpers Without Tense

A large group of helping verbs, sometimes called *modal auxiliaries*, is used to show that an action may or may not take place. These are words like *can, could, may, might, must, ought, should*, and *would*. Unlike other verbs and helpers, they have no endings for tense or number.

I can	*We can*	*I might*	*We might*
You can	*You can*	*You might*	*You might*
He, she, it can	*They can*	*She, he, it might*	*They might*

Here's an example of a modal auxiliary used in a sentence: *Juanita may play the oboe.*

The First View

[1]To Conway, seeing it first, it might have been a vision fluttering out of that solitary rhythm in which lack of oxygen had encompassed all his faculties. [2]A group of colored pavilions clung to the mountainside with none of the grim deliberation of a Rhineland castle, but rather with the chance delicacy of flower-petals impaled upon a crag. [3]Beyond that, in a dazzling pyramid, soared the snow slopes of Karakal. [4]It might well be, Conway thought, the most terrifying mountainscape in the world, and he imagined the immense stress of snow and glacier against which the rock functioned as a gigantic retaining wall. [5]Someday, perhaps, the whole mountain would split, and a half of Karakal's icy splendor come toppling into the valley. [6]He wondered if the slightness of the risk combined with its fearfulness might even be found agreeably stimulating. [7]Hardly less an enticement was the downward prospect, for the mountain wall continued to drop, nearly perpendicularly, into a cleft that could only have been the result of some cataclysm in the far past.

—James Hilton, *Lost Horizon*

■ What is terrifying about Conway's first look at Karakal? Write your answer in a sentence. _____

_____

■ Several of the compound verbs in this excerpt are formed with modal auxiliaries. Some have more than one helping verb. Find them, then write them on the lines below, as shown in the example.

Modal Auxiliary	Other Auxiliary (if there is one)	Verb
1. *might*	*have*	*been*
2.		
3.		
4.		
5.		

■ Think of the most exciting natural wonder view you have ever seen—a mountain, an ocean, or some other scenic place. Write a sentence explaining how you felt when you first saw it. _____

_____

LESSON 9a
More Helpers Without Tense

Very often helpers form contractions with their verbs. An interesting example is *would have*, which becomes *would've*. Sometimes this is mistakenly written *would of* because that is what it sounds like. Be careful about this.

The Umpire's Brush

[1]Probably the most important piece of equipment the umpire has is the whisk brush which he uses to clean home plate. [2]These brushes are not easy to find in stores because they have to be wide, but must have very short handles so they will fit into a back pocket. [3]Brushes last for many years and umpires become very emotional about them. [4]If an umpire can't find his brush before a big game he might go crazy. [5]Gugie had a brush that should be in the Hall of Fame. [6]He must've used it for twenty seasons and by the time I worked with him it only had a few stumpy bristles left on it; because of this it took him a long, long time to clean the plate. [7]He'd be scratching the dirt off home and the batter or catcher would suggest he buy a new brush. [8]To Gugie this was like insulting his best friend.

—Ron Luciano, *The Umpire Strikes Back*

■ Combine these sentences:

Umpires are very attached to their whisk brushes. The right kind is hard to find.

_____

■ In the excerpt above underline the verbs formed with modal helpers and write them below. Be sure to note that some of them are contractions, like *he'd be* for *he would be.*

	Helper	**Verb**
1.	*must*	*have*
2.		
3.		
4.		
5.		
6.		
7.		

■ Write a sentence about a sporting event you attended at which your favorite team was defeated at the last minute. _____

_____

LESSON 9b
Helpers and Their Verbs

• • • • • • • • •

Unlike helping verbs that are combined with past and present participles, those without tense are combined with the infinitive form of the verb, the form without any changing endings. *To go, to look, to walk, to understand, to seek* are just a few examples of the infinitive form. For example, *we want to take the bus to the game.*

After the Concentration Camp

[1]Even though conditions such as lack of sleep, insufficient food and various mental stresses may suggest that the inmates of concentration camps were bound to react in certain ways, in the final analysis it becomes clear that the

sort of person the prisoner became was the result of an inner decision, and not the result of camp influences alone. [2]Fundamentally, therefore, any man can, even under such circumstances, decide what shall become of him— mentally and spiritually. [3]He may retain his human dignity even in a concentration camp. [4]I became acquainted with martyrs whose behavior in camp, whose suffering and death, bore witness to the fact that the last inner freedom cannot be lost. [5]It is this spiritual freedom—which cannot be taken away—that makes life meaningful and purposeful.

—Viktor E. Frankl, *Man's Search for Meaning*

■ What example does the writer give of inner freedom? Write your answer in a sentence. _____

_____

■ Underline the modal helpers in the passage above. Use them to complete the sentences below.

1. To do well in school one ___*must*___ study.

2. We _____ decide to go to the ball game.

3. Matt _____ take us in his car.

4. _____ we pack a picnic lunch?

■ Think of a proverb or wise saying that you hear people using frequently, like *Early to bed, early to rise. . . .* Write a sentence about the usefulness of that statement. _____

_____

For more about helping verbs, see Review Exercises 8, 10, 16, 44.

L E S S O N   1 0
A Special Kind of Helper

Two very familiar helping verbs, *shall* and *will*, combine with the verb to form the future tense. Unlike many other languages, English has no ending to indicate that a verb is in the future tense. Instead it uses these helpers to show that an action is to take place at a later time: *Sam will arrive on the ten o'clock train.*

A New Dark Age

[1]"The Dark Ages that are to come will cover the whole world in a single pall; there will be neither escape nor sanctuary, save such as are too secret to be found or too humble to be noticed. [2]And Shangri-La may hope to be both of these. [3]The airman bearing loads of death to the great cities will not pass our way, and if by chance he should he may not consider us worth a bomb. [4]I believe that you will live through the storm. [5]And after, through the long age of desolation, you may still live, growing older and wiser and more patient. [6]You will conserve the fragrance of our history and add to it the touch of your own mind. [7]You will welcome the stranger and teach him the rule of age and wisdom; and one of these strangers, it may well be, will succeed you when you are yourself very old. [8]Beyond that, my vision weakens, but I see, at a great distance, a new world stirring in the ruins, stirring clumsily but in hopefulness, seeking its lost and legendary treasures. [9]And they will all be here, my son, hidden behind the mountains in the valley of Blue Moon."

—James Hilton, *Lost Horizon*

■ Combine these sentences:

The Dark Age will end. The new world will seek the lost treasures. _____

_____

■ The excerpt above is predicting things to happen in the future. Find the future tense verbs and write them below, as shown in the example.

Auxiliary	Verb
1. *will*	*cover*
2. _____	_____
3. _____	_____
4. _____	_____

Auxiliary	Verb
5. _____	_____
6. _____	_____
7. _____	_____
8. _____	_____

▪ Write a sentence explaining one of the qualities you would include if you could design an ideal world. _____

_____

LESSON 10a
Future Tense Verbs

• • • • • • • • •

The future tense is most often expressed by the helping verb *will* and the simple present tense form of the verb: *will see, will talk, will remember, will swim.* For example, *Commencement will take place next Sunday.*

The Knight's Vigil

[1]What happens when you are made a knight? Only a lot of fuss. [2]You will have to undress him and put him in a bath hung with rich hangings, and then two experienced knights will turn up—probably Sir Ector will get hold of old Grummore and King Pellinore—and they will both sit on the edge of the bath and give him a long lecture about the ideals of chivalry, such as they are. [3]When they have done, they will pour some of the bath water over him and sign him with the cross, and then you will have to conduct him into a clean bed to get dry. [4]Then you dress him up as a hermit and take him off to the chapel, and there he stays awake all night, watching his armour and saying prayers. [5]People say it is lonely and terrible for him in this vigil, but it is not at all lonely really, because the vicar and the man who sees to the candles and an armed guard and probably you as well, as his esquire, will have to sit up with him at the same time.

—T. H. White, *The Sword in the Stone*

▪ Why is it necessary for the knight-to-be to have a lecture about the ideals of chivalry? Write your answer in a sentence. _____

_____

- Underline the future tense verbs in *The Knight's Vigil* and write them below.

1. _____*will have*_____ 4. _____

2. _____ 5. _____

3. _____

- Did you ever have to go through a test or initiation to join a club or other organization? Write a sentence about what happened. _____

_____

LESSON 10b
More Future Tense Verbs

. . . .

One of the common contractions of verbs adds *'ll* to the subject, as in *The class'll start later* or *We'll see you tomorrow.*

A Friendlier World

[1]If you don't like people, put up with them as well as you can. [2]Don't try to love them; you can't, you'll only strain yourself. [3]But try to tolerate them. [4]On the basis of that tolerance a civilized future may be built. [5]For what it will most need is the negative virtues: not being huffy, touchy, irritable, revengeful. [6]I have lost all faith in positive militant ideals; they can so seldom be carried out without thousands of human beings getting maimed or imprisoned. [7]Phrases like "I will purge this nation," "I will clean up this city," terrify and disgust me. [8]They might not have mattered when the world was emptier; they are horrifying now, when one nation is mixed up with another, when one city cannot be organically separated from its neighbours. [9]Tolerance, I believe, will be imperative after the establishment of peace. [10]It is wanted in the street, in the office, at the factory, and it is wanted above all between classes, races, and nations.

—E. M. Forster, *Tolerance*

- Combine these sentences:

We don't have to like people to tolerate them. We can live peacefully only with

tolerance. _____

_____

■ For each of the subjects below, write its future tense verb from the passage above.

Subject	Verb
1. You	*will strain*
2. It	
3. I	
4. Tolerance	

■ What do you consider the most important quality to ensure that people in a group get along with each other? Write your answer in a sentence. _____

LESSON 11
The Many Forms of *Do*

· · · · · · · · ·

The verb *to do*, like *to have* and *to be*, can sometimes be a helper. *Does* Joey play hockey? I *do* like ice cream.

Do is also used with *not* to turn a verb into a negative. A positive sentence, *We listen to the radio in the car*, becomes negative with the addition of *do not: We do not listen to the radio in the car.*

Lo-Tsen

[1]There was a fragrance about Lo-Tsen that communicated itself to his own emotions, kindling the embers to a glow that did not burn, but merely warmed. [2]And suddenly then he realized that Shangri-La and Lo-Tsen were quite perfect and that he did not wish for more than to stir a faint and eventual response in all that stillness. [3]For years his passions had been like a nerve that the world jarred on; now at last the aching was soothed, and he could yield himself to love that was neither a torment nor a bore. [4]As he passed by the lotus-pool at night he sometimes pictured her in his arms, but the sense of time washed over the vision, calming him to an infinite and tender reluctance. [6]He did not think he had ever been so happy, even in the years of his life before the great barrier of the War.

—James Hilton, *Lost Horizon*

■ Combine these sentences:

Passion can cause an ache. His love for Lo-Tsen was soothing. _____

_____

■ Rewrite each of the sentences below to make it negative, as in the example shown.

1. Alana swims on Tuesdays.   *Alana does not swim on Tuesdays.*

2. Students like to take exams.   _____

3. We lost the map of the campus.   _____

4. Mike travels during the summer.   _____

5. Some flowers bloom in the fall.   _____

■ Think of a romantic novel you have read or movie you have seen. Write a sentence explaining what you like about it. _____

_____

LESSON 11a
Negatives with *Do*

· · · · · · · · ·

Most negatives are formed with *do* as a helper followed by *not* and the infinitive form of the verb. Example: *Jasmine does not enjoy horror movies.*

A Royal Marriage

[1]A charming lady of twenty-nine may fascinate a youth of eighteen, but after fifteen years their marriage will be severely tested. [2]That was the fate of the marriage between Henry and Eleanor. [3]To begin with they were excellent friends. [4]The evidence suggests that though the royal couple did not meet very often, when they were together they were passionately in love. [5]Even the difficult question of the government of Aquitaine did not make a breach between them. [6]In her private life Eleanor was more discreet as Queen of England than she had been when Queen of France; probably because her lusty second husband satisfied her as the pious Louis could not. [7]Henry's casual infidelities were no more than might be expected from any King; it does not seem that Eleanor minded them, since the unimportant harlots concerned possessed neither social position nor political power. [8]It is significant that in later years Rosamund Clifford was a lady of good family, and that the King lived with her openly. [9]For the first time in her second marriage Queen Eleanor was faced with a genuine rival, instead of a harlot who might be ignored.

—Alfred Duggan, *Devil's Brood: The Angevin Family*

■ Combine these sentences:

The King had mistresses of low rank. The Queen did not mind. _____

_____

■ Identify the negative statements in *A Royal Marriage*. Write them below.

Auxiliary	Negative	Verb
1. _____did_____	_____not_____	_____meet_____
2. _____	_____	_____
3. _____	_____	_____

■ Do people today care about social rank as much as they once did? Write a sentence giving the reason for your answer. _____

_____

LESSON 11b
More About *Do* as a Helper

. . . .

Do and *not* together form a negative, but *do* can also be combined with the verb to intensify its meaning, as in *Professor Jones does believe in a lot of homework*. It also helps ask a question: *Do you know the teacher's name?* And, of course, it can also be a simple verb: *Antoine does his homework every day*.

Who's the Boss?

[1]The producer said, "The first thing I always do when I arrive on my set is fire someone." [2]I was stunned. [3]The idea that firing someone could be regarded as either fun or strategic had never occurred to me. [4]Since I don't go to such extreme measures, I wondered, do my crews think I'm a wuss? [5]Absolutely not. [6]Do they know who's boss? [7]Absolutely. [8]Somehow, although I am a short female who does not fire people the first week without cause, my crews *still* know that I am the boss because I make it my business to know what they're doing. [9]And my reputation, for better or for worse, precedes me. [10]This need to scream, berate, fire a lowly employee, demonize, or terrorize is fake power. [11]Most powerful people don't need to coerce; their mere presence is coercive.

—Lynda Obst, *Hello, He Lied and Other Truths from the Hollywood Trenches*

■ Why would a movie producer want to fire someone the first day of filming? Write your answer in a sentence. _____

_____

■ The passage above uses *do* to form a negative or to ask a question, and as a simple verb. Find each of these uses and write them below, indicating which category they are in.

	Verb	Function
1.	I do	simple verb
2.		
3.		
4.		
5.		
6.		
7.		

■ Misusing power is also called *bullying*. Write a sentence that illustrates an example of bullying. _____

_____

For more on *do* as a helper, see Review Exercises 13, 35.

YOUR WRITING
Developing the Thesis

So now you've written your thesis sentence. You've checked to be sure it is a statement that makes a point. You know there is much more to be said about it. What comes next? Why, more sentences, of course.

And here's where the real challenge comes in. You must be sure that these sentences are about, and *only* about, the statement you've made in your thesis. This is when it's easy to get off the track of what you want to say, and once you've lost your way it's not easy to find it again. So let's take an example of sticking to the point by making a statement about preserving natural resources.

Wasting energy threatens our sources of power.

Now, there are three ideas in that sentence that will have to be in *all* the sentences that follow although not necessarily in the same words: (1) *wasting energy*, (2) *sources of power*, and (3) *threat*. Ways in which we waste energy are easy to think of; they can be anything from leaving lights on in empty rooms to driving cars that use a lot of gas. The same is true of sources of power, from coal and oil to nuclear energy. What are some of the sentences we can write as follow-ups to our thesis, the sentences that will become *topic sentences* for the paragraphs that follow?

Leaving lights on in empty rooms can make power plants run out of the fuel they need to produce electricity.

Throwing out plastic containers instead of recycling them means manufacturers will need more of the petroleum products that are their raw materials.

Driving to the movies instead of riding a bike uses up gasoline.

The thing to notice about each of these sentences is that they give an instance of *wasting energy* while posing a *threat* of diminishing our *sources of power*. If your thesis is *Wasting energy threatens our sources of power*, however, you will have little chance of producing a successful paper by following it with, *SUVs use a lot of gas, but the Explorer is an awesome car*. What's wrong with the sentence about the Explorer? First, only a part of the sentence is about saving energy. Next, we're not comparing cars but looking at practices that waste power. The three key ideas—*waste*, *threat*, and *power*—aren't there.

In the spaces below, write a thesis statement followed by five sentences that give specific instances of the thesis. You may be tempted to say at this point, "Why all this endless writing of sentences? I want to write something more substantial than that!" The reason is the same as that for practicing a swimming stroke over and over, or a tennis serve, or a guitar chord: to do anything well requires practice, and practice by its very nature is repetitious.

So, think of this not as producing polished prose but as a step on the way to achieving that aim.

Thesis Statement _____

_____

1. _____

2. _____

3. _____

4. _____

5. _____

UNIT III

Endings and Their Meaning

Nearly a thousand years ago the people of England lived in great fear of sea raiders from Scandinavia called Vikings. Some of the Vikings, though, proved to be not so fierce after they invaded the country. They settled down beside the English and became neighbors. In fact, they got along rather easily because the English and Scandinavian, or *Old Norse,* languages were much alike, both coming from an old form of German. So where the English said *brothor* for *brother* and *thrie* for *three*, the Old Norse said *brothir* and *thrir.*

The biggest difference between the two languages is easy to spot: in the endings of the words. Such endings were used at that time not to show what a word meant, but how it was used in a sentence: perhaps as a subject or an object, or to show possession.

Eventually the Vikings and the English compromised, choosing one or another form of word ending to serve for both languages, and sometimes dispensing with endings altogether. Today English has evolved into a language with a fixed set of endings, endings that are essential to our understanding one another clearly.

Many of the old endings fell into disuse and were lost. A few remained in either English or Old Norse: in English the third-person singular present tense ended in *-th*, the Norse in *-s.* Eventually the *-s* prevailed and today we say *she does* instead of *she doth.* So, now we have in English far fewer word endings that have meaning, but failure to use them, especially when we write, can make for a good deal of confusion. There is a big difference between "I am excit*ed*" and "I am excit*ing.*"

It certainly comes as no surprise to hear that parts of words have meaning; you may even know that these parts are called *morphemes.* You have probably learned about *prefixes*, letters before the root word, and *suffixes*, letters that come after, and the ways they change meanings. But have you ever

57

thought about how the simple letter -*s* changes the meaning of the word it is added to? It can, in fact, turn an apple into two apples or six hundred apples. It can change a person, *her*, into something belonging to a person, *hers*. What -*s* can do to change a word's meaning will be the matter of our next lesson.

LESSON 12
The *-s* Ending and Its Uses: Singular and Plural Nouns

· · · · · · · · ·

We all know that one person, place, or thing requires a *singular* form and that more than one person, place, or thing requires the *plural*. Most nouns show that they are plural by adding *-s*, for example, *one shoe/two shoes*, *one book/many books*, *one car/a parking lot full of cars*.

Rachel Carson's *The Sea Around Us*, published in 1951, awakened interest in the environment and led to the activism of today. Here are some examples of her writing, which uses endings that have meaning.

The Sea's Origins

[1]Beginnings are apt to be shadowy, and so it is with the beginnings of that great mother of life, the sea. [2]Many people have debated how and when the earth got its ocean, and it is not surprising that their explanations do not always agree. [3]For the plain and inescapable truth is that no one was there to see, and in the absence of eyewitness accounts there is bound to be a certain amount of disagreement. [4]So if I tell here the story of how the young planet Earth acquired an ocean, it must be a story pieced together from many sources and containing whole chapters the details of which we can only imagine. [5]The story is founded on the testimony of the earth's most ancient rocks, which were young when the earth was young; on other evidence written on the face of the earth's satellite, the moon; and on hints contained in the history of the sun and the whole universe of star-filled space.

—Rachel Carson, *The Sea Around Us*

■ Why do we need the evidence of heavenly bodies to learn about the beginnings of the sea? Write your answer in a sentence. _____

_____

■ Go back and look at all the words in the excerpt above that end in *-s*; if the *-s* makes a singular noun plural—*shoe, shoes*—write the word below:

1. _____*Beginnings*_____   6. _____

2. _____   7. _____

3. _____   8. _____

4. _____   9. _____

5. _____

■ Write a sentence about something we can learn from observing nature.

_____

LESSON 12a
More Plural Nouns

Although most plural nouns end in *-s* or *-es*, a few, like *children*, have irregular endings or even no plural ending at all, like *sheep*. You will find more about these in Lesson 41.

The Dance

¹Reality was also Binetou, who went from night club to night club. ²She would arrive draped in a long, costly garment, a gold belt, a present from Modou on the birth of their first child, shining round her waist. ³Her shoes tapped on the ground, announcing her presence. ⁴The waiters would move aside and bow respectfully in the hope of a royal tip. ⁵The couples held each other or danced apart depending on the music, sometimes slow and coaxing, sometimes vigorous and wild. ⁶When the trumpet blared out, backed by the frenzy of the drums, the young dancers, excited and untiring, would stamp, jump and caper about, shouting their joy. ⁷Modou would try to follow suit. ⁸The harsh lights betrayed him to the unpitying sarcasm of some of them, who called him a "cradle-snatcher." ⁹What did it matter! ¹⁰He had Binetou in his arms. ¹¹He was happy.

—Mariama Bâ, *So Long a Letter*

■ How is Binetou treated at the night club? Write your answer in a sentence.

_____

■ Find the plural nouns that end in *-s*. Write them below, followed by their singular form, as the example shows.

1. ___*shoes/shoe*___   5. _____

2. _____   6. _____

3. _____   7. _____

4. _____

▪ Write a sentence about a party at which you had a wonderful time.

_____

LESSON 12b
More Plurals with -s

· · · · · · · · ·

Most nouns that end in -y change their endings to -ies in the plural. _Parties, butterflies,_ and _centuries_ are examples.

Gandhi's Travels

[1]For seven months Gandhi toured the countryside in torrid, humid weather, moving in hot, crowded, dirty trains and addressing mass assemblies of a hundred thousand or more, who, in those premicrophone days, could only hope to be reached by his spirit. [2]Clamoring multitudes everywhere demanded a view of the Mahatma; it hallowed them. [3]The inhabitants of one place sent word that if his train did not halt at their tiny station they would lie down on the tracks and be run over by it. [4]The train did stop, and when Gandhi, roused out of a deep sleep, appeared, the crowd, theretofore boisterous, sank to their knees on the railway platform and wept. [5]During those strenuous seven months of travel, all his meals, three a day, were the same and consisted of sixteen ounces of goat's milk, three slices of toast, two oranges, and a score of grapes or raisins. [6]They filled him with energy.

—Louis Fischer, _Gandhi: His Life and Message for the World_

▪ Combine these sentences:

Gandhi ate very lightly. His meals filled him with energy. _____

_____

▪ Find the plural nouns in the passage above. Choose five of them and write a sentence using the singular form. Then write the plural word from the passage.

Sentence	**Plural Word**
It took me a month to finish Chapter 10 in the textbook.	
1. _____	_months_
2. _____	_____

Sentence	Plural Word
3. _____	_____
4. _____	_____
5. _____	_____
6. _____	_____

▪ Think of a meal you had while traveling. Write a sentence explaining what was good or bad about it. _____

_____

For more on plural endings, see Review Exercises 23, 25, 31.

LESSON 13
The -s Ending and Its Uses: The Third-Person Exception

• • • • • • • • •

Unlike many languages, English has only one verb ending that changes in the present tense to agree with the subject, the third person singular. That means the subject can be *she, he,* or *it,* or any noun for which these pronouns can be substituted. For example: *Tonya goes to class. She goes to class.*

Life in the Sea

[1]Sea life in the tropics, then, is intense, vivid, and infinitely varied. [2]In the cold seas it proceeds at a pace slowed by the icy water in which it exists, but the mineral richness of these waters (largely a result of seasonal overturn and consequent mixing) makes possible the enormous abundance of the forms that inhabit them. [3]For a good many years it has been said categorically that the total productivity of the colder temperate and polar seas is far greater than the tropical. [4]Now it is becoming plain that this is not necessarily true. [5]In many tropical and subtropical waters, there are areas where the sheer abundance of life rivals the Grand Banks or the Barents Sea or any antarctic whaling ground. [6]These are the places, as in the Humboldt Current or the Benguela Current, where upwelling of cold, mineral-laden water from deeper layers of the sea provides the fertilizing elements to sustain the great food chains.

—Rachel Carson, *The Sea Around Us*

■ Combine these sentences:

It was once thought that cold seas were more productive. Many tropical waters

have an abundance of life. _____

_____

■ Look for the words in the excerpt above that end in -*s*. If they are present tense verbs, decide whether they agree with a third person subject—*he, she, it*—and write them below together with their subjects.

1. _____*it proceeds*_____   3. _____

2. _____   4. _____

5. _____   8. _____

6. _____   9. _____

7. _____   10. _____

▪ Have you visited a body of water—seashore, lakeside, riverbank—where you had a particularly good time? Write a sentence describing what happened.

_____

LESSON 13a
Another Look at Person

Grammatically, the *first person* is *I*, the speaker, and the *second person* is *you*, the one spoken to. The *third person* is the one spoken about, that is, any person or thing for whose name *he, she,* or *it* can be substituted. For example, *The marathon runner trains by running. She trains by running every morning.*

The Crook's Conscience

[1]Both Raffles and Bunny, of course, are devoid of religious belief, and they have no real ethical code, merely certain rules of behavior which they observe semi-instinctively. [2]Raffles and Bunny, after all, are gentlemen, and such standards as they do have are not to be violated. [3]Certain things are "not done," and the idea of doing them hardly arises. [4]Raffles will not, for example, abuse hospitality. [5]He will commit a burglary in a house where he is staying as a guest, but the victim must be a fellow-guest and not the host. [6]He will not commit murder, and he avoids violence wherever possible and prefers to carry out his robberies unarmed. [7]He regards friendship as sacred, and is chivalrous though not moral in his relations with women. [8]He will take extra risks in the name of "sportsmanship," and sometimes even for aesthetic reasons. [9]And, above all, he is intensely patriotic.

—George Orwell, *Raffles and Miss Blandish*

▪ Why does Raffles prefer to carry out his burglaries unarmed? Write your answer in a sentence. _____

_____

■ Find the present tense verbs with third person singular subjects in the excerpt above. Write them below, then write them with a plural noun for the subject, as shown in the example.

1. _____*idea arises*_____   _____*students arise*_____

2. _____   _____

3. _____   _____

4. _____   _____

5. _____   _____

■ Have you ever seen a movie comedy with bumbling burglars? Write a sentence about why they are funny. _____

_____

LESSON 13b
The Present Tense—Subjects and Verbs

· · · · · · · · ·

While languages like Spanish and French have different endings for singular and plural verbs and for those in which the subject is *I* or *you*, English changes the verb ending only for singular verbs with *she, he,* or *it* as subject: *the clock* (or *it*) *shows the date and the time.*

Mountain Climber

[1]As Jeff Mathy hunkers down in base camp on Mount Everest, waiting through the days before his attempt at the summit later this month, he resides in a land full of dreams. [2]Mathy is well on his way to becoming the youngest person to reach the seven summits, the highest mountains on each continent, of which he has climbed five. [3]It is an adventure now financed by an American corporation to the tune of about $150,000. [4]A tea company made sense because that is what mountain climbers drink, believing it keeps them better hydrated than water. [5]Sherpas, the Himalayan natives who live at these extreme altitudes, drink it almost exclusively. [6]But no one knows why. [7]The climb will take two months from start to finish. [8]Camp 4, at 26,000 feet, is the last before the summit, which they should attempt to reach in late May.

—Lynn Zinser, *Mount Everest Is the Highest, But Not the Only One to Climb*

▪ What is Jeff Mathy's climbing goal? Write your answer in a sentence.

_____

▪ Look for the present tense verbs above with third person singular subjects. Write each of them with a plural subject, as shown in the example below.

1. _____*hunkers*_____   _____*the climbers hunker*_____

2. _____   _____

3. _____   _____

4. _____   _____

5. _____   _____

6. _____   _____

▪ What adventure have you undertaken? Write a sentence explaining what made it an adventure. _____

_____

For more about endings in -s, see Review Exercises 23, 25, 31.

LESSON 14
The -s Ending and Its Uses: Possessives

· · · · · · · · · ·

A *possessive* is a word used to indicate that something belongs to some-one. It is written as -'s. Wait. Did you look carefully at that? For the possessive of nouns we put an apostrophe, an upside down comma, before the -s that ends the noun. *Cella's* is a possessive noun. There is *no* apostrophe in posses-sive pronouns like *hers, his,* and *its.* See Lesson 50 for more about this.

How Climates Change

[1]Pettersson's fertile mind evolved a theory of climatic variation. [2]Marshalling scientific, historic, and literary evidence, he showed that there are alternat-ing periods of mild and severe climates which correspond to the long-period cycles of the oceanic tides. [3]The world's most recent period of maximum tides, and most rigorous climate, occurred about 1433, its effect being felt, however, for several centuries before and after that year. [4]During the latest period of benevolent climate, snow and ice were little known on the coast of Europe and in the seas about Iceland and Greenland. [5]Then the Vikings sailed freely over northern seas, monks went back and forth between Ireland and "Thyle" or Iceland, and there was easy intercourse between Great Britain and the Scandinavian countries. [6]Eric the Red "came from the sea to land at the middle glacier. [7]The first year he wintered on Erik's Island." [8]This was probably in the year 984.

—Rachel Carson, *The Sea Around Us*

▪ Why did the Vikings make their voyages in the tenth century? Write your answer in a sentence. _____

_____

▪ Look again at the -s endings in the excerpt above. Pick out those nouns and pronouns that are possessives and write them here along with what it is they possess.

1. _____*Pettersson's mind*_____   3. _____

2. _____   4. _____

■ Think of a winter you can remember that was colder than usual. Write a sentence about how it affected you. _____

_____

LESSON 14a
Plural Possessives

. . . .

When a plural noun ending in *-s* is also a possessive, the apostrophe follows the plural *-s*. *Florida is a three days' journey by car.*

Naming a Hurricane

[1]*Storm*, a novel published in 1941, surely deserves some of the credit for the practice of giving women's names to storms in the Northern Hemisphere. [2]The novel follows the career of a Pacific storm that eventually affects much of North America; a "Junior Meteorologist" plotting the storm on a weather map gives it the name "Maria" without telling his boss or his colleagues. [3]"Not at any price would the Junior Meteorologist have revealed to the Chief that he was bestowing names—and girls' names at that—upon these great moving low-pressure areas." [4]The first official naming of storms in the Atlantic Basin began in 1950. [5]Six-year lists of only female names continued through 1978. [6]The following year the policy was changed to include both men's and women's names, as it was for typhoons in the Pacific.

—Dr. Bob Sheets and Jack Williams, *Hurricane Watch*

■ Where did the idea of naming storms in the Atlantic Basin originate? Write your answer in a sentence. _____

_____

■ In the spaces below write all of the possessive nouns or pronouns from the excerpt above.

1. _____*women's*_____   3. _____

2. _____   4. _____

- Sometimes, watching a storm can be exciting. Write a sentence about a thunderstorm or other violent kind of weather you have seen. _____

_____

LESSON 14b
More Possessives

· · · · · · · · ·

Don't forget that pronouns as well as nouns can be possessives, but that they don't have apostrophes before the *-s*. *The boy's eyes were on his shoes.* The noun *boy* has an apostrophe before the *-s*, but the pronoun *his* does not.

Possessive Pronouns

my, mine	*our, ours*
your, yours	*your, yours*
his, her, hers, its	*their, theirs*

Meeting the Pony

[1]They crossed a stubble-field to shortcut to the barn. [2]Jody's father unhooked the door and they went in. [3]They had been walking toward the sun on the way down. [4]The barn was black as night in contrast and warm from the hay and from the beasts. [5]Jody's father moved over toward the one box stall. [6]Jody could begin to see things now. [7]He looked into the box stall and then stepped back quickly. [8]A red pony colt was looking at him out of the stall. [9]Its tense ears were forward and a light of disobedience was in its eyes. [10] Its coat was rough and thick as an airedale's fur and its mane was long and tangled. [11]Jody's throat collapsed in on itself and cut his breath short. [12]Jody couldn't bear to look at the pony's eyes anymore. [13]He gazed down at his hands for a moment, and he asked very shyly, "Mine?"

—John Steinbeck, *The Red Pony*

■ Why is Jody's breath cut short when he sees the pony? Write your answer in

a sentence. _____

_____

■ Find the possessive pronouns and nouns in the excerpt above and write
them on the lines below, noting whether the word is a noun or a pronoun.

1. _____ *Jody's [noun]* _____   4. _____

2. _____   5. _____

3. _____   6. _____

■ Write a sentence about a time when you were surprised to get something

you had wanted very much. _____

_____

LESSON 15
The -s Ending and Its Uses: Spelling

The -s at the end of a word doesn't always have a special meaning. Sometimes it is just the way the word is spelled, like *stress* or *impress*. *Can you guess whether you will pass the exam?* In *guess* and *pass* the final -s is the words' spelling.

The Power of the Tide

[1]There is no drop of water in the ocean, not even in the deepest parts of the abyss, that does not know and respond to the mysterious forces that create the tide. [2]No other force that affects the sea is so strong. [3]Compared with the tide the wind-created waves are surface movements felt, at most, no more than a hundred fathoms below the surface. [4]So, despite their impressive sweep, are the planetary currents, which seldom involve more than the upper several hundred fathoms. [5]The masses of water affected by the tidal movement are enormous, as will be clear from one example. [6]Into one small bay on the east coast of North America—Passamaquoddy—2 billion tons of water are carried by the tidal currents twice each day, into the whole Bay of Fundy, 100 billion tons.

—Rachel Carson, *The Sea Around Us*

- Combine these sentences:

Waves are surface movements. Tides are felt in the deepest part of the ocean.

_____

- Some words, like *glass* and *press*, end in -s because of their spelling, not because of any significance of the -s ending. Look again at *The Power of the Tide* and find those words that end in -s because they are spelled that way. Write them in the spaces below.

1. _____*abyss*_____   3. _____
2. _____   4. _____

- Write a sentence about a natural phenomenon you have observed. It might be the tide going out or coming in, or a shooting star, or a thunderstorm.

_____

LESSON 15a
Review of *-s* Endings

. . . .

We have seen that *-s* at the end of a word can mean

- more than one of something
- a present tense verb with a subject that can be replaced by *she, he,* or *it*
- a word showing possession

Sometimes an *-s* may have no meaning, and just be part of the word's spelling.

Poverty

[1]Most of Morocco is so desolate that no wild animal bigger than a hare can live on it. [2]Huge areas which were once covered with forest have turned into a treeless waste where the soil is exactly like broken-up brick. [3]Nevertheless a good deal of it is cultivated, with frightful labour. [4]Everything is done by hand. [5]Long lines of women, bent double like inverted capital Ls work their way slowly across the fields, tearing up the prickly weeds with their hands, and the peasant gathering lucerne [alfalfa] for fodder pulls it up stalk by stalk instead of reaping it, thus saving an inch or two on each stalk. [6]The plough is a wretched wooden thing, so frail that one can easily carry it on one's shoulder, and fitted underneath with a rough iron spike which stirs the soil to a depth of about four inches.

—George Orwell, *Marrakesh*

■ Combine these sentences:

The land in Morocco is dry and unproductive. Farming requires enormous work.

_____

■ Find all the words in the excerpt above that end in -s. Write them in the appropriate column below.

Plural	Present Tense Verb	Possessive	Spelling
1. _areas_	_is_	_one's_	_treeless_
2. _____	_____	_____	_____
3. _____	_____	_____	_____
4. _____	_____	_____	_____

Plural	Present Tense Verb	Possessive	Spelling
5. _____	_____	_____	_____
6. _____	_____	_____	_____
7. _____	_____	_____	_____

- Write a sentence about an extremely hard job you have done or have watched someone else do. _____

_____

LESSON 15b
Another Look at -s Endings

You remember that a word ending in -s can be a plural noun, a third person present tense singular verb, or, with an apostrophe, a possessive noun. Sometimes the -s is just the spelling of the word.

Here are more words ending in -s for you to identify. Find plural nouns, third person singular present tense verbs, possessives, and words whose spelling ends in -s.

The Magic Bottle

[1]By this time Alice had found her way into a tidy little room with a table in the window, and on its top (as she had hoped) a fan and two or three pairs of tiny white kid-gloves: she took up the fan and a pair of the gloves, and was just going to leave the room, when Alice's eye fell upon a little bottle that stood near the looking-glass. [2]There was no label this time with the words "DRINK ME," but nevertheless she uncorked it and put it to her lips. [3]"I know *something* interesting is sure to happen," she said to herself, "whenever I eat or drink anything: so I'll just see what this bottle does. [4]I do hope it'll make me grow large again, for really I'm quite tired of being such a tiny little thing!"

—Lewis Carroll, *Alice in Wonderland*

- Why does Alice drink the liquid in the bottle? _____

_____

■ Find all the words ending in -s in the excerpt above. Write them in the appropriate column below.

	Plural	Present Tense Verb	Possessive	Spelling
1.	*pairs*	*does*	*its*	*looking-glass*
2.				
3.				
4.				
5.				
6.				

■ *Alice in Wonderland* is a favorite story of many children. Write a sentence about your favorite children's story. _____

_____

YOUR WRITING
Filling in the Details

As we have seen, the whole point of your composition should be included in your thesis statement. Does this make you think there is nothing further to be said on the subject? Look at this paragraph from *The Sea Around Us*.

> Neither the Pacific Ocean nor the Indian Ocean has any submerged mountains that compare in length with the Atlantic Ridge, but they have their smaller ranges. The Hawaiian Islands are the peaks of a mountain range that runs across the central Pacific basin for a distance of nearly 2000 miles. The Gilbert and Marshall islands stand on the shoulders of another mid-Pacific mountain chain. In the eastern Pacific, a broad plateau connects the coast of South America and the Tuamotu Islands in the mid-Pacific, and in the Indian Ocean a long ridge runs from India to Antarctica, for most of its length broader and deeper than the Atlantic Ridge.

What is the thesis here? It is that the Pacific and Indian Oceans have smaller mountain ranges than those to be found in the Atlantic. How does the writer go on to illustrate her thesis? She provides examples. And this is one of the ways in which you can continue your composition after you have stated your thesis. Try it on this question:

> What aspect of protecting the environment concerns you most: pollution, natural resources, genetic engineering?

Write a thesis statement explaining why one of these is a particular concern. For example, you might write, *Air pollution contributes to breathing problems in humans.* Next, think about what some of these problems are. *Children may develop asthma. Older people may suffer from shortness of breath. Almost everyone runs the risk of being stricken by a disease of the lungs.* Each of these offers a possibility for a paragraph giving further information about the condition. *What are the symptoms, the treatments, the prospects for recovery? Why is a particular age group especially susceptible? What kind of pollution poses the greatest threat for each?*

You can see how keeping what you write focused on your thesis will bring up questions, the answers to which will provide abundant material for an interesting and informative paper.

Try this: Write a thesis sentence based on one of the ideas above or on one of your own choosing. Then, write five sentences that are about *all* of that thesis statement and that could serve as topic sentences for the paragraphs of your composition.

Thesis _____

_____

1. _____

2. _____

3. _____

4. _____

5. _____

LESSON 16
The Meanings of the *-d* Ending

Just as *-s* endings can change the meaning of a word, sometimes *-d* can also signal a change in meaning. For example, we know this ending can often mean that something happened in the past: *we look* (now), *we looked* (last evening). In this case it changes the verb to *past tense*. It can also be used to turn a verb into an adjective, and, of course, it can have no meaning at all when it is simply the way a word is spelled.

Here are some examples of *-d* endings taken from the classic suspense thriller, *Dracula*.

The Body in the Crypt

¹Then I stopped and looked at the Count. ²There was a mocking smile on the bloated face which seemed to drive me mad. ³A terrible desire came upon me to rid the world of such a monster. ⁴There was no lethal weapon at hand, but I seized a shovel which the workmen had been using to fill the cases, and, lifting it high, struck, with the edge downward, at the hateful face. ⁵But as I did so the head turned, and the eyes fell full upon me, with all their blaze of basilisk [a mythical monster] horror. ⁶The shovel fell from my hand across the box, and hid the horrid thing from my sight.

—Bram Stoker, *Dracula*

■ Write a sentence explaining what the narrator feels about the Count. _____

_____

■ Find all the verbs in the excerpt above that end in *-d*. Which of them is past tense? Write the past tense verbs below followed by their present tense forms.

Past Tense Verb	Present Tense Verb
1. _____ *stopped* _____	_____ *stop* _____
2. _____	_____
3. _____	_____
4. _____	_____
5. _____	_____
6. _____	_____

■ Write a sentence about a scene from the scariest movie you have seen or book you have read. _____

_____

LESSON 16a
Past Tense Verbs Ending in *-d*

· · · · · · · · · ·

The past tense of *regular* verbs ends in *-ed*. The past tense of the irregular verb *have*, often used as a helping verb, is *had*, which also ends in *-d*. See Lesson 7 for more about this topic.

A Giant's World

[1]Neither the birds nor the mammals, however, were quite what they seemed. [2]They were waiting for the Age of Flowers. [3]They were waiting for what flowers, and with them the true encased seed, would bring. [4]Fish-eating, gigantic leather-winged reptiles, twenty-eight feet from wing tip to wing tip, hovered over the coasts that one day would be swarming with gulls. [5]Inland the monotonous green of the pine and spruce forests with their primitive wooden cone flowers stretched everywhere. [6]No grass hindered the fall of the naked seeds to earth. [7]Great sequoias towered to the skies. [8]The world of that time has a certain appeal but it is a giant's world, a world moving slowly like the reptiles who stalked magnificently among the boles of its trees.

—Loren Eiseley, *How Flowers Changed the World*

■ Combine these sentences:

Plants and animals were gigantic. The landscape was monotonous. _____

_____

■ Find the past tense verbs that end in *-d* or *-ed* in the excerpt above. Write them below, then use their present tense forms in a sentence.

	Past Tense	Present Tense
1.	*seemed*	*Harry seems very happy today.*
2.	_____	_____
3.	_____	_____

Past Tense	Present Tense

4. _____   _____

5. _____   _____

6. _____   _____

■ Write a sentence about how trees and other plants make the world a more pleasant place to live in. _____

_____

LESSON 16b
More Past Tense Verbs

· · · · · · · · · ·

While a great many past tense verbs end in -*d*, *irregular* verbs have other forms like *break/broke, begin/began,* and *choose/chose.* See Lesson 40 for more about this topic.

The Secrets in the Palm

[1]Wilson began to study Luigi's palm, tracing life lines, heart lines, head lines, and so on, and noting carefully their relations with the cobweb of finer and more delicate marks and lines that enmeshed them on all sides; he felt of the fleshy cushion at the base of the thumb, and noted its shape; he felt of the fleshy side of the hand between the wrist and the base of the little finger, and noted its shape also; he painstakingly examined the fingers, observing their form, proportions, and natural manner of disposing themselves when in repose. [2]All this process was watched by the three spectators with absorbing interest, their heads bent together over Luigi's palm, and nobody disturbing the stillness with a word. [3]Wilson now entered upon a close survey of the palm again, and his revelations began. [4]He mapped out Luigi's character and disposition, and eccentricities in a way which sometimes made Luigi wince and the others laugh, but both twins declared that the chart was artistically drawn and was correct.

—Mark Twain, *Pudd'nhead Wilson*

■ Combine these sentences:

Wilson examined Luigi's palm. He identified characteristics of Luigi's personality.

_____

■ Identify all of the past tense verbs in the excerpt above, including any that do not end in -d.

1. _____*began*_____   8. _____

2. _____   9. _____

3. _____   10. _____

4. _____   11. _____

5. _____   12. _____

6. _____   13. _____

7. _____

■ Examining fingerprints was once a key tool in crime detection. Write a sentence about the new test that has replaced fingerprinting. _____

For more about -d endings, see Review Exercises 20, 26.

L E S S O N   1 7
The Past Participle

. . . .

The past participle is formed from a verb, but it can never be a verb by itself; it must be combined with a *helping* verb like *has* or *had*. Some examples are *he has walked, people have been, Joaquin had spoken.* Look for past participles in the following paragraph.

Deepening Mystery

[1]During the past two or three days several cases have occurred of young children straying from home or neglecting to return from their playing on the Heath. [2]In all these cases the children were too young to give any properly intelligible account of themselves, but the consensus of their excuses is that they had been with a "bloofer lady." [3]It has always been late in the evening when they have been missed, and on two occasions the children have not been found until early in the following morning. [4]It is generally supposed in the neighbourhood that, as the first child missed gave as his reason for being away that a "bloofer lady" had asked him to come for a walk, the others had picked up the phrase and used it as occasion served. [5]There is, however, possibly a serious side to the question, for some of the children, indeed all who have been missed at night, have been slightly torn or wounded in the throat.

—Bram Stoker, *Dracula*

▪ Combine these sentences:

Children have been missing. They were found with wounds in their throats.

_____

▪ Underline the past participles that are combined with auxiliaries, or helping verbs, to form the main verbs of sentences in the excerpt above. Write them in the spaces below, along with their auxiliaries.

Auxiliaries	Past Participles
1. *have*	*occurred*
2.	
3.	
4.	

Auxiliaries	Past Participles
5. _____	_____
6. _____	_____

■ *Dracula* is a story about a vampire. Write a sentence explaining what a vampire is. _____

_____

_____

LESSON 17a
Past Participles with Helping Verbs

A compound verb is more specific about the time something happened than is a simple past tense verb. For example, *Olga cried when we went to sad movies. She has cried at every movie in which lovers are parted.*

The Flight of the Century

¹The idea for the flight came to Lindbergh above the Illinois prairie, on one of his St. Louis–Chicago mail runs in 1926. ²Raymond Orteig, a French-born hotel owner in New York, had offered a $25,000 prize to the first aviator to cross the Atlantic in an airplane from Paris to New York or vice versa. ³In 1919, two British pilots had flown across from Newfoundland to Ireland, a difficult 1,900-mile trip, but not nearly as challenging as New York to Paris. ⁴The prize had yet to be won. ⁵The Spirit of St. Louis was sufficient to its task, where others had failed. ⁶A tall 25-year-old aviator known as Slim, Lindbergh had taken off from Roosevelt field, outside New York City on Long Island. ⁷Through daylight and dark, fog and sleet and gathering clouds of fatigue, he flew 33 hours 30 minutes and covered 3,610 miles. ⁸After dark on May 21, 1927, he landed at LeBourget Field to the wild cheers of the French crowd.

—John Noble Wilford, *The Man and the Aircraft Were One*

■ Combine these sentences:

Lindbergh took off from Roosevelt field. He reached Paris more than 33 hours later. _____

_____

▪ Use verbs formed with past participles from the passage above to complete these sentences.

1. The kindly neighbor ___*had offered*___ candy to the children on Halloween.

2. The birds _____ north as soon as the weather warmed up.

3. Oriana _____ history that semester.

4. Rory and Joe _____ their sweaters because it was so hot.

▪ Lindbergh's flight is said to have made history. Write a sentence about an accomplishment you consider history-making. _____

_____

LESSON 17b
Irregular Past Participles

A great many past participles end in -*d*, but others end in -*n*, like *broken* and *taken*. Still others, like *brought* or *sung*, have a completely irregular form. See Lesson 40 for more about irregular verb forms.

Westminster Abbey's Beginning

[1]Thorney Island had been a place of holy reputation since the earliest days of Christendom in England. [2]Several churches had been founded there and dedicated to St. Peter; in the seventh century, the saint was said to have appeared in person to bless the latest building. [3]This was the place the King had chosen for what he considered his life's most important work, the creation of the abbey that came to be known, in distinction from St. Paul's cathedral in the city, as the West Minster. [4]He had planned and supervised the work year after year, and while he lay sick the weather vane was mounted on the cupola of the central tower to symbolize completion of the building. [5]On Wednesday, 28 December, Childermas or Holy Innocents' Day, the great new church was consecrated.

—David Howarth, *1066: The Year of the Conquest*

▪ Why was Thorney Island considered a holy place? Write your answer in a sentence. _____

_____

▪ Find the compound verbs in the excerpt above, both those with regular and those with irregular past participles. Write them below, as shown in the example.

Auxiliary	Past Participle
1. _____ had _____	_____ been _____
2. _____	_____
3. _____	_____
4. _____	_____
5. _____	_____

▪ Write a sentence about a building you have seen that impressed you—because it is beautiful or historical or because of the activities that take place there. _____

_____

For more about participles, see Review Exercises 7, 16, 30, 39.

L E S S O N   1 8
Past Participles as Adjectives

Sometimes the past participle form of the verb acts as if it isn't a verb at all. It can appear in a sentence as an adjective. Examples of this are *the whispered message, a hidden treasure.*

Vampire's End

[1]She seemed like a nightmare of Lucy as she lay there; the pointed teeth, the bloodstained, voluptuous mouth—which it made one shudder to see— the whole carnal and unspirited appearance, seeming like a devilish mockery of Lucy's sweet purity. [2]Arthur took the stake and the hammer, and when once his mind was set on action his hands never trembled nor even quivered. [3]He placed the point over the heart, and as I looked I could see its dint in the white flesh. [4]Then he struck with all his might. [5]The thing in the coffin writhed; and a hideous, blood-curdling screech came from the opened red lips. [6]The blood from the pierced heart welled and spurted up around the stake. [7]And then the writhing and quivering of the body became less, and the teeth seemed to champ, and the face to quiver. [8]Finally it lay still. [9]The terrible task was over.

—Bram Stoker, *Dracula*

■ From the information in this passage from *Dracula*, explain in one sentence what steps are necessary to do away with a vampire. _____

_____

■ Find all the verbs that end in *-d* in the excerpt above. Some are past participles acting as adjectives, describing nouns. Write these below along with the nouns they describe.

Past Participle/Adjective	Noun
1. _____ *pointed* _____	_____ *teeth* _____
2. _____	_____
3. _____	_____

■ Do you think it takes courage to destroy a vampire? Write a sentence about it. _____

_____

LESSON 18a
More Past Participles as Adjectives

• • • • • • • • •

Like all adjectives, the past participle used as an adjective can sometimes follow the noun it describes instead of going before it. *The picture painted by Rembrandt is in the museum.*

Awakened by the *Titanic*

[1]Overriding everything else, the *Titanic* also marked the end of a general feeling of confidence. [2]Until then men felt they had found the answer to a steady, orderly, civilized life. [3]For 100 years the Western world had been at peace. [4]For 100 years technology had steadily improved. [5]For 100 years the benefits of peace and industry seemed to be filtering satisfactorily through society. [6]Most articulate people felt life was all right. [7]The *Titanic* woke them up. [8]If wealth meant so little on this cold April night, did it mean so much the rest of the year? [9]If it was a lesson, it worked—people have never been sure of anything since. [10]The unending sequence of disillusionment that has followed can't be blamed on the *Titanic*, but she was the first jar. [11]That is why, to anybody who lived at the time, the *Titanic* more than any other single event marks the end of the old days, and the beginning of a new, uneasy era.

—Walter Lord, *A Night to Remember*

■ Combine these sentences:

People were satisfied with life. The *Titanic* shocked them out of it. _____

_____

■ Find the past participles in the excerpt above. For each of them, write a sentence using the present tense form of the verb.

	Verb	**Sentence**
1.	*had found*	*Maria finds biology fascinating.*
2.		
3.		
4.		

■ *Titanic* is only one of many disaster movies that have been produced. Write a sentence about one you liked—it could be *Titanic*—and why you liked it.

_____

LESSON 18b
Past Participle Adjectives After the Verb

. . . .

Often, when a past participle is used as an adjective, it will follow a form of the verb *to be*, as in *The letter is <u>dated</u> May 20th. Dated* in this sentence describes the letter.

A Solemn Ceremony

[1]On Trinity Sunday, the 10th of June 1172, all the candles were alight in the dark thick-walled cathedral of Poitiers. [2]The vaulted nave was a sea of colour. [3]The Bishop and his chapter were almost hidden by clouds of incense, but on the altar steps two handsome figures showed plain. [4]Queen Eleanor was fifty years old, and still the most beautiful queen in Christendom, so beautiful that poets on the far side of the distant Rhine yet sang her praises. [5]Her face was wrinkled by the fierce southern sun; but her regular features were unblemished, and the grey streaks in her hair were hidden by her silk kerchief. [6]Above her kerchief gleamed the gilded coronet of Aquitaine, which was hers by inheritance from her grandfather; but her scarlet mantle of state was worked all over with the ramping golden leopards of Anjou which she bore by right of marriage. [7]While the long psalms were chanted she stood motionless, her face half-turned; so that while her eyes remained fixed on the altar, as was proper in church, the spectators had a clear view of her flawless profile.

—Alfred Duggan, *Devil's Brood: The Angevin Family*

■ Why does Eleanor have her face half-turned? Answer this question in a sentence. _____

_____

■ Find the past participles used as adjectives in the excerpt above. Write them as shown in the examples below, noting whether they occur before the noun or after the verb.

Past Participle	Noun	Verb
1. _hidden_		_were_
2. _gilded_	_coronet_	_gleamed_
3.		
4.		
5.		
6.		

■ Write a sentence about a ceremony you have witnessed—anything from a graduation to the inauguration of a public official. _____

The -d ending doesn't always have a special meaning. Sometimes it is merely the way the root word is spelled, as in *bread, sound,* and *behold* (not to mention *and*). For example, *The sad child shed tears for the cold redhead.*

Out of the Trance

[1]"Something is going out; I can feel it pass me like a cold wind. [2]I can hear, far off, confused sounds—as of men talking in strange tongues, fierce-falling water, and the howling of wolves." [3]She stopped and a shudder ran through her, increasing in intensity for a few seconds, till, at the end, she shook as though in a palsy. [4]She said no more, even in answer to the Professor's imperative questioning. [5]When she woke from the trance, she was cold, and exhausted, and languid; but her mind was all alert. [6]She could not remember anything, but asked what she had said; when she was told, she pondered over it deeply for a long time and in silence.

—Bram Stoker, *Dracula*

■ Combine these sentences to explain what is happening in the passage:

Mina woke from her trance. She could not remember what she had said. _____

_____

■ Find the words in the excerpt above that end in -d because that is the spelling of the root. Be careful not to confuse them with past tense verbs or past participles. Write the root words below.

1. _____*cold*_____   4. _____

2. _____   5. _____

3. _____   6. _____

■ Did you ever wake up in a strange place, not knowing where you were? Write a sentence about how you felt. _____

_____

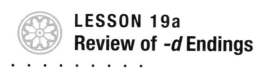

LESSON 19a
Review of -*d* Endings

Be sure to think twice about a word with a spelling that ends in -*d*. The -*d* can mean it is a past tense verb, like *looked*—which can also be a past participle—or it can be the way a word is spelled, like *blind*.

A Woman's Work

[1]And this is how I came to know my mother: she seemed a large, soft, loving-eyed woman who was rarely impatient in our home. [2]Her quick, violent temper was on view only a few times a year, when she battled with the white landlord who had the misfortune to suggest to her that her children did not need to go to school. [3]During the "working" day, she labored beside—not behind—my father in the fields. [4]Her day began before sunup, and did not end until late at night. [5]There was never a moment for her to sit down, undisturbed, to unravel her own private thoughts; never a time free from interruption—by work or the noisy inquiries of her many children. [6]And yet, it is to my mother—and all our mothers who were not famous—that I went in search of the secret of what has fed that muzzled and often mutilated, but vibrant, creative spirit that the black woman has inherited, and that pops out in wild and unlikely places to this day.

—Alice Walker, *In Search of Our Mothers' Gardens*

■ Why does the writer emphasize that her mother worked "beside" her father in the fields? Write your answer in a sentence. _____

_____

■ There are ten past tense verbs or past participles in the passage above. Choose five of them and write a sentence using the verb in the present tense, as shown in the example.

Sentence	Verb
Myrna seems happy with her grade.	
1. _____	*seem* _____
2. _____	_____
3. _____	_____
4. _____	_____
5. _____	_____
6. _____	_____

■ Write a sentence explaining your idea of what "women's work" is. _____

_____

LESSON 19b
Spellings That End in *-d*

If a *-d* ending is not part of the spelling of a word—like the word *word*, for example—it may indicate the past tense, *stepped*, or the past participle, *have talked*.

Eleanor of Aquitaine

[1]The lady Eleanor was a typical daughter of the south, incompatible in every characteristic with her dour and devout northern husband. [2]Her wit was as famous as her beauty. [3]She could read, as was usual with members of the upper class; and write also, a more rare accomplishment. [4]Her complexion was dark, with black eyes and black hair; her figure curved generously, but even in old age she never grew fat. [5]The story goes that she was one of the founders of the "Courts of Love," where the technique of the love-affair was dissected in public by experts. [6]For romantic love is the great contribution of southern France to civilization, and it was then a new idea.

—Alfred Duggan, *Devil's Brood: The Angevin Family*

■ Combine these sentences:

Eleanor was accomplished. She could read and write, and could speak several

languages. _____

_____

■ Give examples from the excerpt above of two past tense verbs ending in *-d* and of two other words that are not verbs with spelling that ends in *-d*.

1. _____*curved*_____   3. _____*old*_____

2. _____   4. _____

■ Eleanor was a celebrity in her day. Write a sentence about what one of to-day's celebrities is famous for. _____

_____

For more on words ending in *-d*, see Review Exercises 20, 26.

YOUR WRITING
Details for Clarity

We have seen that adding examples is a very useful way to *develop* or add to the thesis of your paper. What other means of strengthening your point are there? One easy and profitable way is to pay attention to details. This means providing more than just the simplest kind of reference to a person or object: *The book was next to Marc's computer.* How much more information about why Marc is not getting his homework done do we find in *A new issue of Dragonball II was lying open next to Marc's closed Toshiba laptop.*

Notice how Bram Stoker uses details in this passage from *Dracula*:

> There, in one of the **great** boxes, on a pile of **newly dug** earth, lay the Count! He was either dead or asleep, I could not say which—for the eyes were **open** and **stony,** but without the **glassiness** of death—and the cheeks had the **warmth** of life through all their **pallor**; the lips were as **red** as ever.

Would that picture of the Count lying in a box of soil in a dark basement be as frightening without the highlighted details?

Try getting those telling details into your writing in response to the following thesis: *Young people enjoy being scared by horror stories and movies.* Here are some sentences—the *topic sentences*—that might begin the paragraphs that follow:

1. They find the suspense exciting.
2. They like the strange characters.
3. They try to guess how it will end.
4. They are dazzled by the special effects.

What kinds of details might you add to these sentences to develop the paragraphs in your composition? Suppose you are writing about *Dracula* and want to use details to develop sentence 1 above. You might refer to the suspense of worrying about which girl, Mina or Lucy, will be turned into a vampire next. Or you could discuss why the madman Renfield wants to eat spiders and how garlic can defeat Dracula. Notice that we bring in the names of the characters, the behavior they show after being attacked by a vampire, and some of the weapons that can be used against vampires. Similarly, in sentence 2 we would want to learn about Dracula's black cape, his blazing eyes and sharp, pointed teeth, and his ability to change appearance to that of a bat. All of these details are what makes your writing real communication.

Write a thesis statement about the kind of entertainment you have observed that young people most enjoy. Follow it with four topic sentences that explain why they enjoy it. For each of the topic sentences, list as many details or examples as you can that will support what your sentence says.

Thesis: _____

_____

Sentence 1: _____

_____

Details: _____   _____   _____

_____   _____   _____

Sentence 2: _____

_____

Details: _____   _____   _____

_____   _____   _____

Sentence 3: _____

_____

Details: _____   _____   _____

_____   _____   _____

Sentence 4: _____

_____

Details: _____   _____   _____

_____   _____   _____

LESSON 20
The -ing Ending and Its Uses

Like the past participle, the verb part called the *present participle,* ending in *-ing,* cannot be used as the verb of a sentence unless it is combined with an auxiliary like *am, is, are, was, were.* But it can be used as a noun, *the loud talking,* or an adjective, *running water.* And, of course, sometimes the *-ing* simply represents the spelling of a word—*morning.*

You will find examples of all these in the excerpt below from George Orwell's *Animal Farm,* a fable about totalitarian government in which animals play the leading roles.

Don't forget that the present participle is the verb of a sentence when combined with the auxiliaries *am, is, are, was, were.*

The Battle Begins

[1]As the human beings approached the farm buildings, Snowball launched his first attack. [2]All the pigeons, to the number of thirty-five, flew to and fro over the men's heads and muted upon them from mid-air, and while the men were dealing with this, the geese, who were hiding behind the hedge, rushed out and pecked viciously at the calves of their legs. [3]However, this was only a light skirmishing manoeuvre, intended to create a little disorder, and the men easily drove the geese off with their sticks. [4]Suddenly, at a squeal from Snowball, which was the signal for retreat, all the animals turned and fled through the gateway into the yard. [5]The men gave a shout of triumph. [6]They saw, as they imagined, their enemies in flight. [7]As soon as they were well inside the yard, the three horses, the three cows, and the rest of the pigs, who were lying in ambush in the cowshed, suddenly emerged in their rear, cutting them off.

—George Orwell, *Animal Farm*

▪ How are the animals trying to defeat the humans? Answer in a sentence.

_____

▪ Find the present participles used as verbs in the excerpt above. Write them below along with their auxiliaries and subjects.

Present Participle	Auxiliary	Subject
1. *dealing*	*were*	*men*
2.		
3.		

■ Can you think of an example of an animal behaving with surprising intelligence? Write a sentence about what that animal did. _____

_____

LESSON 20a
More Present Participles with Helpers

· · · · · · · · · ·

The present participle, with a part of the verb *to be* as helper, is often called the *present progressive tense* because it indicates that a movement is continuing. For example, *Emily is wearing new earrings to the dance.*

Shooting in the Rain

[1]By 11:20 P.M. rain was pouring from sprinklers attached to the scissor-lift crane. [2]Tom Hanks was dragging the reluctant dachshund out of the building. [3]Inside, the animal's handler was calling out encouragement. [4]Schwab was talking to a friend who had dropped by the set. [5]DePalma sat in the middle of the downtown lanes of Park Avenue under a giant umbrella. [6]He was watching the monitor, analyzing the composition of the fake rain and the fake lightning and the fake wind. [7]When he felt it worked, he nodded at Chris Soldo, the first assistant director. [8]Soldo yelled, "Save the rain."

—Julie Salamon, *The Devil's Candy*

■ Combine these sentences:

The movie has a scene in the rain. The movie makers are using machinery to

produce fake rain. _____

_____

■ Find the verbs formed with present participles in the excerpt above. Then write each in a sentence of your own.

	Verb	**Sentence**
1.	*pouring*	*Water was pouring from the leaky pipe.*
2.	_____	_____
3.	_____	_____

Verb	Sentence
4. _____	_____
5. _____	_____

■ Write a sentence about a movie scene you found especially effective.

_____

LESSON 20b
More Compound Verbs

· · · · · · · · ·

The present participle with an auxiliary is often called the *present progressive tense* because it indicates that a movement is continuing, as it is in the excerpt below. As we saw with verbs formed with past participles, the verb and helper can sometimes be divided by an adverb: *He had often spoken to me.* Here's what you might find with the present participle: *Molly is always looking for a new brand of jeans.*

A Different World

¹In a movement that was almost instantaneous, geologically speaking, the angiosperms [a class of flowering plants] had taken over the world. ²Grass was beginning to cover the bare earth until, today, there are over six thousand species. ³All kinds of vines and bushes squirmed and writhed under new trees with flying seeds. ⁴The explosion was having its effect on animal life also. ⁵Specialized groups of insects were arising to feed on the new sources of food and, incidentally and unknowingly, to pollinate the plant. ⁶The flowers bloomed and bloomed in ever larger and more spectacular varieties. ⁷Honey ran, insects multiplied, and even the descendants of that toothed and ancient lizard bird had become strangely altered. ⁸Across the planet grasslands were now spreading. ⁹A slow continental upthrust which had been a part of the early Age of Flowers had cooled the world's climates.

—Loren Eiseley, *How Flowers Changed the World*

■ How did the Age of Flowers change the nature of animal life on earth? Write a sentence with your answer. _____

_____

■ Find the compound verbs in the excerpt above formed from present participles. If their subjects are singular, the helper will be *was*; plural subjects will be followed by *were* as a helper. Write the subjects and verbs in the appropriate column below.

Singular Subjects	**Plural Subjects**
1. _____ grass was beginning _____	insects were arising
2. _____	_____

■ People use flowers to beautify their surroundings. Write a sentence about a flower garden that impressed you, either as part of a public place or in someone's yard or even as part of a collection of indoor plants. _____

_____

For more about helping verbs, see Review Exercises 8, 10, 16, 44.

LESSON 21
The Present Participle as a Noun

Although it is a form of the verb, the present participle is often used as a noun in such forms as *painting* or *serving*. You can tell a present participle is being used as a noun if a determiner—another name for the articles *the, a,* and *an*—can be placed before it. Example: *I ordered a serving of fries.*

Marching Pigs

¹It was just after the sheep had returned, on a pleasant evening when the animals had finished work and were making their way back to the farm buildings, that the terrified neighing of a horse sounded from the yard. ²Startled, the animals stopped in their tracks. ³It was Clover's voice. ⁴She neighed again, and all the animals broke into a gallop and rushed into the yard. ⁵Then they saw what Clover had seen. ⁶It was a pig walking on his hind legs. ⁷And a moment later, out from the door of the farmhouse came a long file of pigs, all walking on their hind legs. ⁸And finally there was a tremendous baying of dogs and a shrill crowing from the black cockerel, and out came Napoleon himself, majestically upright, casting haughty glances from side to side, and with his dogs gambolling round him.

—George Orwell, *Animal Farm*

- Combine these sentences:

Clover was terrified. A pig was walking on his hind legs. _____

_____

- We can tell that some of the words in the excerpt above that end in *-ing* are used as nouns because they have a determiner. Write these words in the appropriate spaces below.

1. _____*the neighing*_____   3. _____

2. _____

- Do you have a pet that does tricks? Or do you know someone who has? Write a sentence about the cleverest trick you have seen. _____

_____

LESSON 21a
The Present Participles as Subject or Object

A present participle is used as a noun when it is the subject or object of a sentence or the object of a preposition such as *at, by, for, in, to*. For example, *Speaking is a way of communicating.*

Concentration Camp Life

[1]We could hold endless debates on the sense or nonsense of certain methods of dealing with the small bread ration, which was given out only once daily during the latter part of our confinement. [2]There were two schools of thought. [3]One was in favor of eating up the ration immediately. [4]This had the twofold advantage of satisfying the worst hunger pangs for a very short time at least once a day and of safeguarding against possible theft or loss of the ration. [5]The second group, which held with dividing the ration up, used different arguments. [6]The most ghastly moment of the twenty-four hours of camp life was the awakening, when, at a still nocturnal hour, the three shrill blows of a whistle tore us pitilessly from our exhausted sleep and from the longing in our dreams. [7]We then began the tussle with our wet shoes, into which we could scarcely force our feet, which were sore and swollen with edema. [8]And there were the usual moans and groans about petty troubles, such as the snapping of wires which replaced shoelaces.

—Viktor E. Frankl, *Man's Search for Meaning*

■ Why did some people in the camp choose to eat their ration immediately? Answer this question in a sentence. _____

_____

■ In the spaces below write the present participles that are used as nouns in the excerpt above.

1. _____*[the] dealing*_____   5. _____

2. _____   6. _____

3. _____   7. _____

4. _____   8. _____

■ We have to make decisions, large and small, all the time. Write a sentence about a difficult decision you have made. _____

_____

LESSON 21b
Present Participles with Adjectives

Sometimes, when a present participle is used as a noun, it may be modified by an adjective. For example: *Marti's excellent playing of the clarinet won him a place in the band.* Look for adjectives before the present participles in the following excerpt.

A Moviemaker's Problem

[1]Though all of De Palma's artistic training had taken place in the theater and in movies, he too found endings to be nearly impossible. [2]It wasn't all that different from life. [3]Beginnings were thrilling, the opening up of all kinds of possibilities. [4]But endings, endings implied some kind of resolution, an epiphany or a summing up—and such moments seemed elusive to him, and false. [5]He could rarely see how to sum up a story without trivializing it. [6]The idea of the Magic Hour made so much more sense, an acknowledgment that it was difficult to pinpoint the exact moment when day ended and night began, that endings and beginnings were linked in some mutable, magical way.

—Julie Salamon, *The Devil's Candy*

▪ Why does the director find endings difficult? Answer this question in a sentence. _____

_____

▪ In the spaces below write the present participles that are used as nouns. If they follow adjectives, write the adjectives as well.

1. _____*[artistic] training*_____   4. _____

2. _____   5. _____

3. _____

▪ Do you find it easier to begin writing a paper than to end it? Write a sentence explaining why or why not. _____

_____

LESSON 22
The Present Participle as an Adjective

Used as an adjective, the present participle describes a noun. Remember that it cannot be the verb of a sentence without a helper, or auxiliary. But as an adjective it can provide descriptions—for example, *deafening applause* or *Anya, laughing happily.*

The End of the Windmill

[1]In their spare moments the animals would walk round and round the half-finished mill, admiring the strength and perpendicularity of its walls and marvelling that they should ever have been able to build anything so imposing. [2]November came, with raging south-west winds. [3]Finally there came a night when the gale was so violent that the farm buildings rocked on their foundations and several tiles were blown off the roof of the barn. [4]The hens woke up squawking with terror because they had all dreamed simultaneously of a gun going off in the distance. [5]The animals came out of their stalls to find that the flagstaff had been blown down and an elm tree at the foot of the orchard had been plucked up like a radish. [6]They had just noticed this when a despairing cry broke from every animal's throat. [7]The windmill was in ruins.

—George Orwell, *Animal Farm*

■ Why are the animals so upset to find the windmill in ruins? Write your answer in a sentence. _____

_____

■ Find the words ending in *-ing* in the excerpt above that are used as adjectives. Write them below along with the nouns they modify.

Present Participle	**Noun**
1. _____*admiring*_____	_____*animals*_____
2. _____	_____
3. _____	_____
4. _____	_____
5. _____	_____
6. _____	_____

■ Have you ever had something you prized destroyed by the weather? Write a sentence about what happened. _____

For more about participles, see Review Exercises 7, 16, 30, 39.

LESSON 22a
The Present Participle as Adjective Again

Used as an adjective, the present participle is usually found before the noun, but it sometimes follows the noun, as it does in this sentence: *Annie, reading the letter, nearly fainted at the news. Reading* here is an adjective describing Annie.

Introduction to the Hotel X

[1]The Hotel X was a vast, grandiose place with a classical facade and at one side a little, dark doorway like a rat-hole, which was the service entrance. [2]The assistant manager led me down a winding staircase into a narrow passage, deep underground and so low that I had to stoop in places. [3]There seemed to be miles of dark labyrinthine passages that reminded one queerly of the lower decks of a liner; there were the same heat and cramped space and warm reek of food, and a humming, whirring noise (it came from the kitchen furnaces) just like the whir of engines. [4]We passed doorways which let out sometimes a shouting of oaths, sometimes the red glare of a fire, once a shuddering draught from an ice chamber. [5]The kitchen was like nothing I had ever seen or imagined—a stifling, low-ceilinged inferno of a cellar, red-lit from the fires, and deafening with oaths and the clanging of pots and pans.

—George Orwell, *Down and Out in Paris and London*

■ Combine these sentences:

The front of the hotel is grand and imposing. The kitchen is an inferno. _____

■ Find the present participles in the excerpt above that are used as adjectives. Write them below next to the nouns they modify.

Present Participle	Noun
1. _winding_	_staircase_
2. _____	_noise_
3. _____	_draught_
4. _____	_inferno_

■ Think of a place you've visited that was either very hot or very cold. Now write your own sentence about the experience. _____

_____

LESSON 22b
More Participle-Adjectives
• • • • • • • • •

Sometimes the present participle as an adjective will follow the noun it describes. *The actress, checking her makeup, walked onstage* is an example. Look for more present participles like this in the excerpt below.

Homework Before Practice

[1]On a typical afternoon at the Williams house, practicing French comes before practicing tennis. [2]Venus Williams and her sister Serena can see their three private practice courts from the bedroom window. [3]But the courts at the family's 10-acre compound will remain empty today. [4]Venus and Serena have homework to do. [5]Most young pros spend grueling days honing their backhands, not their French accents. [6]Missing practice might mean missing out on ranking points, paychecks and endorsement deals. [7]Venus is nonchalant about skipping practice, and tournaments. [8]The traveling circus of the women's tennis tour has encamped at a Hilton Head resort this week without her. [9]While her would-be opponents perform before cheering crowds, she hears cows mooing on the neighbors' property.

—Linda Robertson, *On Planet Venus*

■ What does Venus Williams find more important than practicing her tennis game? Answer this question in a sentence. _____

_____

■ For each of the present participle/adjectives in the excerpt above, find another noun to fit the meaning of the adjective.

Present Participle	Noun
1. _____ranking_____	_____Points_____
2. _____traveling_____	_____
3. _____cheering_____	_____
4. _____mooing_____	_____

■ Did you ever practice especially hard for some event or competition? Write a sentence about it. _____

_____

LESSON 23
The -*ing* Ending as Spelling

Sometimes the -*ing* ending has no meaning; it is just the way a word is spelled. Or we might explain its use in another way: the -*ing* means *nothing*.

The Bitter Winter

[1]In January food fell short. [2]For days at a time the animals had nothing to eat but chaff and mangels [animal food]. [3]One Sunday morning Squealer announced that the hens, who had just come in to lay again, must surrender their eggs. [4]When the hens heard this, they raised a terrible outcry. [5]They were just getting their clutches ready for the spring sitting, and they protested that to take the eggs away now was murder. [6]For the first time since the expulsion of Jones, there was something resembling a rebellion. [7]Led by three young pullets, the hens made a determined effort to thwart Napoleon's wishes. [8]Whymper heard nothing of this affair, and the eggs were duly delivered, a grocer's van driving up to the farm once a week to take them away.

—George Orwell, *Animal Farm*

■ Combine these sentences:

The hens were angry. Squealer planned to take their eggs away. _____

_____

■ In the excerpt above, find those words ending in -*ing* that are not a verb form and write them below.

1. _____*nothing*_____   3. _____

2. _____

■ Write a sentence about a time you or someone you know took action to prevent what you saw as injustice. _____

_____

LESSON 23a
More Words Spelled with *-ing*

One of the most common nouns in the language, *thing*, ends in *-ing*. Some other nouns with this ending are *ring* and *swing;* verbs ending in *-ing* include *fling* and *sing*.

Arthur's Arrival

¹It was a quiet morning, so still that you could not tell where the mist ended and the surface of the lake began. ²It seemed a kind of desecration to break the hush and plunge into that virgin water, but the fresh chill of it washed away the clinging strands of the night, and when I came out and was dry again and dressed, I ate my breakfast with pleasure, then settled down with my fishing rod to wait for the morning rise, and hope for a breeze at sun-up to ruffle the glassy water. ³No ring or ripple broke the glassy water, no sign of a breeze to come. ⁴I had just decided that I might as well go, when I heard something coming fast through the forest at my back. ⁵I had been wrong in thinking that nothing could come through the forest as fast as a fleeing deer. ⁶Arthur's white hound, Cabal, broke from the trees exactly where the stag had broken, and hurled himself into the water. ⁷Seconds later Arthur himself, on the stallion Canrith, burst out after it. ⁸He shouted something, and came cantering along the shingle.

—Mary Stewart, *The Hollow Hills*

■ Combine these sentences:

The morning was quiet. Arthur's coming shattered the stillness. _____

_____

■ Underline those words from the excerpt above that end in *-ing* because that is part of the spelling. Then for each find another word that expresses nearly the same meaning.

1. _____*a quiet dawn*_____   4. _____

2. _____   5. _____

3. _____

■ Write a sentence about eating outdoors, while camping, having a picnic, or

cooking a backyard barbecue. _____

_____

LESSON 23b
Other Words Ending in -*ing*

. . . .

Most words ending in -*ing* are present participles, but we find verbs like *sing* and nouns like *anything* where the -*ing* is just the way the word is spelled.

Chimps Out!

[1]There was one particular week I'll never forget. [2]It began one morning when someone in the compound shouted "Chimps out!" [3]I ran to the seven-acre handling facilities and saw three chimps walking on top of the wall. [4]Patrick ran around shouting at the chimps and they scrambled back into the enclosure. [5]We searched all around The Wall looking for a hole, then went down to the river to see if they had got out that way, but could find nothing. [6]One of our staff fled down to the river, and Rita must have gone down there after him. [7]I do not know what happened next, but I think the man must have hit Rita with something or at least taken a swing at her, because we suddenly heard that Rita was attacking him. [8]Dave announced that the only way to keep the chimps in was to run another strand of electrical wiring along the top of the wall. [9]The escapes stopped promptly and we all caught a much-needed rest while the chimps took some time to find another way out.

—Sheila Siddle, *In My Family Tree: A Life with Chimpanzees*

■ Why would the chimpanzees keep looking for a way out of their enclosure? Write your answer in a sentence. _____

_____

■ On the lines below write those words in the excerpt above that end in -*ing* because they are spelled that way.

1. _____*morning*_____   3. _____

2. _____   4. _____

■ Have you ever had a problem with a pet that had a mind of its own? Write a sentence about what happened. _____

_____

YOUR WRITING
Using Anecdotes

Sometimes telling a little story or *anecdote* will provide further development to your composition. In George Orwell's *Animal Farm*, Moses the raven does this:

> Moses, who was Mr. Jones's especial pet, was a spy and a tale-bearer, but he was also a clever talker. He claimed to know of the existence of a mysterious country called Sugarcandy Mountain, to which all animals went when they died. In Sugarcandy Mountain it was Sunday seven days a week, clover was in season all the year round, and lump sugar and linseed cake grew on the hedges.

The story Moses tells is meant to make the animals forget their plans for a rebellion with the promise of a glorious future. Some of them even believed the story and lost part of their enthusiasm for the revolt. So, even though it is a story, it adds to the point of Orwell's tale.

Think about a class trip you have taken. Write a thesis sentence that makes a statement about either the educational value of the trip, the entertainment you enjoyed, or the responsibility it required of you. Whichever you choose, write topic sentences for three paragraphs that will follow. Here are some suggestions:

> The trip taught me the value of another country's money.
>
> I had some lessons in getting along with others.
>
> I found out how to use public transportation in a new city.

Once you have written your own sentences, write a brief anecdote for each paragraph. Each anecdote should be no longer than three sentences.

Thesis: _____

_____

Sentence 1: _____

_____

Anecdote: _____

_____

_____

Sentence 2: _____

_____

Anecdote: _____

_____

_____

Sentence 3: _____

_____

Anecdote: _____

_____

_____

LESSON 24
Endings That Form Nouns

· · · · · · · · ·

We saw at the beginning of this unit how word endings were lost on many root words long ago when the Vikings and English needed to communicate. But English has continued, like many other languages, to change the *parts of speech* of words by adding *suffixes*, an ending syllable added to a verb, noun or adjective. Think about the adjective *brave* in the following example: *His saving the child was a brave action.* You can change the adjective to a noun meaning the quality of being brave by adding the suffix *-ry* which gives you the word *bravery*: *His bravery saved the child.*

Endings that produce a noun of quality

-ance	rely. . .	reliance
-dom	king. . .	kingdom
-ence	provide. . .	providence
-ism	cynic. . . .	cynicism
-ity	generous. . .	generosity
-ment	govern. . .	government
-ness	happy. . .	happiness
-ship	friend. . .	friendship
-tion	admire. . .	admiration

The *Titanic* Sinks

[1]As the cries died away the night became strangely peaceful. [2]The *Titanic*, the agonizing suspense, was gone. [3]The shock of what had happened, the confusion and excitement ahead, the realization that close friends were lost forever had not yet sunk in. [4]A curiously tranquil feeling came over many of those in the boats. [5]With the feeling of calm came loneliness. [6]Lawrence Beesley wondered why the *Titanic*, even when mortally wounded, gave everyone a feeling of companionship and security that no lifeboat could replace. [7]In No. 3, Elizabeth Shutes watched the shooting stars and thought to herself how insignificant the *Titanic's* rockets must have looked, competing against nature. [8]In Boat 4, Miss Jean Gertrude Hippach also watched the shooting stars—she had never seen so many. [9]She recalled a legend that every time there's a shooting star, somebody dies.

—Walter Lord, *A Night to Remember*

▪ Why did people in the boats feel calm after the ship sank? Write your answer in a sentence. _____

_____

▪ Several nouns in the excerpt above have been formed by affixing endings on other parts of speech. Write them below along with the word they were formed from.

Noun	Original Word
1. _suspense_	_suspend_
2. _____	_____
3. _____	_____
4. _____	_____
5. _____	_____
6. _____	_____

▪ Think of an exciting event you have been present at—a championship game, a concert, a celebrity's appearance. Write a sentence explaining how you felt then. _____

_____

LESSON 24a
Suffixes Forming Nouns

Many of the nouns formed by suffixes are derived from verbs—for example, *talker* from *talk* and *education* from *educate*. A few, however, come from adjectives—for example, *weakness* from *weak* and *loyalty* from *loyal*.

The Back of the Bus

[1] On December 1, 1955, Rosa Parks propelled the civil rights movement into a new stage of activism when she refused to give up her seat and move to the back of a Montgomery, Alabama, bus, so a white rider could sit down. [2] It

wasn't the first time she'd done so, but it was the first time a bus driver had her arrested for it. [3]Her arrest set off the yearlong boycott in which hundreds of African-Americans walked or carpooled to work rather than ride the buses. [4]Pressure on local authorities to change their policies spawned a lawsuit that ultimately made its way to the U.S. Supreme Court. [5]In November 1956, the court ruled in *Browder v. Gayle* that Alabama's bus segregation laws were unconstitutional.

—Constance Jones, *1001 Things Everyone Should Know About Women's History*

▪ What led to the end of Alabama's bus segregation laws? Write a sentence explaining your answer. _____

_____

▪ Identify those nouns in the excerpt above that are formed from verbs or adjectives. Write them below together with the verb or adjective from which they come, indicating the suffix, as *confine-ment* from the verb *confine*.

Noun	Verb or Adjective/Suffix
1. *movement*	*move-ment*
2. _____	_____
3. _____	_____
4. _____	_____

▪ Have you ever observed a protest? Explain, in a sentence, what form it took.

_____

LESSON 24b
More Suffixes Forming Nouns
· · · · · · · · ·

In addition to verbs and adjectives, some nouns can also form new nouns. One example of this is seen in the suffix *-ship*: the noun *fellow* can become the noun *fellowship*, a group of fellows.

Baseball Vacation

[1]The last traces of my baseball neutrality disappeared during the month of August, which I passed on vacation in Maine, deep in Red Sox country. [2]Far from any ballpark and without a television set, I went to bed early on most

nights and lay there kept almost awake by the murmurous running thread of Bosox baseball from my bedside radio. [3]I felt very close to the game then—perhaps because I grew up listening to baseball over the radio, or perhaps because the familiar quiet tones and effortless precision of the veteran Red Sox announcers invited me to share with them the profound New England seriousness of Following the Sox. [4]I have spent many summers in this part of the world, but this was the first year I could remember when the Red Sox were in first place all through August—a development that seemed only to deepen the sense of foreboding that always afflicts the Red Sox faithful as the summer wanes.

—Roger Angell, *Late Innings*

■ Combine these sentences:

New Englanders root for the Red Sox. The team is seldom in first place. _____

_____

■ Find the nouns formed from verbs, adjectives, and other nouns and write them below. Be sure to indicate what part of the noun is the suffix and the original word from which the noun is formed.

Noun	Verb, Adjective, or Noun
1. _____*neutral—ity*_____	_____*neutral, adjective*_____
2. _____	_____
3. _____	_____
4. _____	_____
5. _____	_____
6. _____	_____

■ Often people like to root for the underdog. In a sentence explain why you think this is so. _____

_____

For more about suffixes, see Review Exercises 15, 18, 28, 45.

LESSON 25
Endings That Show Who or What Performs an Action

· · · · · · · · ·

The heading above includes the verb *performs*; people who perform are called *performers*. An *-er* or *-or* ending can change a verb, an action word, into a noun—a person or thing—that performs the action. For example: *Josh loves to act, so he became an actor.*

On the March

[1]On Friday morning, October 26, a group of us gather on the outskirts of New Orleans to begin walking the 80 miles to Baton Rouge. [2]Several TV and radio stations and newspaper reporters show up. [3]Reflecting back I realize now, even more than I did then, just how crucial the media are to public education on this issue, and I am struck by how many reporters and journalists become sympathetic to the cause once they become knowledgeable about the issue. [4]We're an interesting assortment: black and white, ex-cons and nuns, secretaries and teachers, housewives, students, a carpenter, a woman whose sister was murdered but who opposes capital punishment, some family members with sons on death row, a Vietnam vet. [5]We arrive in Baton Rouge as the sun is setting. [6]A young man, one of the marchers, touches my arm and points to the bottom of the steps where the counter-demonstrators are and says that the man down there wants to talk to me.

—Helen Prejean, C. S. J., *Dead Man Walking*

- Combine these sentences:

A group is marching to Baton Rouge. Many different kinds of people are in the group. _____

_____

- Find the nouns in the excerpt above that show by their endings the performer of an action. Write them below with the words from which they are formed.

Performer	Verb
1. _____*reporter*_____	_____*reports*_____
2. _____	_____

114

Performer	Verb
3. _____	_____
4. _____	_____

- Think of a long walk you have taken. Write a sentence about why you did it—to prove a point, to reach a place you wanted to be, or just because it was a nice day for walking. _____

_____

 ## LESSON 25a
Suffixes That Turn Verbs into Agents

· · · · · · · · ·

The person who performs an action is sometimes called an agent. One who *writes* is a *writer*, one who *orates* is an *orator*. Note that the suffix for these words is sometimes spelled *-er* and sometimes *-or*.

An Ambitious Doctor

[1]Does it seem incongruous to you that a Middlemarch surgeon should dream of himself as a discoverer? [2]Most of us, indeed, know little of the great originators until they have been lifted up among the constellations and already rule our fates. [3]Lydgate would be a good Middlemarch doctor, and by that very means keep himself in the track of far-reaching investigation. [4]This was an innovation for one who had chosen to adopt the style of general practitioner in a country town, and would be felt as offensive criticism by his professional brethren. [5]But Lydgate meant to innovate in his treatment also, and he was wise enough to see that the best security for his practicing honestly according to his belief was to get rid of systematic temptations to the contrary. [6]Perhaps that was a more cheerful time for observers and theorizers than the present; we are apt to think it the finest era of the world when America was beginning to be discovered, when a bold sailor, even if he were wrecked, might alight on a new kingdom; and about 1829 the dark territories of pathology were a fine America for a spirited young adventurer.

—George Eliot, *Middlemarch*

■ How does Lydgate hope to make his mark on the world? Write your answer in a sentence. _____

_____

■ Find the nouns in the excerpt above in which verbs are turned into agents by the suffixes *-er* or *-or*. For five of them, write a sentence using the verbs from which they are formed, as shown in the first example.

	Noun	**Sentence**
1.	*discoverer*	*Did you discover the date the paper is due?*
2.		
3.		
4.		
5.		
6.		

■ Write a sentence about a goal you have achieved. It might be the ability to cook, to run for a touchdown, or to play the guitar. _____

_____

LESSON 25b
Changing More Verbs into Nouns

· · · · · · · · · ·

Remember that you can recognize a verb if it has an infinitive form such as *to think, to shout, to row*. Nouns formed from these verbs are *thinker, shouter*, and *rower*.

Captain Cook's Misjudgment

[1]Cook learned much about Fiji, but evinced no curiosity to visit it and its neighbouring islands. [2]He did not so much as point his prow in Fiji's known direction. [3]Instead he courted disaster to his sloops when sailing carelessly through a channel, was nearly assassinated, caused more distress than happiness among these child-like islanders, showed a new side of his nature to

his concerned officers, lost a large number of his precious livestock, and experienced a lowering in the morale of his sailors. [4]William Bligh was among those who could not understand his commander's inaction. [5]If he had been in command he would soon have sought out these islands. [6]And by a strange chance of fate, Bligh was to do just that. [7]In these same waters, a group of his men led by Fletcher Christian was to rise up against him and cast him and eighteen of his men—that admirable tough gunner William Peckover and the amiable gardener David Nelson among them—into the ship's launch. [8]He then headed for those islands, sailed through them in the most masterly piece of navigation in history, charted them as well as he could from his tiny overloaded vessel, and thus became, instead of Cook, their famed discoverer.

—Richard Hough, *The Last Voyage of Captain James Cook*

■ Combine these sentences:

Cook lost an opportunity. He might have discovered Fiji. _____

_____

■ Find the nouns in the excerpt above indicating performers that are formed from a verb with the suffix *-er* or *-or* and write what they do, as the example shows.

Noun	**Verb**
1. _____ *a sailor* _____	_____ *sails* _____
2. _____	_____
3. _____	_____
4. _____	_____
5. _____	_____
6. _____	_____

■ Think of someone you admire for making a discovery of a place or thing. Write a sentence explaining why you admire this person. _____

_____

LESSON 26
Endings That Form Adjectives

Adjectives, the words that indicate *what kind,* are frequently formed from nouns and verbs by adding endings. For example, *question* can become *questionable, depend* becomes *dependent,* and *zeal* becomes *zealous.*

Endings That Form Adjectives

-able	love...	lovable
-al	condition...	conditional
-ant	triumph...	triumphant
-ary	custom...	customary
-ent	depend...	dependent
-ful	peace...	peaceful
-ible	contempt...	contemptible
-ic	photograph...	photographic
-ish	girl...	girlish
-ly	friend...	friendly
-less	friend...	friendless
-ous	harmony..	harmonious

In the Lifeboats

[1]The crew did their best to make the women more comfortable. [2]In No. 5 a sailor took off his stockings and gave them to Mrs. Washington Dodge. [3]When she looked up in startled gratitude, he explained, "I assure you, ma'am, they are perfectly clean. [4]I just put them on this morning." [5]In No. 13, Fireman Beauchamp shivered in his thin jumpers, but he refused to take an extra coat offered him by an elderly lady, insisting it go to a young Irish girl instead. [6]Besides the cold, the number of lady oarsmen dispelled the picnic illusion. [7]In No. 6 the irrepressible Mrs. Brown organized the women, two to an oar. [8]One held the oar in place, while the second did the pulling. [9]In this way Mrs. Brown, Mrs. Meyer, Mrs. Candee and others propelled the boat some three or four miles, in a hopeless effort to overtake the light that twinkled on the horizon most of the night.

—Walter Lord, *A Night to Remember*

■ Combine these sentences:

Everyone was cold. Everyone in the boats tried to help the others. _____

_____

■ Find the adjectives in the excerpt above that have been formed from other words. Write them in the column below, then write a sentence for each using the words from which they are formed, as the example shows.

<table>
<tr><td></td><td align="center">**Adjectives**</td><td align="center">**Sentence**</td></tr>
<tr><td>1.</td><td align="center">*comfortable*</td><td align="center">*The socks were a comfort to Mrs. Dodge.*</td></tr>
<tr><td>2.</td><td></td><td></td></tr>
<tr><td>3.</td><td></td><td></td></tr>
<tr><td>4.</td><td></td><td></td></tr>
</table>

■ Write a sentence about a generous action you have seen someone do for another person. _____

LESSON 26a
Suffixes That Form Adjectives

Many adjectives are formed from nouns, such as *sorrowful* from *sorrow* and *marvelous* from *marvel*. Some can be made from verbs, like *different* from *differ*.

All-Purpose Cells

[1]The human body looks and works like a seamless whole, but it is constructed of individual units too small to be seen, some 100 trillion living cells. [2]Stem cells have recently burst from the obscurity of the research laboratory into the arena of national politics, propelled by assertions that they are either the fruits of murder or the panacea for the degenerative diseases of age. [3]Obtained from the surplus embryos generated in fertility clinics, human embryonic stem cells have not yet been much studied because many biomedical researchers were forbidden to work on them. [4]Embryonic stem cells are of great interest because of their all-purpose nature. [5]But the body's adult stem cells also hold high medical promise. [6]The promise of stem cell research is that it may allow doctors to bend the rules of this harsh game just a little, by using the vast generative power of stem cells to extend life and health.

—Nicholas Wade, *In Tiny Cells, Glimpses of Body's Master Plan*

▪ Combine these sentences:

Stem cells have not been studied much. They hold medical promise. _____

_____

▪ Match the list of nouns and verbs below with the adjectives that you can find in the excerpt above.

Nouns and Verbs	Adjectives
1. seam	_seamless_
2. nation	_____
3. degenerate	_____
4. embryo	_____
5. medicine	_____
6. generate	_____

▪ What recent scientific discovery do you find most exciting? Write a sentence explaining what it is. _____

_____

LESSON 26b
Adjectives and Adverbs
• • • • • • • • •

We have seen a number of adjectives formed from nouns. These adjectives, in turn, are often turned into adverbs—words that tell how—by adding -*ly* to an adjective. For example, *natur-al*, an adjective formed from the noun *nature* and the suffix -*al*, can become the adverb *natur-al-ly*, the way in which one acts. Some others are *use-ful-ly, plenti-ful-ly,* and *beauti-ful-ly*.

A Dictionary Maker

[1]Noah Webster (1758–1843) was by all accounts a severe, correct, humorless, religious, temperate man who was not easy to like, even by other severe, religious, temperate, humorless people. [2]All Webster's work was informed by a passionate patriotism and the belief that American English was at least as good as British English. [3]He worked tirelessly, churning out endless hectoring books and tracts, as well as working on the more or less

constant revisions of his spellers and dictionaries. [4]In between time he wrote impassioned letters to congressmen, dabbled in politics, proffered unwanted advice to presidents, led his church choir, lectured to large audiences, helped found Amherst College, and produced a sanitized version of the Bible. [5]Like Samuel Johnson, he was a better lexicographer than a businessman. [6]Instead of insisting on royalties he sold the rights outright and never gained the sort of wealth that his tireless labors merited.

—Bill Bryson, *The Mother Tongue: English and How It Got That Way*

■ What in this excerpt indicates the reason Webster could be called "not easy to like"? Answer the question in a sentence. _____

_____

■ Find the adjectives in the excerpt above that are formed from nouns or verbs and list them on the lines below. If there are any adverbs formed from adjectives, list them too.

Adjective	Noun or Verb	Adverb
1. *humorless*	*humor*	*humorlessly*
2.		
3.		
4.		
5.		
6.		

■ People who achieve remarkable things are not always pleasant human beings. Can you think of anyone famous who has a reputation for being hard to get along with? Write your answer in a sentence. _____

_____

For more on suffixes, see Review Exercises 15, 18, 28, 45.

LESSON 27
Endings That Show More or Most

Adjectives not only indicate the quality of a person or thing; they can also show the *degree* of this quality, as in the familiar *good, better, best.* Thus a glass of lemonade can be *cold*, another glass can be *colder,* and still another glass can be *coldest*. These forms are called the *positive*, the *comparative*, and the *superlative.* We can use these endings on nearly all adjectives to show more or most of the quality. We can also write that some sunsets are *beautiful*, others are *more beautiful*, and that last night's was the *most beautiful* of all. We use this form when the adjective formed by *-er* or *-est* would be more difficult to say or write.

After the Sinking

[1]In the case of the living, the Register carefully ran the phrase, "Arrived *Titan-Carpath*, April 18, 1912." [2]The hyphen represented history's greatest sea disaster. [3]What troubled people especially was not just the tragedy—or even its needlessness—but the element of fate in it all. [4]If the *Titanic* had heeded any of the six ice messages on Sunday . . . if ice conditions had been normal . . . if the night had been rough or moonlit . . . if she had seen the berg 15 seconds sooner—or 15 seconds later . . . if she had hit the ice any other way . . . if her watertight bulkheads had been one deck higher . . . if she had carried enough boats . . . if the *Californian* had only come. [5]Had any one of these "ifs" turned out right, every life might have been saved. [6]But they all went against her—a classic Greek tragedy.

—Walter Lord, *A Night to Remember*

- Combine these sentences:

People were troubled by the sinking of the *Titanic*. There was an element of fate in what happened. _____

_____

- Underline all the adjectives in the excerpt above that end in *-er* or *-est*. Write them below in their positive, comparative, and superlative forms, as shown in the example.

Positive	Comparative	Superlative
1. *great*	*greater*	*greatest*
2.		

Positive	Comparative	Superlative
3. _____	_____	_____
4. _____	_____	_____

- Think of a time when the weather affected your mood. Write a sentence about how much of a change it made in the way you felt. _____

_____

LESSON 27a
More Adjectives of Degree

· · · · · · · · · ·

Although most adjectives add -*er* or -*est* to show degree, note that some must use *more* or *most* to signal such changes.

Paris in the Spring

[1]I bade adieu to Paris the twenty-fifth of February, just as we had had one fine day. [2]This one fine day brought out the Parisian world in its gayest colors. [3]I never saw anything more animated or prettier, of the kind, than the promenade that day in the *Champs Elysées*. [4]But a French crowd is always gay, full of quick turns and drolleries; most amusing when most petulant, it represents what is so agreeable in the character of the nation. [5]We have now seen it on two good occasions, the festivities of the new year and just after we came was the *mardi gras*. [6]An immense crowd thronged the streets this year to see it, but few figures and little invention followed the emblem of plenty; indeed few among the people could have had the heart for such a sham, knowing how the poorer classes have suffered from hunger this Winter. [7]All signs of this are kept out of sight in Paris.

—Margaret Fuller, *These Sad but Glorious Days: Dispatches from Europe*

- Combine these sentences:

Spring in Paris is beautiful. The poor are kept out of sight. _____

_____

■ Some of the adjectives that appear in the excerpt above can show changes in degree with *-er* or *-est*, while others need *more* or *most*. Choose five adjectives, and show how they can be compared, as shown in the example.

Adjective	Comparative	Superlative
1. *clear*	*clearer*	*clearest*
2.		
3.		
4.		
5.		
6.		

■ Write a sentence about a beautiful spring day that had something sad about it, as thoughts of the poor affect the writer's feeling about the day in Paris. _____

_____

LESSON 27b
Adjectives Having Irregular Degree Forms

· · · · · · · · · ·

While many adjectives show comparative and superlative degree by adding *-er* or *-est*, others do this by preceding the adjective with *more* or *most*, and still others are completely irregular, like *bad*, *worse*, and *worst*.

The Discovery of Hawaii

[1]At dawn on 18 January Cook could just make out the shape of the first of the Hawaiian islands he was to note in his log and describe in his journal. [2]They were clearly on the brink of making the greatest discovery of this voyage so far. [3]Oahu bore almost due east, its mountains sharply defined in the clear air, but no nearer than before. [4]Kauai was directly ahead, mountainous, too, and already giving evidence of rich fruitfulness. [5]Gore "saw a high hummock of land" at 5:30 p.m., rising straight from the sea at the east end of the island, then gentler slopes along the south side with trees higher up, and along the shore and hinterland villages, plantations

of some root crop, sugar and plantains. ⁶The natives were massing in groups on favourable headlands and staring out wonderingly at the strange sight of these great vessels running before the wind half a league off the shore.

—Richard Hough, *The Last Voyage of Captain James Cook*

▪ Why does the writer believe that this was to be the greatest discovery of the voyage? _____

_____

▪ Underline the adjectives in the excerpt above. Choose three and write them below in all three forms, as shown in the example.

Adjective	Comparative	Superlative
1. _____ *fine* _____	_____ *finer* _____	_____ *finest* _____
2. _____	_____	_____
3. _____	_____	_____
4. _____	_____	_____

▪ Are any voyages of discovery being made today? Write a sentence about one you have read of. _____

_____

YOUR WRITING
Being Specific

The movie was exciting. What goes through your mind when you read a sentence like this? Chances are you'll have questions immediately: What was the name of the movie? What was exciting about it? At what theater is it playing? In order to communicate information it is essential to provide details like these. Yet very often sentences, while accurate enough, are not informative enough. What can you do to produce writing that gives a reader a clearer picture of what you want to say? There are several ways, the ones you have been practicing throughout this unit.

- Be as specific as you can. Does Lora have a new top? Make it a fire-engine red sleeveless cotton T-shirt. How about the car Hari's brother is lending him to go to the beach? It's a black Mustang convertible with five speeds, isn't it? Don't be shy about including information; it's almost impossible to have too much.
- Use examples to provide information. Are you telling someone how difficult a science class can be? Don't just say biology or chemistry is tough. Be specific: *The hardest part is memorizing the periodic table of the elements.* Or perhaps *Preparing a slide for the microscope is extremely difficult.*
- Make your examples more interesting with an *anecdote* or brief story. (Be careful here to keep it *brief.*) It could be something like, *For the fourth morning in a row Maybelle didn't hear the alarm clock and walked into her Spanish class just ten minutes before the period ended.*
- Be sure to include plenty of details to provide a clear picture: brand names: not just *toothpaste,* but *Crest Tartar Control Toothpaste;* colors: *magenta, burnt orange;* places: *Sam's Pizzeria, the Fifty-Ninth Street station, Lake of the Woods;* titles: *Bridget Jones's Diary, Of Mice and Men;* flavors: *mint chocolate chip* . . . this list could go on indefinitely.

Notice that the people in the examples above have names, the classes have titles. and the car has a transmission as well as a brand name. These are ways of providing specific information to your reader.

It's time now to write a paragraph.

Sister Helen Prejean's book, *Dead Man Walking,* is written to support a cause in which she believes deeply. If you have ever supported a cause, whether collecting clothing for the homeless or campaigning for better traffic signals, write a topic sentence that explains your reason for supporting it. (If you haven't, write about a cause you've heard about.) Now go on to write a paragraph of at least five sentences.

_____

_____

_____

_____

_____

_____

_____

_____

_____

_____

Read your paragraph again, making as many words as possible more specific and adding as many details as you can think of.

UNIT IV

What We *Really* Say: Idiomatic Uses

We saw in Unit 3 that English once had many more word endings that changed meanings than it now has. A word's ending signaled whether it was the subject or object of a sentence, for example. Thus the poet of *Beowulf* could write *Tham wife tha word wel licodon*—literally *To the woman the words well pleased*. *Tham wife* indicates by the endings *-m* and *-e* that the meaning is *to the woman,* and *tha word* signifies a plural noun. Endings also carried information that affected word order, which was much less important than it is in today's English, which would say, *The words pleased the woman well.*

But endings affected more than word order; they provided such information as *where, when,* and *whose.* For example, *to the king* was *thaem cyninge* and *belonging to the king* was *thaes cyninges.* What happened after these endings were lost to make clear what was being said? People began to use prepositional phrases like *after the game, across the river,* and *the point of the assignment* (the assignment's point). Read this:

> It was only hours since I had last seen them, but they had changed and I had changed. *In the very front rank*, two men were wounded and staggered along, trailing blood *behind them.* No drummers here, no pipers, and the red coats were covered *with a fine film of dust.* They marched *with bayonets fixed*, and as fixed *on their faces* was anger, fear, and torment.
>
> —Howard Fast, *April Morning*

You probably identified several prepositional phrases in that excerpt. Something else to notice is that while prepositions show time, direction, and possession, the phrases they produce often fall into the category known as *idioms*—expressions in a language that are peculiar to themselves and cannot be reduced to rules. It is the reason we say that some people wait *in line* and

129

others wait *on line*, and it accounts for expressions like *to the store* but *to Macy's* and *around town* but *around the block*. Idioms also make use of prepositions to form two-word verbs like *put on, take off, go out, wash up* and many more, as we'll see.

But before we go on (notice the idiomatic two-word verb), let's look at how *determiners* or *articles* are used idiomatically. You know that *the* is used for one or more specific things and that *a* and *an* refer to something that is not specified. *The dog* [my friend Spot] *chased the stick. A dog* [a stranger whose name I don't know] *chased me down the street.*

We'll be looking for examples of these idioms in Howard Fast's *April Morning,* a novel about the beginning of the American Revolution as seen by a teenaged boy.

LESSON 28
Prepositions That Indicate
Where and *When*

Prepositions are usually small words—*to, by, at, of*—but they are words we cannot do without. They show us many things: when and where things happen—*after the game, we went to the picnic*; how they happen—*we watched the movie with excitement*; and who makes them happen—*the class read the story by Stephen King*. In the passage below look for prepositions that give you information about *when* and *where*.

A Brother's Comfort

¹We sat quietly in the darkness for a few minutes. ²Levi pressed close to me, pushing his face into my jacket. ³He felt small and helpless, and I was filled with guilt for all the times we had quarreled and all the names we had called each other, and I told myself that from now on, I would take care of him just as if I were his own father. ⁴But when Levi slipped out of the smokehouse, I was alone again and afraid again, and had no one to come between myself and my fear and grief.

—Howard Fast, *April Morning*

▪ Combine these sentences:

Levi is my younger brother. I reassured him. _____

_____

▪ Underline the prepositional phrases in the excerpt above. Decide which ones describe *when* and *where* something is happening. Write them below, as shown in the example.

Phrase	**Where or When**
1. *in the darkness*	*where*
2.	
3.	
4.	
5.	
6.	

131

Phrase	Where or When
7. _____	_____
8. _____	_____

■ Write a sentence about a time when you felt especially close to a friend or a member of your family. _____

_____

LESSON 28A
More Prepositional Phrases

We depend so much on prepositional phrases to show us directions—*over, under, between*—that we may forget how frequently they occur in our writing. See how many you find in the passage below.

New Chimp in Town

[1]Milla appeared to be most taken with The Babies in the cage next to her. [2]Most were about two years of age and, in addition to the Rwandan chimps, all arrived within an eighteen-month period. [3]Milla would sometimes lie on the ledge next to their cage and pretend to be asleep, allowing the braver souls like Pan to sneak up and grab or bite any part of her that seemed to stick through the bars—a finger or foot, or even just a toe. [4]Though Milla was fully awake, she never showed any reaction to this nasty behavior. [5]In fact, Milla often encouraged Dora to approach and groom her through the bars, sometimes even turning her back, and with a finger indicating to Dora a spot she'd like scratched. [6]Milla blossomed in the fourteen-acre enclosure.

—Sheila Siddle, *In My Family Tree: A Life with Chimpanzees*

■ Combine these sentences:

Milla liked The Babies. She let them tease her. _____

_____

▪ Fill in the blanks below with prepositional phrases that show direction. Your answers need not be in the exact words of the excerpt.

1. The Babies were ___*in the cage*___, _____ Milla. She liked to lie

_____ and let her arm or leg stick _____. She really

enjoyed being _____.

▪ Have you ever watched puppies or kittens or other baby animals? Write a sentence about how they behave. _____

_____

LESSON 28B
Prepositional Phrases That Tell *When*

Many of our common prepositional phrases indicate *when* something happened—or will happen. For example, *I'll meet you after the movie* or *That happened before my time.* Look for some of these phrases in the following paragraph.

Women Writing Sports

[1]The arrival of the first female reporters in the Yankee clubhouse last September had perfectly predictable results. [2]On the night that Judge Motley's order took effect, the Yankee clubhouse was suddenly crowded with strangers, male and female, who had come to report on the new socio-journalistic phenomenon. [3]After the first night, however, the clubhouse was a much quieter place, and the players, caught up in their excruciating race, talked mostly baseball. [4]On Friday night, the Yankees announced that the clubhouse would be closed to all reporters for forty-five minutes after the game, to permit the players to shower and dress. [5]The reporters were badly upset.

—Roger Angell, *Late Innings*

▪ Combine these sentences:

Reporters interview players after the game. They get the best story in the clubhouse. _____

_____

■ Find the prepositions in the excerpt above that indicate *when*. Write them in the spaces below to complete the sentences.

1. The Yankee clubhouse was suddenly crowded _____*on the night*_____.

2. The clubhouse was a much quieter place _____.

3. The Yankees announced that the clubhouse would be closed _____

_____.

4. The closing would be _____.

5. It would happen _____.

■ Do you have a favorite sportswriter? Explain in a sentence what you like

about that writer's style. _____

_____

For more on prepositions, see Review Exercises 11, 14.

LESSON 29
Prepositions That Indicate
How and *Why*

. . . .

Some prepositional phrases, like *by chance* or *for the reward,* tell how or why something happens. *Alice explained her research project with a PowerPoint presentation.* Look for this kind of phrase in the following paragraph.

Silence

[1]I was awakened by the silence. [2]I guess it was the first silence in six or seven hours, and it was just unbelievable and a little frightening as well. [3]I don't mean that it was a complete and total silence, or anything unnatural or spooky. [4]There were sounds in the distance and in the background, as there always are, but even these sounds were muffled by the tangled pile of trees; and missing were the violent and awful sounds of battle, the crash of firearms and the savage shouting and swearing of men in anger and pain. [5]It was still daylight outside, but under the windfall was a sort of comforting twilight, and being used to gauging time without a pocket watch, I had a feeling that at least an hour had passed.

—Howard Fast, *April Morning*

▪ Why would anyone be awakened by silence? Write your answer in a sentence. _____

_____

▪ Find the prepositional phrases in the excerpt above. Write them in the spaces below to answer the following questions.

1. How is the narrator awakened? _____*by the silence*_____

2. By what are the sounds muffled? _____

3. What is the crash? _____

4. What is the savage shouting and swearing? _____

5. How do the men shout? _____

6. How does the writer gauge time? _____

▪ Now write a sentence about how you felt in a very silent place you have been in. _____

_____

LESSON 29A
Why and *How* Prepositional Phrases

Using a prepositional phrase to indicate how something is done or why someone chooses to do it can be a less complicated way of showing these relationships than writing one or more sentences of explanation: *Jonny uses a dictionary for finding synonyms.*

A Latin Language?

[1]English grammar is so complex and confusing for the one very simple reason that its rules and terminology are based on Latin—a language with which it has precious little in common. [2]In Latin, to take one example, it is not possible to split an infinitive. [3]So in English, the early authorities decided, it should not be possible to split an infinitive either. [4]But there is no reason why we shouldn't any more than we should forsake instant coffee and air travel because they weren't available to the Romans. [5]Making English grammar conform to Latin rules is like asking people to play baseball using the rules of football. [6]It is a patent absurdity. [7]The early authorities not only used Latin grammar as their model, but actually went to the almost farcical length of writing English grammars in that language.

—Bill Bryson, *The Mother Tongue: English and How It Got That Way*

▪ Combine these sentences:

Some people try to apply Latin rules to English. English is an entirely different language. _____

_____

▪ Identify the prepositional phrases in the excerpt above that help to answer the following:

1. Why English is confusing   *for the one very simple reason* _____

2. To whom was air travel not available?   _____

3. On what did early authorities base English rules _____

4. What Latin grammar was used as 　　　_____

5. How some English grammars are written　　_____

■ What might happen if a language had no rules? Write your own sentence to answer this question. _____

_____

LESSON 29B
More on *How* and *Why*

· · · · · · · · · ·

　We have seen prepositional phrases that answer *when, where, how,* and *why.* In the following passage look for more prepositional phrases that answer these questions.

Black Comedy

[1]In the postwar years, as the civil rights movement gained force and the pop culture universe expanded, black comedians seized the moment. [2]So just what is black humor and, by extension, its entertainment offshoot, black comedy? [3]Mr. Watkins describes certain characteristics that sound remarkably like those mentioned by the comedians. [4]Foremost among them are realism, a willingness to poke fun at the predicaments of life, and delivery, owing to the more expressive and flamboyant styles of Black America. [5]Generally speaking, the black comedians agreed that the spread of urban culture, and rap music in particular, was helping to bridge the sensibility gap between black and white audiences, further blurring distinctions between black and white comedy.

—Fletcher Roberts, *Explosive, Realistic, but Most of All Funny*

■ How can the development of urban culture benefit our society? Write your answer in a sentence. _____

_____

■ Find a prepositional phrase in the excerpt above that answers each of the following questions, as shown in the example.

1. When?   *In the postwar years* _____

2. How?   _____

3. What?   _____

4. Where?   _____

■ Write a sentence explaining why your favorite comedian makes you laugh.

_____

For more about prepositional phrases, see Review Exercises 24, 27.

L E S S O N   3 0
Prepositions That Show Possession

Much of the time we indicate that something belongs to someone or something by adding -'s. Another way of doing it is by a prepositional phrase beginning with *of: the roof of the house* means the same as *the house's roof.* Here are some examples.

The Return

[1]When I saw the tower of the meetinghouse, I felt better, and then I saw the Parker barns on the outskirts of town, and I told myself that if they had burned one, they would have burned the other too. [2]You might think we would run in our haste to be there and see what had happened, but you don't hurry for bad news. [3]Also, we were tired, all three of us. [4]So we came up to the town slowly, and bit by bit we realized that it still stood, only the three houses that I spoke of before burned down. [5]It was the ending of a day when I had seen many bodies, bodies of redcoats and bodies of Committeemen.

—Howard Fast, *April Morning*

■ What feeling do you get from this passage? Write a sentence explaining why you feel this way. _____

_____

■ Among the prepositional phrases in the excerpt above are some that show possession. Write them below, followed by the form with an apostrophe, as shown in the example.

1. *the tower of the meetinghouse*   *the meetinghouse's tower*

2. _____   _____

3. _____   _____

4. _____   _____

5. _____   _____

139

▪ Sometimes we can see that something unusual has happened nearby—a fire engine, a police car's flashing lights, a gathering crowd. Write a sentence about such a scene that you have come upon. _____

_____

LESSON 30A
More Possessive Prepositional Phrases
· · · · · · · · · ·

You can determine if a prepositional phrase is a possessive simply by turning it around: *the face of the clock* can be rewritten as *the clock's face.*

The Stranger in the Water

¹The side of the ship made a belt of shadow on the glassy shimmer of the sea. ²But I saw at once something elongated and pale floating very close to the ladder. ³Before I could form a guess a faint flash of phosphorescent light, which seemed to issue suddenly from the naked body of a man, flickered in the sleeping water with the elusive, silent play of summer lightning in a night sky. ⁴With a gasp I saw revealed to my stare a pair of feet, the long legs, a broad livid back immersed right up to the neck in a greenish cadaverous glow. ⁵One hand, awash, clutched the bottom rung of the ladder. ⁶He was complete but for the head. ⁷A headless corpse! ⁸At that I suppose he raised up his face, a dimly pale oval in the shadow of the ship's side.

—Joseph Conrad, *The Secret-Sharer*

▪ Combine these sentences:

The narrator thinks he sees a headless corpse. He sees a face. _____

_____

▪ Find the prepositional phrases that serve as possessives in the excerpt above and write them as they would be formed with an apostrophe, as shown in the example.

1. _____*the ship's side*_____   4. _____

2. _____   5. _____

3. _____   6. _____

▪ Write a sentence about a scene in a horror movie that made you jump in your seat. _____

_____

LESSON 30B
Still More Possessive Prepositional Phrases
• • • • • • • • •

Sometimes we choose to write a possessive as a prepositional phrase because a simple -'s would sound awkward. For example, in sentence 2 below we would wind up with *the eighteenth-century ruined fortresses' shelter.*

Laundry and Civilization

[1]At Acre, the stronghold of the Crusaders on the Mediterranean, west of Galilee, the fortifications stand in golden ruins, piled on the foundations of earlier ruins. [2]Arabs lived in the shelter of the eighteenth-century ruined fortresses, and even now in the years of the establishment of Israel, burning with its mixture of religion, hygiene, and applied sociology, the poor Arabs still hung out their washing on the battlements, so that it fluttered all along the antique sea-front, innocent of the offense it was committing in the eyes of the seekers of beautiful sights and spiritual sensations, who had come all the way from the twentieth century, due west of Acre. [3]Indeed, the washing draped out on the historic walls was a sign of progress, enlightenment, and industry, as it had been from time immemorial; it betokened a settlement and a society with a sense of tomorrow, even if it was only tomorrow's clean shirt, as against the shifty tent-dwelling communities of the wilderness.

—Muriel Spark, *The Mandelbaum Gate*

▪ Why does the writer find the washing hung on the city walls a sign of civilization? Write a sentence explaining your answer. _____

_____

▪ Find the prepositional phrases in the excerpt above that show what possesses each of the following:

1. the stronghold   *of the Crusaders*

2. foundations   _____

3. shelter   _____

4. establishment   _____

5. eyes   _____

6. communities   _____

▪ What kind of scene represents civilization for you? Write your answer in a sentence. _____

_____

For more on prepositional phrases, see Review Exercises 11, 14, 24, 27.

LESSON 31
Two-Word Verbs

Some prepositions are an integral part of what we call *two-word verbs*—*put down, take up, make over,* and many more. Each of these two-word verbs has a meaning of its own distinct from the meaning of the verb alone. (Think about the difference between *put down* and *put.*) Prepositions used like this are called *particles.*

The Night Rider

[1]I heard it now, and Levi was right. [2]The sound was of a horse being raced through the night, and clearer and clearer came the drumbeat of its hoofs. [3]I strained my eyes toward the Menotomy Road, but it was too dark and there were too many trees obstructing my vision for me to make out a rider. [4]But the rider was nearer now, and the hoofbeats echoed through the whole village; and then he pulled up in front of Buckman's, and I heard him shouting at the top of his lungs, although I couldn't make out his words. [5]We heard him shouting again. [6]Mother came in, carrying a candle. [7]Lights were beginning to flicker in some of the houses. [8]Middle of the night or not, the village was up and awake, and every man and boy in town was either already at the common or heading for it. [9]I dashed out of the house and took off for the common.

—Howard Fast, *April Morning*

- Combine these sentences:

A horseman has arrived. The village is excited. _____

_____

- Find the two-word verbs in the excerpt above.

1. _____*make out*_____   3. _____

2. _____   4. _____

- Think of a time you were surprised when an unexpected visitor arrived at your home or school. Write a sentence about it. _____

_____

LESSON 31A
More Two-Word Verbs

One way to recognize a two-word verb is by testing to see if a pronoun can appear between the verb and the preposition. For example, we can *take it off* but we can't *take off it*. Here's another example: *Wally wants to take up snowboarding as a hobby. He would really like to take it up.*

Danger at Sea

[1]Sometimes a storm would hit the Grand Banks and half a dozen ships would go down, a hundred men lost overnight. [2]On more than one occasion, Newfoundlanders woke up to find their beaches strewn with bodies. [3]The Grand Banks are so dangerous because they happen to sit on one of the worst storm tracks in the world. [4]In the old days, there wasn't much the boats could do but put out extra anchor cable and try to ride it out. [5]As dangerous as the Grand Banks were, though, Georges Bank was even worse. [6]Currents ran in strange vortexes on Georges, and the tide was said to run off so fast that ocean bottom was left exposed for gulls to feed on.

—Sebastian Junger, *The Perfect Storm*

■ Why is Georges Bank more dangerous than the Grand Banks? Write your answer in a sentence. _____

_____

■ Identify the two-word verbs in the excerpt above and write them below.

1. ____*go down*____ 4. _____

2. _____ 5. _____

3. _____ 6. _____

■ What is the most dangerous place you have ever seen? Write a sentence about that place. _____

_____

LESSON 31B
Two-Word Verbs and Prepositional Phrases

Another way to recognize two-word verbs is to note whether they are followed by a prepositional phrase, as in *Oscar looked out over the sea. Looked out* is a two-word verb and *over the sea* is a prepositional phrase.

The First Practice

[1]The coaches stand there looking at us the way a mechanic eyes his socket wrenches, as tools to be picked up, used, and thrown aside. [2]There is only this simple equation: as a ballplayer, I am expected to do as I'm told, lay my body on the line or else get out of the way for somebody who will. [3]Everybody in the room knows and understands this and, when asked, will put himself in harm's way with the dim, deluded hope that he will come out the other end a star. [4]The speech begins, and it's like every other coach's speech. [5]He lays down the rules about how we're here to win and anything less is simply unacceptable.

—Elwood Reid, *My Body, My Weapon, My Shame*

■ Combine these sentences:

A football player must use his body. His only purpose is to win. _____

_____

■ Two-word verbs may be followed by a direct object or by a prepositional phrase. On the lines below write the two-word verbs you find in the passage, along with either the direct object or the prepositional phrase that follows.

Two-Word Verb	Direct Object or Prepositional Phrase
1. *look at*	*us (direct object)*
2. _____	_____
3. _____	_____

Two-Word Verb	**Direct Object or Prepositional Phrase**
4. _____	_____
5. _____	_____

■ The writer of the excerpt on the previous page puts his body through pain to play football. Write a sentence about some other activity that is painful but rewarding. _____

_____

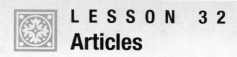

LESSON 32
Articles

Think about some of the smallest most frequently used words in English—for example, *the, a,* and *an.* These are called *articles,* and they indicate whether a noun is a particular one of its kind, a definite article—*the hat Sandy wore yesterday*—or any of a larger group of things, an indefinite article—*A hat is necessary in cold weather.* Before a vowel *a* becomes *an: Alyce wore an orange skirt.* Articles are also called determiners.

The Blockade

[1]There was a place our people had in mind where the Menotomy Road dips between two banks of earth, with a great tangle of wild blackberry bushes on one side and a windfall of dead trees on the other. [2]I knew the place well, because the bramble patch made for the best rabbit hunting in the whole neighborhood, and many was the time Father and I hiked down there for an early morning's shooting. [3]Now the plan was to drag enough fallen trees across the road to block it, and then back the trees up with rocks and dirt. [4]With such a breastwork, we felt we could hold the British long enough for a considerable army of Essex men, who were said to be marching in under the leadership of Colonel Pickering, to lead us.

—Howard Fast, *April Morning*

■ Write a sentence explaining what the people are planning. _____

_____

■ Underline all of the articles, with their nouns, in the excerpt above. Then, for five of them, write a sentence using the noun with another article, as shown in the example.

1. _____*the Menotomy Road*_____   _*Our town has a Menotomy Road.*_

2. _____   _____

3. _____   _____

4. _____   _____

5. _____   _____

6. _____   _____

■ Write a sentence about a special place you go to when you want to think things over. _____

_____

LESSON 32A
Recognizing Articles

A, an, and *the* are sometimes called *determiners* because they provide information, such as number, about their nouns. *An apple* tells us that there is only one piece of fruit, while *the apples* tells us there are two or two dozen pieces.

You Name It

[1]Whether you call a long cylindrical sandwich a hero, a submarine, a hoagy, a torpedo, a garibaldi, a poor boy, or any of at least half a dozen other names tells us something about where you come from. [2]Whether you call it cottage cheese, Dutch cheese, pot cheese, smearcase, clabber cheese, or curd cheese tells us something more. [3]If you call the playground toy in which a long plank balances on a fulcrum a dandle you almost certainly come from Rhode Island. [4]If you call a soft drink tonic, you come from Boston. [5]If you call a small naturally occurring object a stone rather than a rock you mark yourself as a New Englander. [6]If you have a catch rather than play catch or stand on line rather than in line clearly you are a New Yorker. [7]Whether you call it pop or soda, bucket or pail, baby carriage or baby buggy, scat or gesundheit, the beach or the shore—all these and countless others tell us a little something about where you come from.

—Bill Bryson, *The Mother Tongue: English and How It Got That Way*

■ Combine these sentences:

People use different words and expressions in different places. Your speech can tell others where you are from. _____

_____

■ Pick out five nouns in the passage above and write them, without any adjectives, first with the definite article, *the,* then with the appropriate form of the indefinite article, *a* or *an.* The first one is an example:

Noun	Definite Article	Indefinite Article
1. _sandwich_	_the sandwich_	_a sandwich_
2. _____	_____	_____
3. _____	_____	_____
4. _____	_____	_____
5. _____	_____	_____
6. _____	_____	_____

■ Now write your own sentence about an expression that is used in your family or your neighborhood but not usually by other people. _____

_____

LESSON 32B
More Articles

· · · · · · · · ·

For students whose native language is not English, it is often difficult to determine when to use *the,* when to use *a* or *an,* and when not to use an article at all. Unfortunately, there are no rules for this; students must listen to native speakers and read to determine when to use articles.

Sports Overload

[1]We are heading toward sports overload. [2]Screens are melting down. [3]Remotes are imploding. [4]Then comes Saturday. [5]Viewers will face a menu of events that appears to have been conjured by beer sponsors desperate to keep people homebound and unsuspecting of competitive nonsports programming. [6]The viewing commences at 11 a.m., Eastern, with the French Open women's final on NBC. [7]It reaches a late afternoon crescendo on NBC with the Belmont Stakes and will conclude around midnight with the Mike Tyson–Lennox Lewis pay-per-view circus. [8]"I look at Saturday and think

every indication says, 'Buy stock in La-Z-Boy,'" said Robert J. Thompson, a professor of media and popular culture at Syracuse University. [9]"All of a sudden, the lounge chair becomes something you inhabit, not just something you sit in."

—Richard Sandomir, *For Saturday, Buy the Chips and the Visine*

■ Combine these sentences:

There are many sports events on television. People can spend the entire day watching them. _____

_____

■ Identify the nouns and their determiners in the excerpt above. Following the examples shown, write two nouns that are a particular kind of thing (following *the*), two that are one of a larger group (following *a* or *an*), and two that have no article before them.

Particular Kind	One of a Group	No Article
1. _____ *the viewing* _____	_____ *a menu* _____	_____ *viewers* _____
2. _____	_____	_____
3. _____	_____	_____

■ Write a sentence about whether it is better to be present at a sporting event or to watch it on television. _____

_____

YOUR WRITING
Making Connections

In Lesson 31 you were asked to combine the following sentences:

A horseman has arrived.
The village is excited.

You may have written, "Because a horseman has arrived, the village is excited" or "Ever since a horseman arrived the village has been excited" or "Now that a horseman has arrived the village is excited." You will notice that each of these well-formed compound sentences conveys a slightly different meaning. In the first, it is the arrival of the horseman that *causes* the village to be excited; in the second, the excitement starts *when* the horseman arrives; in the third, there is a suggestion that the village *has been waiting* for the horseman. Changes in just a word or two have shifted the emphasis of the combined sentences from cause to time to anticipation. Changes like these can clarify your points by making your sentences more informative.

You've had practice combining sentences in many of the exercises in this book. It's time now to test your skills in a paragraph.

Have you ever been part of some dramatic event: winning a big game, taking part in a rally, watching a fierce storm? Write a topic sentence that makes clear why you consider the event important, then go on to complete a paragraph of at least five sentences. In each of these sentences be sure to include as many details as possible. If you decide to write about a game, don't just say what the game is. Name the teams, and at least some of the players and describe the color of their uniforms. How many fans are in the crowd? What is the name of the stadium? What do the banners say?

Topic Sentence: _____

_____

_____

_____

_____

_____

Go through your paragraph, deciding which sentences can be combined and making whatever changes are necessary to produce informative statements that clarify the point, making as many words as possible more specific and adding as many details as you can think of.

UNIT **V**

Making Connections

$\blacksquare$n Unit 1 we saw that a sentence must have at least *one* subject and *one* verb. We also saw that one sentence, or *clause*, can be joined to another to form a longer and more informative sentence. Doing this can clarify your ideas as well as provide more details about your subject. Consider these sentences:

> The weather was steaming hot.
> Hanna and Lulu were wearing jeans.
> They ate delicious burritos at the snack bar.
> The pool opened at ten.
> They went swimming.
> They ran into their friend.
> Roberto made a date.
> The movie started at seven.

What do we have here? Well, we have a nice list of sentences, each with at least one subject and one verb but without much to do with the other sentences. In fact, the sentences don't seem to have *anything* to do with each other. And what information do we learn from these sentences? Very little when you come right down to it. Something seems to be happening, but it's hard to figure out exactly what. One reason is that we have very few details to fill out the meaning of these sentences. Another is that these sentences are *unconnected*, all by themselves with nothing to pull them into a meaningful whole. Let's see what happens if we add a few words:

> Although the weather was steaming hot, Hanna and Lulu were wearing jeans as they ate the delicious burritos at the snack bar while they waited for the pool to open at ten. Later, after they finished swimming, they ran into their friend, Roberto, who made a date to meet them at the movie, which started at seven.

Is the picture getting clearer? Even without the name of the movie or the brand of the jeans, we have the beginnings of a story. Events happen in a certain order. Even more important, the ideas are related to one another so we can see the *how* and *why* of what's happening through the use of just a few small words: *although, as, later, after, which.* Words like these—we know them as conjunctions, relative pronouns, conjunctive adverbs, and sometimes transition words and phrases—pull ideas together and thus create a narrative or a scene rather than a list.

Conjunctions in Action

Some conjunctions join two or more clauses, either of which could stand alone: *Josie wants to shop, but Leon wants to play basketball.* Each of these is a perfectly good sentence by itself, telling what Josie and Leon want to do, so they are joined by the coordinating conjunction *but.* If we change this to *Josie wants to shop while Leon plays basketball,* we have an independent clause, *Josie wants to shop,* and a dependent or subordinate clause in *while Leon plays basketball.* This second clause tells us *when* Josie wants to shop—*while Leon plays*—and thus needs the independent clause to make sense.

The Relative Clause

Another kind of dependent clause uses a relative pronoun—*who, which, that*—to be joined to the independent clause: *Anthony slipped on the stairs, which had just been polished.* Notice that in this case the relative pronoun *which* refers to *stairs* and acts as the subject of *had just been.*

Although we use conjunctions and relative pronouns to join clauses, we use transitional words and phrases to introduce ideas and to show how these ideas are connected. For example, we may contrast one assertion with another by writing *on the other hand.* Similarly, to present more facts in our argument, we may write *in addition,* and we might add *finally* to conclude a statement.

The psychologist B. F. Skinner created a utopia for the twentieth century in his *Walden Two.* Here are some examples of words that connect ideas from that book.

L E S S O N   3 3
Coordinating Conjunctions

Independent clauses—clauses that can stand as sentences on their own—are connected by the coordinating conjunctions, *and, but, or, no, for, so, yet.* Thus we can have the sentence, *It rained all night,* an independent clause, connected to another independent clause, *We canceled the picnic,* by the conjunction *so: It rained all night so we canceled the picnic.*

Individuals and Groups

[1]Our interests conflict with the interests of everybody else. [2]That's our original sin, and it can't be helped. [3]Now, "everybody else" we call "society." [4]It's a powerful opponent, and it always wins. [5]Oh, here and there an individual prevails for a while and gets what he wants. [6]Sometimes he storms the culture of a society and changes it slightly to his own advantage. [7]But society wins in the long run, for it has the advantage of numbers and of age. [8]It enslaves one almost before he has tasted freedom. [9]Considering how long society has been at it, you'd expect a better job. [10]The behavior of the individual has been shaped according to revelations of "good conduct," never as the result of experimental study.

—B. F. Skinner, *Walden Two*

■ Does Skinner believe that individuals have little chance of changing "society"? Explain your answer in a sentence. _____

_____

■ Find the independent clauses in the excerpt above. Underline the subject and verb of each clause and the coordinating conjunction that connects them, then write them below. For example: <u>He was working</u> on faith <u>and it bothered him.</u>

Subject/Verb	Conjunction	Subject/Verb
1. *that is our original sin*	*and*	*it can't be helped*
2.		
3.		
4.		
5.		

▪ Write a sentence explaining why you believe—or don't believe—that an individual can make a difference in society. _____

_____

LESSON 33A
Independent Clauses

Sometimes independent clauses are sentences by themselves; sometimes they are joined to other independent clauses by a coordinating conjunction or a semicolon. For example, *The comedian told a joke, but we didn't laugh.* We use a semicolon when ideas are closely related but cannot easily be joined by a coordinating conjunction. *The temperature was high for January; it made us think of spring.*

Another Chance

[1]Michelle Kwan didn't even win. [2]But even with a silver medal around her neck, Michelle Kwan couldn't lose. [3]Four years later, she is held to a different standard. [4]But in Salt Lake City she will have the advantage of skating before an American crowd. [5]The crowd can only do so much, however. [6]Although elegant as ever, Kwan has been painfully inconsistent on jumps all season, falling in competition on several occasions. [7]She still hasn't mastered an important triple-triple combination, and it's unlikely she will in time for the Olympic long program.

—Sam Weinman, *Kwan Goes It Alone*

▪ What is lessening Michelle Kwan's chance at a gold medal? Write your answer in a sentence. _____

_____

▪ Underline the independent clauses in the excerpt above. Write them below, indicating whether they are single sentences or part of a compound sentence joined by a conjunction. You need show only the subject and verb of the independent clause.

Clause	Conjunction, If Any
1. _____*Kwan didn't win*_____	_____*Single Sentence*_____
2. _____	_____

Clause	Conjunction, If Any
3. _____	_____
4. _____	_____
5. _____	_____
6. _____	_____
7. _____	_____

■ Write a sentence about a time you had a second chance to improve your performance at some sport or other accomplishment. _____

_____

LESSON 33B
More Independent Clauses

· · · · · · · · ·

Remember that an independent clause can be a sentence by itself, it can be connected to another independent clause, or it can be connected to a dependent clause:

Marsha likes peanuts.
Marsha likes peanuts, but Jojo likes potato chips.
Marsha likes peanuts because they are salty.

Freedom

[1]The body has fewer inhibitions than the mind. [2]It made good use of the new freedom from the first moment on. [3]It began to eat ravenously, for hours and days, even half the night. [4]It is amazing what quantities one can eat. [5]One day, a few days after the liberation, I walked through the country past flowering meadows, for miles and miles, toward the market town near the camp. [6]Larks rose to the sky and I could hear their joyous song. [7]There was no one to be seen for miles around; there was nothing but the wide earth and sky and the larks' jubilation and the freedom of space. [8]I stopped, looked around, and up to the sky—and then I went down on my knees.

—Viktor E. Frankl, *Man's Search for Meaning*

■ Combine these sentences:

Freedom affects the body as well as the mind. Former prisoners ate ravenously.

_____

■ Choose two pairs of independent clauses in the excerpt above, then combine them as either independent or dependent clauses. The first is done for you.

1. _Because the body has fewer inhibitions than the mind, it made good use_

   of the new freedom.

2. _____

3. _____

■ Were you ever hungry enough to eat something you don't like? Write a sentence about it. _____

_____

For more about conjunctions, see Review Exercises 21, 34.

LESSON 34
Subordinating Conjunctions

A *subordinate* or *dependent clause*, introduced by a subordinating conjunction, does not make sense by itself. It needs an independent clause to complete the idea of the sentence. For example, *while I was taking a nap* doesn't make sense until you join it to *I had a funny dream*. The subordinating conjunctions include *as, if, although, because, since, when, whereas, while, which, that,* and many others.

Smoking Permitted?

[1]Very few people smoked in Walden Two—Frazier not at all, so far as I could tell, though I remembered him as a heavy pipe-smoker in graduate school. [2]In such company my own consumption of tobacco had fallen off. [3]At first this was because I had felt conspicuous when smoking, and rather guilty, although not the slightest objection was made or implied. [4]Later I found that my interest had weakened. [5]I was surprised to note that I was still on the pack of cigarettes I had slipped into my pocket Wednesday morning. [6]I had smoked only twice since breakfast. [7]I began to wonder whether I might not be able to give it up, after all.

—B. F. Skinner, *Walden Two*

■ Does the writer really want to stop smoking? Write a sentence explaining your answer. _____

_____

■ Underline the subordinate clauses in the excerpt above. Write five of them below with an independent clause of your own to complete the sentence. The first is an example.

Subordinate Clause	Independent Clause
1. *Though I remembered him as a heavy pipe-smoker,*	*he did not smoke now.*
2. _____	_____
3. _____	_____
4. _____	_____
5. _____	_____
6. _____	_____

▪ Write a sentence about a habit you managed to put an end to. _____

_____

LESSON 34A
Dependent Clauses

· · · · · · · · · ·

Complex sentences contain at least one independent and one dependent clause, but some may also contain more than one of each, like this one: *When the train was late, I decided to go by bus although I knew that it would take longer.* We have here one independent clause, *I decided to go by bus,* and three dependent clauses: (1) *when the train was late,* (2) *although I knew,* and (3) *that it would take longer.*

A Strange Population

[1]This was a good opportunity to see the country, too, and the more I saw of it, the better I liked it. [2]We rolled through many villages and towns, and I soon saw that the parklike beauty of our first-seen city was no exception. [3]We stopped for lunch in quite a sizable town, and here, rolling slowly through the streets, we saw more of the population. [4]They had come out to look at us everywhere, but here were more; and when we went in to eat, in a big garden place with little shaded tables among the trees and flowers, many eyes were upon us. [5]And everywhere, open country, village, or city— were only women. [6]Old women and young women and a great majority who seemed neither young nor old, but just women; young girls also, though these, and the children, seeming to be in groups by themselves generally, were less in evidence. [7]We caught many glimpses of girls and children in what seemed to be schools or in playgrounds, and so far as we could judge there were no boys.

—Charlotte Perkins Gilman, *Herland*

▪ Combine these sentences:

Children were in playgrounds. All of them were girls. _____

_____

■ Choose two sentences in the excerpt above that contain dependent clauses. Rewrite them as two separate sentences, making the necessary changes in wording so that they will be independent clauses. The first is an example from sentence 4.

1. _____*We went in to eat.*_____ _____*Many eyes were upon us.*_____

2. _____ _____

3. _____ _____

■ Think of the first time you saw a new place. Write a sentence about your reaction. _____

_____

LESSON 34B
More Dependent Clauses

· · · · · · · · ·

A dependent clause must always be attached to an independent clause to form a sentence. *When I was a child.* What about it? Did something happen then? Was there a difference in beliefs, in appearance, in friends? As you can see, this clause is asking for further information to make sense. That information might be *When I was a child, I went barefoot at the beach,* or it might be *I liked ice pops when I was a child.* Be sure that your dependent clauses are attached to independent clauses.

A Northern Language

[1]The Eskimo language reaches its apogee in describing the land and man's activity in it. [2]Young people in modern Eskimo villages, especially in the eastern Arctic, say that when they are out on the land with their parents, they find it much more difficult to speak Inuktitut, though they speak it at home all the time. [3]It is not so much a lack of vocabulary as a difficulty with constructions, with idioms, a lost fluency that confuses them. [4]It is out on the land, in the hunting camps and traveling over the ice, that the language comes alive. [5]The Eskimo language is seasonal—terms for the many varieties of snow emerge in winter, while those for whaling come into use in the spring.

—Barry Lopez, *The Country of the Mind*

▪ What parts of the Eskimo language are used only at certain times? Answer this question in a sentence. _____

_____

▪ For each *dependent* clause in this passage write the conjunction that connects it to an *independent* clause as well as the subject and verb.

	Conjunction	Subject	Verb
1.	when	they	are
2.			
3.			
4.			
5.			

▪ Do you speak a different language with your friends at school than you do at home? Write a sentence about how it is different. _____

_____

For more about clauses, see Review Exercises 5, 9, 12, 21, 46.

LESSON 35
Dependent Clauses with Relative Pronouns

Very often a dependent clause will be connected to the independent clause by one of the relative pronouns—*which, that,* or *who.* When this happens, the relative pronoun may become the subject of that clause: *Gary finished the paper that is due next Friday. That* functions as a pronoun representing *paper*; it is also the subject of *is.*

Labor and the Good Life

[1]That's the fatal flaw in labor reform. [2]The program calls for a long, dreary campaign in which the leaders not only keep their men dissatisfied but stir up additional and often spurious grounds for dissatisfaction. [3]No man knows how much heavier the lot of the worker is made by the very people who are trying to make it lighter. [4]Here, there's no battle. [5]We can freely admit that we like to work. [6]Can you believe that we don't need to keep an accurate account of each man's contribution? [7]Or that most of us have stored up enough spare credits to take a long vacation if we liked? [8]We have time for sports, hobbies, arts and crafts, and most important of all, the expression of that interest in the world which is *science* in the deepest sense.

—B. F. Skinner, *Walden Two*

- Combine these sentences:

Workers are dissatisfied with their jobs. Labor leaders want them to oppose management. _____

_____

- Find the clauses in the excerpt above that are connected by relative pronouns. For each relative pronoun, write a sentence with a dependent clause of your own.

Independent Clause	Relative Pronoun	Dependent Clause
1. *We need a quiet room*	*in which*	*we can study our chemistry formulas.*
2. _____	_____	_____
3. _____	_____	_____
4. _____	_____	_____

■ Have you had a job you really enjoyed doing? Write a sentence about it.

_____

LESSON 35A
Relative Pronouns

• • • • • • • • •

When joining a dependent clause to an independent clause, a relative pronoun often becomes the subject of the clause. *Sampson found the keys that opened the locked closet.* The relative pronoun *that* refers to *keys* and also acts as the subject of *opened.*

Madonna and Evita

[1]Unlike Madonna—the daughter of a technician who designed tanks, and who enjoyed a middle-class childhood in a whites-only neighborhood of middle America—Evita was the illegitimate daughter of a servant who grew up in grinding poverty in the Argentinian countryside, coming to Buenos Aires as an impoverished teenager in the hope of finding work. [2]She lived as a prostitute and worked as a radio actress before meeting and marrying a rising politician, Juan Perón, who became the nation's president in 1946. [3]Together they made a golden couple on the national stage, enhancing Perón's charisma, and thus his power, for which he had an insatiable appetite. [4]Like other stars who died young, nothing in her life became her like the leaving it. [5]As hard as Madonna tried to soften Evita's image, the truth is that the two women had essential qualities in common: a driving ambition and a craving for the adoration of the masses.

—Andrew Morton, *Madonna*

■ Although Madonna did not think highly of Evita Perón's background, she was like her in some ways. Describe them in a sentence. _____

_____

_____

■ Find the relative pronouns in the excerpt above that are subjects of dependent clauses. Write them below together with the nouns to which they refer.

Dependent Clause	Noun
1. _who designed tanks_	_technician_
2. _____	_____

Dependent Clause	Noun
3. _____	_____
4. _____	_____
5. _____	_____
6. _____	_____

- Think of a celebrity who has been the subject of a movie. Write a sentence about your reaction to the film. _____

_____

LESSON 35B
Relative Clauses

Dependent clauses that are joined to the rest of the sentence by a relative pronoun are called *relative clauses*. *Jana found a history book, which she brought to the lost and found office.* The clause beginning with *which* is a relative clause.

Behind Football

[1]Football is about hard work, pain, and losing. [2](Messages that the game is all about winning—such as "Just win, baby," which is the Raiders owner Al Davis's hipster re-statement of Vince Lombardi's famous remark "Winning isn't everything, it's the only thing"—are actually less than half the story.) [3]Football is the only common language we have in which to talk about the pitiless, hit-or-be-hit side of America. [4]The game's origins lie in a hazing ritual that was practiced at Ivy League colleges in the 1820s. [5]Freshmen would be summoned to a field to play a rugby-like game during which the upperclassmen would welcome them to school by beating the crap out of them.

—John Seabrook, *Tackling the Competition*

- How do the game's origins tell us that football is about pain? Write your answer in a sentence. _____

_____

■ Underline the relative clauses in the excerpt above. Write the relative pronouns they begin with below, then write another clause using the same relative pronoun.

Relative Pronoun	**Clause**
1. _____*which*_____	_the third question which was very complicated_
2. _____	_____
3. _____	_____
4. _____	_____
5. _____	_____

■ Think of a game, or some other activity, that can be painful. Write a sentence describing the pain. _____

_____

LESSON 36
Transitions That Connect

Among a writer's most useful devices is the transitional word or phrase that shows how one sentence is connected to another. Some of these are adverbs like *before* and *after*, some are prepositional phrases like *at that time*. They indicate additional material, emphasis, contrast, time sequence, location, and conclusion.

Frequently Used Transitional Words

To add facts
additionally
also
as well as
for example
for instance
further
furthermore
moreover

To emphasize
actually
in any case
indeed
in fact
in other words
it is true
that is to say
therefore

To show contrast
evidently
however
instead
merely
nevertheless
on the contrary
on the other hand
otherwise
yet

To show time
after
at last
before
in the meantime
later
next
often
subsequently
temporarily
thereafter

To show result or conclusion
as a result
certainly
consequently
finally
in conclusion
in the end

Freedom and Control

[1]Control is necessary for the proper functioning of the community. [2]Certainly our elite do not command a disproportionate share of the wealth of the community; on the contrary, they work rather harder, I should say, for what they get. [3]"A Manager's lot is not a happy one." [4]And in the end the Planner or

167

Manager is demoted to simple citizenship. [5]Temporarily, they have power, in the sense that they run things—but it's limited. [6]They can't compel anyone to obey, for example. [7]A Manager must make a job desirable. [8]He has no slave labor at his command, for our members choose their own work. [9]His power is scarcely worthy of the name. [10]What he has, instead, is a job to be done. [11]Scarcely a privileged class, to my way of thinking.

—B. F. Skinner, *Walden Two*

■ Combine these sentences:

People at Walden Two choose their own work. Managers have no power. _____

_____

■ Find the transitional words and phrases in the excerpt above and write them below, indicating whether they add, emphasize, show contrast, time, or result.

	Transitional Word(s)	**Function**
1.	*certainly*	*result*
2.		
3.		
4.		

■ Think of a job you have had with an understanding boss. Write a sentence about why it was easier than another job. _____

_____

LESSON 36A
Phrases That Connect

. . . .

Don't overlook the simple words *and, but,* and *now* as connectives. They are the ones we use most often, as in *The weather was bad, but class was not canceled.*

Meeting the Producer

[1]What producers do is rarely understood and seldom appreciated. [2]Simpson's stock-in-trade, we had been told, was trying to intimidate writers, and he, in fact, considered himself the coauthor of any script he produced.

³In general, however, we prefer doing business with the bully boys than with the smoothies. ⁴We, in fact, had gone to school with perhaps the all-time top-seeded Hollywood bully boy, Otto Preminger. ⁵As neophyte screenwriters in 1970, we were the fourth of eight writers on Otto's production of *Such Good Friends,* and right off learned that if Otto thought he could beat up on you, then he would beat up on you without mercy. ⁶Although Otto's rage was never far beneath the surface, we always found him rather engaging.

—John Gregory Dunne, *Monster: Living Off the Big Screen*

■ Combine these sentences:

Producers intimidate writers. Writers can do business with them. _____

_____

■ Find the transitional words and phrases that connect the ideas in the excerpt above. Write them below, indicating whether they show time, cause, addition, or emphasis.

	Transition	Function
1.	*in fact*	*emphasis*
2.		
3.		
4.		
5.		

■ Have you ever had difficulty dealing with someone who bullied others? Write a sentence about it. _____

_____

LESSON 36b
More Phrases That Connect

Note that, with the exception of *and* and *but*, transitional words and phrases do not always occur at the beginning of a sentence. For example, *My mother likes to garden. My father, however, prefers fishing.*

A Fisherman's Place

[1]Herman Melville wrote his masterpiece, *Moby Dick,* based on his own experience aboard a South Seas whaling ship. [2]It starts with the narrator, Ishmael, stumbling through a snowstorm in New Bedford, Massachusetts, looking for a place to spend the night. [3]Finally he comes to the Spouter Inn. [4]"I thought that here was the very spot for cheap lodging and the best of pea coffee." [5]His instincts were sound, of course; he was given hot food and a bed to share with a South Seas cannibal called Queequeg. [6]Queequeg became his adopted brother and eventually saved his life. [7]Since the beginning of fishing, there have been places that have taken in the Ishmaels of the world—and the Murphs, and the Bugsys, and the Bobbys. [8]Without them, conceivably, fishing wouldn't even be possible.

—Sebastian Junger, *The Perfect Storm*

▪ Why wouldn't fishing be possible without a place for fishermen to stay on land? Write your answer in a sentence. _____

_____

▪ Listed below are transitional phrases from *A Fisherman's Place*. For each, continue with a sentence of your own, following the example of the first.

1. Finally, _____ *the day of the big game arrived.* _____

2. Of course, _____

3. Eventually, _____

4. Conceivably, _____

▪ Write a sentence about a time you stayed away from home—at a friend's house, at camp, at a motel, or in some other place. _____

_____

YOUR WRITING
Combining Sentences

When you're writing about your thesis, do you sometimes find that your sentences are more alike than you want them to be? You may have a series of short, declarative sentences something like these:

1. Recycling soda cans helps the environment.
2. There is less to go into the landfill.
3. Riding a bicycle to the beach helps the environment.
4. It means using less gas.
5. Gas is a petroleum product or fossil fuel.
6. Fossil fuels are nonrenewable resources.

Now, if your thesis statement is, *Conserving natural resources contributes to a healthy environment,* these are all perfectly good sentences for expanding your thesis. They may seem, though, like so many odd pieces of wood in a pile with nothing to hold them together until someone with a hammer and nails builds a table out of them.

What serves as hammer and nails to pull your sentences together for a well-shaped paragraph? One of the most effective ways is to combine sentences so that a reader can see how they are related, as we did in Unit 3. For example, *Because recycling soda cans means less refuse goes into the landfill, putting your used can into the bin helps the environment.* Try this kind of combining with sentences 3 to 6 above.

_____

_____

_____

_____

_____

_____

Throughout history people have imagined perfect societies. What one element would you consider essential to a perfect society? Write a thesis statement followed by a topic sentence that begins a paragraph explaining your choice.

_____

_____

_____

_____

Go carefully through the sentences you have just written to see if any will be clarified by combining them or adding connective words. If so, make the changes.

UNIT VI

How to Tell One Look-Alike Word From the Other

Complaints about English spelling have been around for a long time. Some say it's not phonetic. . .and often it isn't. Others say it hasn't kept up with changes in the language. That, too, is frequently the case. The playwright George Bernard Shaw once claimed that the word *fish*, if it followed the logic of English spelling rules, should be spelled *ghoti*: the *gh* as in *cough*, the *o* as in *women*, and the *ti* as in *nation*. He was exaggerating, of course, but his example demonstrates how we can be confused by spelling.

Webster's Word Book

In the nineteenth century Noah Webster proposed to simplify the language by introducing spellings like *thru* instead of *through*. Some of his reforms caught on; as a result today we write *color* and *honor* instead of *colour* and *honour*. He put all of his reforms in the first American dictionary and now his name has become almost synonymous with the word *dictionary*.

Part of the reason for irregular spelling is that long ago, before the invention of printing, no standardized system existed; scribes, who copied long texts by hand, wrote words as they pronounced them—but very often they pronounced them according to where they lived, which was different from the way they were pronounced by other scribes. Printing was invented in the fifteenth century and, along with it, efforts to spell words in a more regulated way.

Despite all that the reformers have done, much confusion remains in the way English words are spelled. You'll probably agree that the most common difficulty is with what we call *homophones*, words that sound the same but have different spellings and different meanings. Some of the most familiar of these are *to, two, too; there, their, they're;* and *bear, bare*. Another bit of confusion comes from the irregularity of verb forms, and this also goes back to the early days of the English language, hundreds of years ago.

You will find many of these easy-to-mistake words in Toni Morrison's *The Bluest Eye*, a story that shows what tragic results may come from racism.

Words That Look Alike

Many words that are spelled the same way can function as different parts of speech. One that we use often is *look*. As a noun, it might appear in a sentence like *Did you take a look at the new TV show?* Notice that as a noun it usually follows *a, an,* or *the*. But, of course, it is also a verb: *I always look at the new shows.* One way of checking whether a word is being used as a verb is to check whether it can be used with the word *to* to form the infinitive: *to look.*

Living with the Grown-Ups

¹Our house is old, cold, and green. ²At night a kerosene lamp lights one large room. ³The others are braced in darkness, peopled by roaches and mice. ⁴Adults do not talk to us—they give us directions. ⁵They issue orders without providing information. ⁶When we trip and fall down, they glance at us; if we cut or bruise ourselves, they ask us are we crazy. ⁷When we catch colds, they shake their heads in disgust at our lack of consideration. ⁸How, they ask us, do you expect anybody to get anything done if you all are sick? ⁹We cannot answer them. ¹⁰Our illness is treated with contempt, foul Black Draught, and castor oil that blunts our minds.

—Toni Morrison, *The Bluest Eye*

- Combine these sentences:

Children are bewildered. Adults do not explain things to them. _____

_____

- Some words in the excerpt above can be either verbs or nouns. Choose five of them; for those used as verbs write a sentence in which the word is used as a noun and for those used as nouns write a sentence in which the word is used as a verb. The first one below is an example.

Verb or Noun	Sentence
1. *trip [verb]*	*Our trip [noun] to the beach will be on Saturday.*
2. _____	_____
3. _____	_____
4. _____	_____

Verb or Noun	Sentence

5. _____   _____

6. _____   _____

▪ Write a sentence about a time in your childhood when an adult was not able to explain something you asked about. _____

_____

LESSON 37a
Verbs That Can Be Nouns

· · · · · · · · · ·

Here's a test you can use to distinguish look-alike words that can be verbs or nouns: a verb can take the infinitive form with *to* as in *to risk*, while a noun can be preceded by an article such as *a risk* or *the risk*.

Fan-tastic

[1]While the game is hugely important to the players and coaches, there is, at the same time, an absence of urgency in the air. [2]I have covered games in Ann Arbor, Columbus, South Bend, and Tallahassee. [3]I have seen the ugliness born of high hopes dashed. [4]I have smiled at the sight of Alabama fans holding a roll of toilet paper and a box of Tide detergent—Roll Tide, get it? [5]I have seen Florida State fans cheer the sight of Miami mascot Sebastian the Ibis being roughed up by Tallahassee police. [6]I have talked to an Arkansas couple who vacationed in Fayetteville every August in order to watch Razorbacks two-a-days. [7]I have thought, but lacked the courage to suggest to these super-fans: *Get a Life!*

—Austin Murphy, *The Sweet Season*

▪ In one sentence explain why the writer wants to tell super-fans to get a life.

_____

▪ Choose three nouns in the excerpt above that can be changed to verbs. For each, write a sentence using the word as a verb. For example, the noun *time* becomes a verb in *The coach will time the runner's speed around the track.* Then do the same for three verbs that can be nouns.

1. _____ *air [noun]* _____   *We air [verb] the winter clothes when they come out of storage*

2. _____   _____

3. _____   _____

4. _____   _____

5. _____   _____

6. _____   _____

7. _____   _____

- Think of something silly you have seen a fan do at a sports event. Write a sentence about it. _____
_____

LESSON 37b
More Words That Can Be Nouns or Verbs
· · · · · · · · · ·

Sometimes when nouns turn to verbs or verbs to nouns, the meaning becomes entirely different. *To play*, for example, is to take part in a sport or game, while *a play* is usually a performance on a stage. We may *watch* a race while wearing a *watch* to keep time.

An African Village

[1]Nicoboozu was a clean little town, the huts wide apart, and the chief was old, hospitable and incurious. [2]He dashed us a chicken and a hamper of rice, saw that the hut we were to sleep in was swept, and then retired to his hammock and shade from the midday sun. [3]Nicoboozu was as favourable an example as one would find of a village touched by the Buzie culture. [4]Here the women wore little silver arrows in their hair and twisted silver bracelets, beaten by the blacksmith out of old Napoleon coins brought from French Guinea, and heavy silver anklets; the men wore rings, primitive signet rings with a flattened side, and decorative beaded rings and rings twisted to match the bracelets. [5]The weavers were busy, and every piece of craftsmanship one saw was light and unself-conscious. [6]There was an air of happiness about the place.

—Graham Greene, *Journey Without Maps*

- Combine these sentences:

The village displayed Buzie culture. The people wore silver jewelry. _____

_____

■ Write in column 1 the nouns in the excerpt above that can be verbs and in column 2 the verbs that can be nouns. Remember the test of a noun is that it can be preceded by *a* or *the,* and of a verb that it can be an infinitive with *to.*

	Column 1—Nouns	**Column 2—Verbs**
1.	shade	sleep
2.		
3.		
4.		
5.		

■ If you could travel to Africa, what souvenir would you like to bring back? Write your answer in a sentence. _____

_____

LESSON 38
Look-Alikes That Have Different Meanings

Some words that are spelled alike, pronounced alike, and are the same part of speech have different meanings depending on the context in which they occur. For example, if we're talking about a boat ride, we may refer to the *river bank*, while a need for more cash will take us to the *savings bank*. *Head, bed, pen,* and *book* are just a few more words of this type.

The Breedlove House

¹The plan of the living quarters was as unimaginative as a first-generation Greek landlord could contrive it to be. ²The large "store" area was partitioned into two rooms by beaverboard planks that did not reach to the ceiling. ³There was a living room, which the family called the front room, and the bedroom, where all the living was done. ⁴In the front room were two sofas, an upright piano, and a tiny artificial Christmas tree which had been there, decorated and dust-laden, for two years. ⁵The bedroom had three beds: a narrow iron bed for Sammy, fourteen years old, another for Pecola, eleven years old, and a double bed for Cholly and Mrs. Breedlove. ⁶In the center of the bedroom, for the even distribution of heat, stood a coal stove. ⁷Trunks, chairs, a small end table, and a cardboard "wardrobe" closet were placed around the walls. ⁸The kitchen was in the back of this apartment, a separate room. ⁹There were no bath facilities, only a toilet bowl, inaccessible to the eye, if not the ear, of the tenants.

—Toni Morrison, *The Bluest Eye*

- Explain, in one sentence, what makes the Breedlove home sound unpleasant.

_____

- In excerpt above some of the words can be used with a different meaning from the ones they have here. Write them in column 1 below, and write their second meaning in column 2.

Column 1	Column 2
1. *bed for sleeping*	*flower bed*
2. _____	_____
3. _____	_____

	Column 1	Column 2
4.	_____	_____
5.	_____	_____
6.	_____	_____

■ Think of a room that makes you feel happy or sad and write a sentence about why it has that effect. _____

_____

LESSON 38a
Look-Alike Words with Two Meanings

. . . .

What do you think of when you see the word *plant?* You can't be sure whether it means something growing in a pot or a place where computers are manufactured unless the context—the sentence in which it appears—gives you the answer. For example, *The demand for laptop computers was so great that the* <u>plant</u> *was operating 24/7*. Or it might be, *For my birthday I received a beautiful cactus* <u>plant</u>.

The Reading Lesson

[1]The male speaker began to read. [2]He was a young man, respectably dressed, and seated at a table, having a book before him. [3]His handsome features glowed with pleasure, and his eyes kept impatiently wandering from the page to a small white hand over his shoulder, which recalled him by a smart slap on the cheek, whenever its owner detected such signs of inattention. [4]Its owner stood behind; her light shining ringlets blending, at intervals, with his brown locks, as she bent to superintend his studies; and her face—it was lucky he could not see her face, or he would never have been so steady.

—Emily Brontë, *Wuthering Heights*

■ Combine these sentences:

His reading earned the pupil a kiss. He gladly returned it. _____

_____

■ Underline the words in the excerpt above that can have two meanings. Write three of these words in the first column, then write the meaning each word has in the passage and the second meaning it can have, as shown in the example.

Word	First Meaning	Second Meaning
1. _table_	_a piece of furniture_	_an arrangement of data_
2. _____	_____	_____
3. _____	_____	_____
4. _____	_____	_____

■ Write a sentence about something that distracts you when you are trying to study. _____

LESSON 38b
Words with Multi-Meanings: Figures of Speech

• • • • • • • • •

The words that concern us in this lesson like *table* or *bed* have the same part of speech but can be used to mean different things. Often such words are *figures of speech*. A figure of speech is a word or phrase whose primary meaning is extended to a person or thing that has similar qualities. *That baby is an angel* means that the baby's behavior is exceptionally pleasing. For example, similarly, *neck* is used to name a narrow strip of land, or the place where a river flows into the sea is called its *mouth*.

The City Game

[1]The Hawk, the Goat, the Destroyer, and the Fly are legends of the asphalt city game, epic players in a pastime that is itself legendary, an offshoot of the indoor sport that Dr. James Naismith invented in 1891. [2]It's a fact that the city game is played when and where it was designed not to be played: outdoors, in the sweltering heat, when the gentler games of summer should rule. [3]But the only thing that rules year-round in the canyons of the inner city is the rock-solid stuff beneath your feet. [4]Just now the tiny, fence-enclosed court at West 4th Street in Greenwich Village is rocking. [5]A tournament is under way, one of the dozens of outdoor hoops programs that run all summer long in New York City.

—Rick Telander, *Asphalt Legends*

■ What is wrong with playing city basketball in the summer? Write your answer in a sentence. _____

_____

■ Underline all of the nouns in the excerpt above that can have more than one meaning. For four of them, write a meaning that is different from the one in *The City Game.*

Noun	Another Meaning
1. _____game_____	_____animals taken in hunting_____
2. _____	_____
3. _____	_____
4. _____	_____
5. _____	_____

■ Most sports have special places in which they are played: football fields, running tracks, baseball diamonds. Write your own sentence about a time you took part in some sport that was played in an unusual place. _____

_____

For more about words with multiple meanings, see Review Exercise 43.

LESSON 39
Words That Sound Alike: Homophones

. . . .

Many words sound the same although they are spelled differently and have different meanings. They are called *homophones*. Writers can find it troublesome to determine which spelling to choose in sentences like *The dew was still on the grass,* and *Which bill is due this week?* or even *I don't know what to do during the break.* But a reader can be completely confused by a spelling different from the accepted one. (So can your computer's spell checker, since it doesn't know which meaning you intend.)

Listening to the Grown-Ups

[1]Their conversation is like a gently wicked dance: sound meets sound, curt-sies, shimmies and retires. [2]Another sound enters, but is upstaged by still another: the two circle each other and stop. [3]Sometimes their words move in lofty spirals; other times they take strident leaps, and all of it is punctuated with warm-pulsed laughter—like the throb of a heart made of jelly. [4]The edge, the curl, the thrust of their emotions is always clear to Frieda and me. [5]We do not, cannot, know the meanings of all their words, for we are nine and ten years old. [6]So we watch their faces, their hands, their feet, and listen for truth in timbre. [7]So when Mr. Henry arrived on a Saturday night, we smelled him. [8]He smelled wonderful, like trees and lemon vanishing cream, and Nu Nile Hair Oil and flecks of Sen-Sen.

—Toni Morrison, *The Bluest Eye*

■ What clues do Frieda and her sister use to figure out what adults mean? Write your answer in a sentence. _____

_____

■ Each homophone in the excerpt above has the same sound as another word but is spelled differently. In column 1, write the homophone as it appears above, and in column 2 write a word that sounds the same but is spelled dif-ferently and has a different meaning.

	Column 1	Column 2
1.	*their*	*there, they're*
2.		
3.		

183

Column 1	Column 2
4._____	_____
5._____	_____
6._____	_____
7._____	_____
8._____	_____
9._____	_____
10._____	_____

■ Can you remember a grown-up whose appearance impressed you when you were a child? Write a sentence about that person. _____

_____

LESSON 39a
More Homophone Sound-Alikes

· · · · · · · · ·

Because English has so many homophones, you must be especially careful when using your computer's spell checker. *Son* and *sun* are both correct spellings but a spell checker will not always know which one to use in a sentence: *My mother's son is my brother,* but *The sun rose at six this morning.* The computer will not know which meaning you have in mind.

The Lady of the Castle

[1]The *châtelaine* [the lord's wife] of a castle more often than not had to manage alone when her husband was occupied elsewhere, as he generally was, for the sun never set on fighting in the 14th century. [2]If not fighting, or attending the King, he was generally being held somewhere for ransom. [3]In such case the wife had to take his place, reach decisions, and assume direction, and there were many besides Jeanne de Monfort who did so. [4]Marcia Ordelaffi, left to defend Cesena while her hot-tempered husband (he who had stabbed his son) held a second city against the papal forces, refused all offers to negotiate despite repeated assaults, mining of walls, bombardment day and night by stones cast from siege engines, and the pleas of her father to surrender.

—Barbara Tuchman, *A Distant Mirror: The Calamitous 14th Century*

- Combine these sentences:

The husband was often at war. The lady took charge of the castle. _____

_____

- List five homophones from the excerpt above in column 1. In column 2, write a sentence using its sound-alike with another meaning.

Column 1	Column 2
1. _____*not*_____	_____*The knot was untied.*_____
2. _____	_____
3. _____	_____
4. _____	_____
5. _____	_____
6. _____	_____

- Think of a time when someone you know had to take over in an emergency, perhaps when a family member was sick or injured. Write a sentence about what happened. _____

_____

LESSON 39b
Still More Homophones
• • • • • • • • •

As we have seen, words that sound alike even though they are spelled differently and have different meanings are called *homophones*. Keeping them straight can be confusing. *Will you have two quizzes to study for, too?*

A Mysterious Noise

[1]And then, because of the strange anxiety at her heart, she stole upstairs to her son's room. [2]Noiselessly she went along the upper corridor. [3]Was there a faint noise? [4]What was it? [5]She stood, with arrested muscles, outside his door, listening. [6]There was a strange, heavy, and yet not loud noise. [7]Her heart stood still. [8]It was a soundless noise, yet rushing and powerful. [9]What in God's name was it? [10]She ought to know. [11]She felt that she knew the

noise. ¹²She knew what it was. ¹³Then suddenly she switched on the light and saw her son, in his green pyjamas, madly surging on the rocking-horse. ¹⁴The blaze of light suddenly lit him up, as he urged the wooden horse, and lit her up, as she stood, in her dress of pale green and crystal, in the doorway.

—D. H. Lawrence, *The Rocking-Horse Winner*

■ Write a sentence explaining what has frightened the woman. _____

_____

■ Underline the homophones in the excerpt above. For three of them, give definitions, first of the word in the excerpt, then of its homophone.

	Homophone 1	**Homophone 2**
1.	*heart: an organ of the body*	*hart: male of the red deer*
2.	_____	_____
3.	_____	_____
4.	_____	_____

■ Why is a strange sound in a dark house so frightening? Write a sentence explaining your answer. _____

_____

L E S S O N   4 0
Irregular Verbs

. . . .

You remember that all verbs have four principal parts: (1) present tense (the same form as the infinitive), (2) past tense, (3) present participle, and (4) past participle. The verbs we call *regular* look like this:

walk	*walked*	*walking*	*walked*

You may say, "That's fine, but what about a verb like *teach, taught, teaching, taught?*" The answer is that *teach* is one of many *irregular* verbs. These too go back to the early days of the English language and we recognize most of them by the vowel change in the past tense and past participle. Let's look at some that we find most frequently. These verbs have a vowel change in the past tense *and* the past participle:

drink	*drank*	*drinking*	*drunk*
ring	*rang*	*ringing*	*rung*
sing	*sang*	*singing*	*sang*
sink	*sunk*	*sinking*	*sank*
swim	*swam*	*swimming*	*swum*

These verbs have a past participle ending in *-en*:

break	*broke*	*breaking*	*broken*
eat	*ate*	*eating*	*eaten*
give	*gave*	*giving*	*given*
know	*knew*	*knowing*	*known*
see	*saw*	*seeing*	*seen*
speak	*spoke*	*speaking*	*spoken*
take	*took*	*taking*	*taken*
throw	*threw*	*throwing*	*thrown*

These verbs do not change in the past tense:

cost	*cost*	*costing*	*cost*
let	*let*	*letting*	*let*
put	*put*	*putting*	*put*

These verbs have the same past tense and past participle:

bring	*brought*	*bringing*	*brought*
catch	*caught*	*catching*	*caught*
teach	*taught*	*teaching*	*taught*

These verbs do not fit in any of the above categories:

begin	*began*	*beginning*	*begun*
go	*went*	*going*	*gone*

These verbs (*to be* and *to have*) are extremely irregular:

I am	*I was*	*I was being*	*I have been*
you are	*you were*		
she is	*he was*		
they are	*they were*		
I have	*I had*	*I was having*	*I have had*
you have			
he has			

Outdoors

[1]Outdoors, we knew, was the real terror of life. [2]The threat of being outdoors surfaced frequently in those days. [3]If somebody ate too much, he could end up outdoors. [4]If somebody used too much coal, he could end up outdoors. [5]People could gamble themselves outdoors, drink themselves outdoors. [6]Sometimes mothers put their sons outdoors, and when that happened, regardless of what the son had done, all sympathy was with him. [7]He was outdoors, and his own flesh had done it. [8]To be put outdoors by a landlord was one thing—unfortunate, but an aspect of life over which you had no control, since you could not control your income. [9]But to be slack enough to put oneself outdoors, or heartless enough to put one's own kin outdoors—that was criminal. [10]There is a difference between being put *out* and put out*doors*. [11]If you are put out, you go somewhere else; if you are outdoors, there is no place to go.

—Toni Morrison, *The Bluest Eye*

■ Explain the difference between *out* and *outdoors* in a sentence. _____

_____

■ Find the irregular verbs in the excerpt above. Write them in the columns shown for each of their principal parts.

	Present Tense	Past Tense	Present Participle	Past Participle
1.	*know*	*knew*	*knowing*	*known*
2.				
3.				

Present Tense	Past Tense	Present Participle	Past Participle
4. _____	_____	_____	_____
5. _____	_____	_____	_____

▪ Toni Morrison explains that to be outdoors is to be in disgrace. Write a sentence about what might be considered being in disgrace among your friends.

_____

LESSON 40a
More Irregular Verbs

Some verbs have completely different forms in the past tense, irregularities that go far back in the history of the language. Think about *go/went buy/bought,* and *take/took.* Because there are no easy rules, we have to memorize all the forms of such verbs.

Beginning of an Affair

[1]The chapel bell started to ring and Barbara leapt eagerly out of bed. [2]But as she poured the enamel can of hot water into her basin, she began to wonder how she was going to get through the six long hours before it would be half past two. [3]It was a wonder that she managed to do any work at all these days, for even writing essays for Francis had lost some of its attraction. [4]He didn't seem to listen very attentively now and even stopped her sometimes before she had finished reading, and began talking about things that had really nothing to do with tutorials. [5]Barbara believed that Francis liked talking to her, and that she was able to bring into his life something which had been lacking in it before—sympathy, understanding, perhaps even love.

—Barbara Pym, *Crampton Hodnet*

▪ Combine these sentences:

Barbara is young. Barbara has little knowledge of love. She thinks she loves

Francis. _____

_____

▪ Underline the irregular verbs in the excerpt above, then use one of their principal parts to complete each of the sentences below.

1. The runner was _____*leaping*_____ over the hurdles.

2. The class had just _____ the exam.

3. Marsha and Roy _____ to the movies last night.

4. Have you _____ your homework yet?

5. Manya will _____ a party next weekend.

▪ Did you ever have a crush on a teacher or some other older person? Write a sentence describing that person. _____

_____

LESSON 40b
Irregular Endings

· · · · · · · · · ·

The past tense of some verbs, like *sleep* and *leap*, is spelled with *-t* rather than *-ed, slept, leapt*; this is a result of the way we pronounce them. Other verbs, like *find/found* and *seek/sought,* change their vowels in the past tense.

The New Woman

[1]As an influence on fashion, on manners, on the complex art of civilized living, the vanished lady had been superseded. [2]Her successor, for the American public, was the movie star. [3]The lady's daughter, or granddaughter, was usually being taught some means of earning her livelihood. [4]She was to be found, in increasing numbers, making a career for herself; in the offices of women's magazines, in Hollywood and the theater, among entertainers in nightclubs, among professional models, in fashionable shops; occasionally in the practice of law or medicine, or teaching in a college. [5]Whatever she was doing, it seemed clear that she was seeking that free development irrespective of its bearing on the other sex which announced her final emancipation and declared her refusal to be—as the lady often had been—a ready-made garment, designed to fit the average man.

—Lloyd Morris, *Postscript to Yesterday: American Life and Thought 1896–1946*

■ In a sentence explain what the writer means when he says the lady was "de-signed to fit the average man." _____

_____

■ Find the irregular verbs in the excerpt above and decide whether the form is past or present. If it is present, write a sentence using the past tense form; if it is past, write a present tense sentence.

	Verb	**Sentence**
1.	*taught*	*Mr. Simpson teaches Biology.*
2.	_____	_____
3.	_____	_____
4.	_____	_____
5.	_____	_____

■ What woman or women have a great influence on American life today: rock stars, politicians, sports figures? Write a sentence explaining your choice. _____

_____

LESSON 41
Plural Nouns, Irregular Plurals

. . . .

To indicate more than one, most nouns add an -s or -es. A few, however, are irregular, keeping the forms they had in early forms of English. In some the vowel changes in the plural, giving us *mouse/mice*. Others, like *ox/oxen* have plurals in -*en*, and some have no plural marker at all: *one sheep* and *twenty sheep*.

Women's Life

[1]Everybody in the world was in a position to give them orders. [2]White women said, "Do this." [3]White children said, "Give me that." [4]White men said, "Come here." [5]Black men said, "Lay down." [6]The only people they need not take orders from were black children and each other. [7]But they took all of that and re-created it in their own image. [8]They ran the houses of white people and knew it. [9]When white men beat their men, they cleaned up the blood and went home to receive abuse from the victim. [10]They beat their children with one hand and stole for them with the other.

—Toni Morrison, *The Bluest Eye*

■ Does the author give these details about black women to show how difficult the women's lives were or does she have another reason? Write your answer in a sentence. _____

_____

■ The excerpt above has a number of plural nouns, most of them regular. Find the irregular plural nouns and indicate what type of change it is: in spelling or in form of the word ending.

Noun	Change
1. _____*women*_____	_____*spelling*_____
2. _____	_____
3. _____	_____

■ People in some jobs are never recognized for the hard work they do. Write a sentence about someone who does a job without getting the credit he or she deserves. _____

_____

LESSON 41a
More Irregular Plurals

· · · · · · · · ·

As we have seen, some plurals end in *-n* rather than *-s* or *-es*. These include *child/children* and *ox/oxen*. In others we find a vowel change between the singular and the plural: *foot/feet, goose/geese, louse/lice, mouse/mice, tooth/teeth*. Another group of words remains the same in singular and plural: *cattle, deer, fish, sheep*. Some nouns that retain the *-s* ending in the plural change the final consonant of the root, as in *knife/knives, life/lives, wife/wives,* and *wolf/wolves*.

Country Women

[1]But there is an eternal quality in the life of farmers' wives which allows one to make a reliable guess at the way they lived in Horstede; even now, there are wives in the remotest parts of Britain, for example the highlands and islands of Scotland, who do all the things the women of Horstede must have done, and do them in much the same way. [2]They carded, spun and dyed and wove the wool and made the clothes, boiled the meat and baked the bread, milked the sheep and goats, perhaps the cow, and made the butter and cheese, loved and scolded the children, fed the hens, worked in the fields at harvest, probably made the pots and brewed the beer, and made love or quarrelled with their husbands, or possibly both. [3]And the children, not burdened by school, herded animals, geese or sheep or goats or pigs according to their size.

—David Howarth, *1066: The Year of the Conquest*

■ Combine these sentences:

Farm wives have always worked hard. Today some do chores the same way they

did centuries ago. _____

_____

■ For each of the nouns with irregular plurals in the excerpt above, write both the singular and plural forms, as shown in the example.

Singular	Plural
1. _____ *wife* _____	_____ *wives* _____
2. _____	_____

	Singular	**Plural**
3.	_____	_____
4.	_____	_____

- Have you heard from a grandparent or older neighbor about the way things used to be? Write your own sentence about what you learned. _____

_____

LESSON 41b
Plurals That Change Spelling
· · · · · · · · ·

In addition to those plurals that are formed by changing a vowel, like *women* or *feet*, and those without a plural ending, like *fish* or *sheep*, there are some that change spelling in the plural. *Party, parties,* and *knife, knives* are examples of these words.

A Strange Dream

[1]So I drifted, deep in the autumn forest, unheeded as a wraith of the forest mist. [2]Straining back now in memory, I see it still. [3]Deep aisles of beech, thick with mast, where the wild boar rooted, and the badger dug for food, and the stags clashed and wrestled, roaring, with never a glance at me. [4]Wolves, too; the way through those high woods is known as the Wolf Road, but though I would have been easy meat, they had had a good summer, and let me be. [5]Then, with the first real chill of winter, came the hoar glitter of icy mornings, with the reeds standing stiff and black out of curded ice, and the forest deserted, badger in lair and deer down in the valley-bottom, and the wild geese gone and the skies empty. [6]Then suddenly, one grey dawn, the sound of horses galloping, filling the forest, and the clash of swords and the whirl of bright axes, the yelling and the screams of wounded beasts and men. [7]Silence then, and the scent of apple trees, and the nightmare sense of grief that comes when a man wakes again to feel a loss he has forgotten in sleep.

—Mary Stewart, *The Last Enchantment*

■ Combine these sentences:

The wolves were not hungry. They had eaten a lot during the summer. They did not attack. _____

_____

■ In the excerpt above, underline the plural nouns that have irregular spellings, then choose an appropriate singular form to complete each of the sentences below, as shown in the example.

1. The _____wolf_____ is often a menace in fairy tales.

2. Bambi is a baby _____ .

3. Some people prefer a _____ for a holiday dinner.

4. The captain was the last _____ to leave the ship.

5. The rain fell from the dark _____ .

■ Think about an unusual dream you have had and write a sentence about it.

_____

• • • • • • • • • • • • • •

YOUR WRITING
Putting it Together

So far you've been writing paragraphs with a strong topic sentence and sentences that stick to the point by keeping their content *only* about what has been asserted in the thesis. Of course, you will be expected to write more than a paragraph for your other classes—and for the kinds of writing you will be doing in your future career. Here are three important things to remember when you write more than one paragraph:

• Be sure to follow the pattern of thesis-plus-topic-sentences-about-the-thesis in every paragraph you write.
• Be sure to use some connecting word or phrase to link one paragraph to the one that goes before.
• Be sure to write a sentence at the end that makes clear that you have made your point. This sentence will *not* repeat the words of your thesis statement but will echo its ideas.

Think of an occupation that requires many different activities. Write three paragraphs explaining why such a job involves many diverse abilities.

¶ _____

_____

_____

_____

¶ _____

_____

_____

_____

¶ _____

_____

_____

_____

UNIT VII

Nuts and Bolts

· · · · · · · · · ·

Picky, picky, picky. Why does that teacher have to be so fussy about where I put a comma, you may well ask. The best way to answer that is with another question: what does this sentence mean? *Night was falling so suddenly I ran to the boat.* You might reply that I ran to the boat because night was falling so suddenly. Or you might say I ran suddenly to the boat because night was falling. As the sentence stands, both are right. But did the writer have both meanings in mind? This is the kind of ambiguous sentence that is clear when spoken because of where emphasis falls, and the pause occurs. It is not so obvious in writing, however, unless we use a comma to indicate that the pause comes either after *falling* or after *suddenly.*

Before the Comma

Several hundred years ago, before printing had been invented, when all writing had to be done by hand, there was very little punctuation or capitalization. In fact, even spelling was pretty much left up to the scribe who copied the manuscript; that last word comes from Latin and means simply *written by hand.*

The real reason, then, that teachers are fussy about punctuation is because we need it for meaning. We need it to show where a sentence ends. We need it to show that we are asking a question. Similar reasons explain our need to capitalize some words, to use the accepted spelling, and to follow conventions for abbreviations. These are the *mechanics* of a paper, what we check in our final draft before printing it out to turn in.

Many of our problems with mechanics are made easier by word processing programs that include spelling or grammar checks. Here's a word of

197

warning about these helpers, though. Remember that the spell-check dictionary contains only those words that have been programmed into it. If your composition contains technical words from your subject, or unfamiliar names, the program may mark them incorrect, so it's up to you to do the checking on them. Something else to watch out for is misspellings that would be correct in another context: *ewe no watt eye mien.* Clearly these are not the spellings you intended for *you know what I mean,* but because they are correct spellings of other words, they will not be picked up by your spell checker. The same is true of grammar checks, which can use only the most general rules, rules like ideal sentence length that cannot be applied to all situations. As we've seen, sentences can be two words long or even fifty or more.

There are a few things about sentences that we need to remember before we talk about punctuation:

- A *declarative* sentence is a simple statement—although it can have more than one clause—that usually follows subject-verb-object as word order.
- An *interrogative* sentence is a question. Very often its word order is reversed to object-(*who* or *what*)-verb-subject.
- An *exclamatory* sentence expresses surprise or some other emotion.
- An *imperative* sentence gives a command.

Many examples in this unit are from *All Quiet on the Western Front,* Erich Maria Remarque's novel about World War I and its effect on young lives.

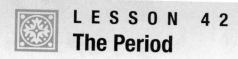

LESSON 42
The Period

Most often we signal the end of a sentence by a period, but it is not the only way to signify that we have come to the end; we might use a question mark, —*What time is dinner?* or an exclamation point —*Her answer shocked me!* For now, let's see how a group of short sentences, ending with a period, can be used to show a mood of urgency. For example: *The sky is dark. The woods are silent. My flashlight is lost. I am frightened.*

Battlefield Gourmet

¹The sucking pigs are slaughtered. ²Kat sees to them. ³We want to make potato-cakes to go with the roast. ⁴But we cannot find a grater for the potatoes. ⁵However that difficulty is soon got over. ⁶With a nail we punch a lot of holes in a pot lid. ⁷There we have a grater. ⁸Three fellows put on thick gloves to protect their fingers against the grater. ⁹Kat takes charge of the sucking pigs, the carrots, the peas, and the cauliflower. ¹⁰I fry the pancakes. ¹¹The sucking pigs are roasted whole. ¹²We all stand round them as before an altar.

—Erich Maria Remarque, *All Quiet on the Western Front*

■ How do you know this dinner is not being prepared in a conventional kitchen? Write your answer in a sentence. _____

_____

■ For each of the sentences in the excerpt above, list below the simple subject and the simple verb.

	Subject	**Verb**
1.	*pigs*	*are slaughtered*
2.		
3.		
4.		
5.		
6.		
7.		
8.		

Subject	Verb
9. _____	_____
10. _____	_____
11. _____	_____
12. _____	_____

■ Write a sentence about cooking outdoors, perhaps over a campfire or on a barbecue grill. _____

_____

For more about periods, see Review Exercise 11.

LESSON 42a
More Periods

· · · · · · · · ·

Many sentences contain more than one clause and will eventually end with a period. *While Ben held the door, Jerry carried out the chair.* Read the paragraph below, identifying the clauses and noting that the sentences end with periods.

The Crowd's Will

[1]But at that moment I glanced round at the crowd that had followed me. [2]It was an immense crowd, two thousand at the least and growing every minute. [3]It blocked the road for a long distance on either side. [4]I looked at the sea of faces above the garish clothes—faces all happy and excited over this bit of fun, all certain that the elephant was going to be shot. [5]They were watching me as they would watch a conjurer about to perform a trick. [6]They did not like me, but with the magical rifle in my hands I was momentarily worth watching. [7]And suddenly I realized that I should have to shoot the elephant after all.

—George Orwell, *Shooting an Elephant*

■ Why does the narrator think he must shoot the elephant? _____

_____

■ Underline the subject(s), verb(s), and conjunctions, if there are any, in each of the sentences in the excerpt above. For each sentence with more than one clause, write a sentence of your own in the same pattern. The example shown is based on sentence 1.

Your Sentence	**Excerpt Sentence #**
1. *I glanced at the clock that had struck seven.*	
2.	
3.	
4.	
5.	

■ Think of a time you did something because the people around you wanted you to do it. Write a sentence about that time. _____

_____

LESSON 42b
Another Use for the Period—Abbreviations

· · · · · · · · · ·

Periods are used at the end of abbreviations of titles such as *Mrs. Hayes* or *Dr. Burton*, and after initials like *J. D. Salinger.* They are also used at the end of common abbreviations such as *a.m.* and *p.m.* and of days of the week, *Fri.*, and months of the year, *Dec.*

TV Medicine

[1]There has always been a place for medicine on television. [2]There was NBC's *Medic* in the 1950s, starring Richard Boone; *Dr. Kildare* and *Ben Casey* in the 1960s; *Marcus Welby, M.D.* and *Medical Center* in the 1970s; and *St. Elsewhere* and *Trapper John, M.D.* in the 1980s. [3]*General Hospital* has been one of daytime's most consistent hits for decades. [4]*Marcus Welby, M.D.* was the father of *ER*—claiming the Number 1 slot for doctors 25 years earlier, during the 1970–71 season. [5]If television has always been drawn to the medical profession, it's because medical dramas take place in a controlled setting that's easy to film. [6]*ER*, which hit the hospital floor running on

Thursdays at 10:00 P.M. on NBC, was Welby plus a gaggle of other medicos passed on to the next generation, as doctor shows continued to deal with controversial topics in an uncontroversial manner.

—Steven D. Stark, *Glued to the Set*

■ Why are there so many medical dramas on television? Write your answer in a sentence. _____

_____

■ Find the abbreviations in the excerpt above that match the reasons shown in the first column.

Reason for Period	Abbreviation
1. _____Professional title_____	_____*Dr.*_____
2. _____Academic degree_____	_____
3. _____Religious title_____	_____
4. _____Time of day_____	_____

■ Have you ever met a doctor as dedicated as some of those we see on television? Write a sentence about that person. _____

_____

The Question Mark

. . . .

The question mark, like the period, signals the end of a sentence. We are most likely to see it in dialogue—conversation among characters—enclosed in quotation marks. Notice that the word order of an interrogative sentence is different than that of a statement. *How are you?* is a simple example of the subject *following* the verb in a question. Others may include the verb *do* in framing the question: *Do freshmen go to the class party?* Questions begin with helpers like *do* or modal auxiliaries (see Unit 2) like *can, must,* and *will* rather than either subject or verb. *Must you keep practicing the drum?*

On Leave

¹After I have been startled a couple of times in the street by the screaming of the tramcars, which resembles the shriek of a shell coming straight for one, somebody taps me on the shoulder. ²It is my German-master, and he fastens on me with the usual question: ³"Well, how are things out there? ⁴Yes, it is dreadful, but we must carry on. ⁵And after all, you do at least get decent food out there, so I hear. ⁶Naturally it's worse here. ⁷The best for our soldiers every time. ⁸That goes without saying." ⁹He drags me along to a table with a lot of others. ¹⁰They welcome me, a head-master shakes hands with me and says: ¹¹"So you come from the front? ¹²What is the spirit like out there?" ¹³I explain that no one would be sorry to be back home.

—Erich Maria Remarque, *All Quiet on the Western Front*

■ Combine these sentences:

People do not know the devastation of war. They greet the soldier as if he has

been on a pleasure trip. _____

_____

■ Find the sentences in the excerpt above that end with a question mark. If their word order is different than it would be in a sentence ending with a period, rewrite it as a declarative sentence.

1. ___*How are things out there?*___   ___*Things out there are fine.*___

2. _____   _____

■ Write five questions someone might ask you about your college experiences.

1. _____

2. _____

3. _____

4. _____

5. _____

■ Do you ever find questions annoying? Write a sentence explaining what bothers you about them. _____

_____

LESSON 43a
Rhetorical Questions

While most questions are asked in an attempt to get information, some are meant only to dramatize a writer's point, without any expectation of receiving an answer. These are called *rhetorical questions. The pitcher caught the ball. Can you believe it?*

Saving Time

[1]The three places Gags spends most of his life—home, office, practice field—form an isosceles triangle no point of which is more than a six-minute walk from the other two. [2]He is not being lazy; he is being time-efficient. [3]You say a six-minute walk, but what about the round trip? [4]That's twelve minutes. [5]Do that five times and you've burned an hour. [6]Who has an hour to burn? [7]What if a man wants to sneak home. . .to do some thinking on his favorite throne? [8]Must that become a twenty-five-minute investment of time? [9]What if John painstakingly makes Jell-O, following the instructions, pouring the mix into the mold, and then puts it in the freezer to harden? [10]This happened a couple weeks ago. [11]Upon learning that the Jell-O goes in the fridge, not the freezer, it was nice for him to be able to speed home and salvage dessert.

—Austin Murphy, *The Sweet Season*

- Combine these sentences:

John likes to be close to home and work. He doesn't like to waste time. _____

_____

- Underline the rhetorical questions in the excerpt above. Rewrite them as statements.

1. ___*A round trip would take twelve minutes.*___   _____

2. _____   _____

3. _____   _____

4. _____   _____

5. _____   _____

- Write a sentence about someone you know who is devoted to his or her job. _____

_____

LESSON 43b
Questions as Requests

• • • • • • • • • •

Sometimes a question is asked not to elicit information but to suggest a course of action. For example, we might say, *Would you like to take a walk?* when we mean, *Let's take a walk.*

A Proposal

[1]Mr. Latimer looked round the room, as if expecting to receive inspiration from the objects in it. [2]Oh, Canon Tottle, he thought, gazing at a faded sepia photograph, how would you do what I have to do this evening? [3]How would you lead up to it? [4]What words would you use? [5]Looking at the heavy, serious face with its determined expression, Mr. Latimer decided that with Canon Tottle there would be no leading up to it. [6]He would plunge straight in and say what he had to say quickly and definitely. [7]That was obviously the right thing to do if one had the courage. [8]He looked round the room again. [9]The sherry and glasses were still on one of the little tables.

[10]"Oh, Miss Morrow—Janie," he burst out suddenly.

[11]"My name isn't Janie. It's Jessie, if you want to know, or Jessica, really."

[12]"Oh, Jessica," continued Mr. Latimer, feeling a little flat by now, "couldn't we escape out of all this together?"

—Barbara Pym, *Crampton Hodnet*

■ Explain in a sentence why Mr. Latimer is nervous. _____

_____

■ There are several questions in the excerpt above. Write them below and note whether they are rhetorical questions, requests, or questions that seek information.

	Question	**Purpose**
1.	*How would you do what I have to do this evening?*	*Rhetorical*
2.	_____	_____
3.	_____	_____
4.	_____	_____

■ Did you ever have to prepare for a difficult meeting with someone? Write a sentence about how you felt before it took place. _____

_____

For more about punctuation, see Review Exercises 29, 40, 43, 44.

LESSON 44
The Exclamation Point

The exclamation point is used to emphasize an important or surprising statement—*What a lovely gift!*—or an interjection—*Holy smoke!* But this mark of punctuation should be used with care; it will lessen the effect the writer wishes to make if it is used too often.

The Bombardment

[1]That moment it breaks out behind us, swells, roars, and thunders. [2]We duck down—a cloud of flame shoots up a hundred yards ahead of us. [3]The next minute under a second explosion part of the wood rises slowly in the air, three or four trees sail up and then crash to pieces. [4]The shells begin to hiss like safety valves—heavy fire. [5]"Take cover!" yells somebody. [6]When we run out again, although I am very excited, I suddenly think: "Where's Himmelstoss?" [7]Quickly I jump back into the dug-out and find him with a small scratch lying in a corner pretending to be wounded. [8]It makes me mad that the young recruits should be out there and he here. [9]"Get out!" I spit.

—Erich Maria Remarque, *All Quiet on the Western Front*

■ Combine these sentences:

The shelling begins. The soldiers run for cover. _____

_____

■ In the above excerpt, there are two sentences ending with exclamation points; both are commands, a construction frequently used with this punctuation mark. For each of these sentences explain why it is appropriate to use an exclamation point for emphasis.

1. _____

_____

_____

2. _____

_____

_____

■ Write a sentence about an exciting event you were part of. _____

_____

LESSON 44a
Exclamations Again

· · · · · · · · ·

Because exclamations and interjections are used to show excitement and emotion, we ordinarily use only one or two at a time. To use more would have the same effect that a room full of loud talk and laughter would have on your ability to hold a conversation.

The Christmas Bicycle

[1]That December, with Christmas approaching, she was out at work and Doris was in the kitchen when I barged into her bedroom one afternoon in search of a safety pin. [2]Standing against the wall was a big, black bicycle with balloon tires. [3]I resolved that between now and Christmas I must do nothing, absolutely nothing, to reveal the slightest hint of my terrible knowledge. [4]Nothing must deny her the happiness of seeing me stunned with amazement on Christmas day. [5]In the privacy of my bedroom I began composing and testing exclamations of delight: "Wow!" "A bike with balloon tires!" "I don't believe it!" "I'm the luckiest boy alive!" and so on. [6]They all owed a lot to movies in which boys like Mickey Rooney had seen their wildest dreams come true, and I realized that, with my lack of acting talent, all of them were going to sound false at the critical moment when I wanted to cry out my love spontaneously from the heart.

—Russell Baker, *Growing Up*

■ Combine these sentences:

He accidentally saw the bike. He didn't want to disappoint his mother. _____

_____

■ Although there are four exclamations of delight in the excerpt above, each is enclosed in separate quotation marks. Why didn't the writer put them all together? _____

_____

■ For each of the exclamations listed below, write an expression that conveys the same kind of reaction. For example, instead of *"Wow!"*, you might say, *"Fantastic!"* or *"Cool!"*

1. A bike with balloon tires! _____

2. I don't believe it! _____

3. I'm the luckiest boy alive! _____

■ What's the most exciting gift you ever received for your birthday or some other special occasion? Write a sentence about how you reacted to seeing it.

_____

LESSON 44b
Exclamatory Words and Phrases

Exclamations are often words or phrases rather than sentences, *"Heat!"*, *"What a day!"*, and they are always followed with an exclamation point to indicate that they express strong emotion. We find these most often in dialogue, the written representation of someone's speech. For example, *"Hooray!" said Lorena when she heard that class was canceled.*

A Day at the Races

[1]He determined to take his nephew with him to the Lincoln races.
[2]"Now, son," he said, "I'm putting twenty on Mirza, and I'll put five for you on any horse you fancy. [3]What's your pick?"
[4]"Daffodil, uncle."
[5]"No, not the fiver on Daffodil!"
[6]"I should if it was my own fiver," said the child.
[7]"Good! Good! Right you are! [8]A fiver for me and a fiver for you on Daffodil."
[8]The child had never been to a race-meeting before, and his eyes were blue fire. [9]He pursed his mouth tight, and watched. [10]A Frenchman just in front had put his money on Lancelot. [11]Wild with excitement, he flayed his arms up and down, yelling *"Lancelot! Lancelot!"* in his French accent.

—D. H. Lawrence, *The Rocking-Horse Winner*

■ In a sentence explain why there is so much excitement at a racetrack. _____

_____

■ For each of the words or phrases with an exclamation point in the excerpt above, rewrite the idea expressed as a complete sentence, as shown in the example.

<table>
<tr><td align="center">**Word or Phrase**</td><td align="center">**Sentence**</td></tr>
<tr><td>1. _No, not the fiver on Daffodil!_</td><td>_No, you shouldn't put the fiver on Daffodil._</td></tr>
<tr><td>2. _____</td><td>_____</td></tr>
<tr><td>3. _____</td><td>_____</td></tr>
<tr><td>4. _____</td><td>_____</td></tr>
</table>

■ When you were a child, were you taken to an exciting sporting event? Write a sentence describing your impression of what was happening. _____

_____

LESSON 45
Capitalization

As we all know, every sentence begins with a capital letter. But there was a time, in the eighteenth century, when almost every noun was capitalized. If you look at a historical document such as the Declaration of Independence, notice how many words are capitalized that would not be today. Still, there do remain many places where we begin words with capital letters—for example, names of people, *Lucy*; of places, *Main Street, San Jose*; of teams, *Mets, Yankees*; of buildings, *Baker Hall*; of academic courses, English 101. These are all called *proper nouns*. Words like *people, place, team, building, course*, which do not refer to a particular person or place, are *common nouns*.

Desperate Times

¹Our lines are falling back. ²There are too many fresh English and American regiments over there. ³We have given up hope that some day an end may come. ⁴We never think so far. ⁵A man can stop a bullet and be killed; he can get wounded, and then the hospital is his next stop. ⁶There, if they do not amputate him, he sooner or later falls into the hand of one of those staff surgeons who, with the War Service Cross in his button-hole, says to him: "What, one leg a bit short? ⁷If you have any pluck you don't need to run at the front." ⁸Kat tells a story that has travelled the whole length of the front from the Vosges to Flanders of the staff surgeon who, when a man comes before him, without looking up, says "A1. ⁹We need soldiers up there."

—Erich Maria Remarque, *All Quiet on the Western Front*

- Combine these sentences:

The soldiers are bitter. The surgeons have no compassion. _____

_____

- Below is a list of reasons for capitalizing proper nouns and adjectives. Match each with the proper noun or adjective in the excerpt above that fits the definition.

Reason	Proper Noun or Adjective
1. Name of a country or nationality	*English*
2. Name of a medal for military service	

	Reason	Proper Noun or Adjective
3.	Name of a person	
4.	Name of a place	

▪ Write a sentence about an interesting place you visited with a friend— maybe a restaurant, a museum, or an athletic stadium. _____

_____

LESSON 45a
Other Uses of Capital Letters

• • • • • • • • • •

In addition to days of the week and months of the year, names of historical events (*Civil War, American Revolution*) are usually capitalized. So are pronouns as well as nouns referring to deities (*God, Buddha*). We also capitalize titles before names: *Professor Smith, President Lincoln, Senator Roberts.*

A Milestone in Journalism

[1]Near the end of the First World War, Captain Joseph Medill Patterson of the famous Rainbow Division paid a visit to London. [2]There he talked with Lord Northcliffe, whose tabloid *Daily Mirror* had won a circulation of some eight hundred thousand copies. [3]Would not Americans, likewise, take to the tabloid press? [4]Late in June, 1919, Patterson brought out the first issue of the *Daily News*—"New York's Picture Newspaper." [5]The American tabloid press was born. [6]Eleven years later, the paper was installed in a ten-million-dollar tower; one of the notable masterpieces of modern business architecture. [7]By 1946, when Patterson died, it had the largest circulation of any newspaper in the world.

—Lloyd Morris, *Postscript to Yesterday: American Life and Thought 1896–1946*

▪ What made the *Daily News* appealing to a mass audience? Write your answer in a sentence. _____

_____

■ List below all the capitalized words—except for first words in sentences—in the excerpt above. In the second column, write the reason for the capitalization, as shown in the example.

Capitalized Words	Reasons
1. _First World War_	_historic event_
2. _____	_____
3. _____	_____
4. _____	_____
5. _____	_____
6. _____	_____
7. _____	_____
8. _____	_____
9. _____	_____
10. _____	_____
11. _____	_____

■ How do you get the news—from a newspaper, radio, television, or the Internet? Write a sentence explaining your preference. _____

_____

LESSON 45b
Capital Letters for Countries and People
• • • • • • • •

We capitalize the names of groups of people whether or not they are part of national groups: _Native Americans, Scandinavians, New Englanders._ The names of religions, such as _Judaism,_ and of organizations like _Amnesty International_ are also capitalized as are adjectives formed from such names: _English, Islamic, Republican._

The Pursuit of Independence

[1]In the early ages of Christianity, Germany was occupied by seven distinct nations, who had no common chief. [2]The Franks, one of the number, having conquered the Gauls, established the kingdom which has taken its name from them. [3]In the ninth century Charlemagne, its warlike monarch, carried his victorious arms in every direction; and Germany became a part of his vast dominions. [4]Charlemagne and his immediate descendants possessed the reality, as well as the ensigns and dignity of imperial power. [5]But the principal vassals, whose fiefs had become hereditary, and who composed the national diets which Charlemagne had not abolished, gradually threw off the yoke and advanced to sovereign jurisdiction and independence.

—James Madison, *The Federalist Papers*

■ Combine these sentences:

The empire could not continue. Individuals sought independence. _____

_____

■ In the excerpt above we have the names of a religion, a country, an emperor, and several peoples. Write them in the appropriate spaces below, as shown in the example.

Name	Category
1. _____*Germany*_____	_____*country*_____
2. _____	_____
3. _____	_____
4. _____	_____
5. _____	_____

■ Write a sentence about someone you met in another state or country that you have visited. _____

_____

For more about capitals, see Review Exercise 22.

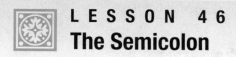

LESSON 46
The Semicolon

The semicolon[;] is a useful mark of punctuation. If you have two clauses, closely related in meaning, but cannot connect them with a conjunction, you may put a semicolon between the two. The second clause will *not* begin with a capital letter. For example, *Winter will soon be here; all of the leaves have fallen.*

Coming Home

[1]There stands the old, square watch-tower, in front of it the great mottled lime tree and behind it the evening. [2]Here we have often sat; we have passed over this bridge and breathed the cool, acid smell of the stagnant water; we have leaned over the still water on this side of the lock, where the green creepers and weeds hang from the piles of the bridge; and on hot days we rejoiced in the spouting foam on the other side of the lock and told tales about our school-teachers. [3]I pass over the bridge, I look right and left; the water is as full of weeds as ever, and it still shoots over in gleaming arches; in the tower-building laundresses still stand with bare arms as they used to over the clean linen, and the heat from the ironing pours out through the open windows.

—Erich Maria Remarque, *All Quiet on the Western Front*

■ In this passage the author uses semicolons between many of the clauses. Why do you think he did this instead of using periods or conjunctions? Give examples in your answer. _____

_____

■ Where did you hang out after school when you were younger? Write a sentence about your favorite place to meet your classmates. _____

_____

LESSON 46a
Another Use for the Semicolon

When we write a series—a list of people, things, or ideas—the items are always separated by commas [see Lesson 47]. But suppose the items in that series, like a date or an address, have commas already in them: *The meeting may take place on December 4, 2002; December 8, 2002; or January 10, 2003.* As you can see, we avoid confusion in such cases by using the semicolon to separate the items.

A Feudal Society

[1]By 1066, the system was elaborate and stable. [2]There were many social strata. [3]At the bottom were serfs or slaves; next cottagers or cottars; then villeins, who farmed as much perhaps as fifty acres; then thanes, who drew rents in kind from the villeins; then earls, each ruling one of the six great earldoms that covered the country; and above all, the King. [4]And in parallel to this secular social ladder was the hierarchy of the church, from village priests to archbishops. [5]None of these people could claim the absolute ownership of land. [6]The villeins, to use the old phrase, "held their land of" the thanes, the thanes held it of an earl or the church or the King, and the King held it all of God's grace. [7]And each of them, without exception, owed duties to the others above and below him.

—David Howarth, *1066: The Year of the Conquest*

■ Why could no one in this society claim absolute ownership of land? Write your answer in a sentence. _____

_____

■ The social ranks in sentence 3 above are separated by semicolons. Rewrite each item in the series as a sentence, following the example below.

1. _____ *After the serfs came the cottagers.* _____

2. _____

3. _____

4. _____

5. _____

6. _____

■ How is the leader chosen in a group you belong to? Write your answer in a sentence. _____

_____

LESSON 46b
More About the Semicolon
· · · · · · · · · ·

The semicolon can pull together ideas that the writer wants to convey in a simple, dramatic way. *The girls wore tankinis, most of the time, at the beach; they wore cut-offs, in the evening, after work; and, most of the time, they wore flip-flops on their feet.*

Grandmother

[1]My grandmother had a reverence for the sun, a holy regard that now is all but gone out of mankind. [2]There was a wariness in her, and an ancient awe. [3]She was a Christian in her later years, but she had come a long way about, and she never forgot her birthright. [4]As a child she had been to the Sun Dances; she had taken part in those annual rites, and by them she had learned the restoration of her people in the presence of Tai-me. [5]She was about seven when the last Kiowa Sun Dance was held in 1887 on the Washita River above Rainy Mountain Creek. [6]Now that I can have her only in memory, I see my grandmother in the several postures that were peculiar to her: standing at the wood stove on a winter morning and turning meat in a great iron skillet; sitting at the south window, bent above her bead-work, and afterwards, when her vision failed, looking down for a long time into the fold of her hands; going out upon a cane, very slowly as she did when the weight of age came upon her; praying. [7]I remember her most often at prayer.

—N. Scott Momaday, *The Way to Rainy Mountain*

■ Combine these sentences:

Grandmother remembered the old rituals. She had a reverence for the sun.

_____

■ In the first column, write each word from the excerpt above that is followed by a semicolon. Indicate whether the punctuation connects clauses or a separates the items in a series.

Words   **Connects or Separates**

1. _____ Sun Dances; _____   _____ Connects two clauses _____

2. _____   _____

3. _____   _____

4. _____   _____

■ Write a sentence naming some things you remember about a grandparent or some other older person. _____

_____

. . . .

The comma is used to *separate*—never connect—words or clauses and to ensure that the sense of a sentence is not lost. As we saw in the introduction to this unit, a sentence can be *ambiguous*—can have two or more possible meanings—when a comma is missing. By the same token, items in a list or series can be confusing if they are not separated by a comma: *for the ski trip I bought boots, hat, and a heavy scarf.* Still another use of the comma is to set off connecting words and phrases like *meanwhile* and *on the other hand* from the rest of the sentence. *Therefore, I stayed home from the party.* When listing several words or phrases, separate them by commas. It is better not to end such a series with *etc.*

A Waste of Youth

[1]I am young, I am twenty years old; yet I know nothing of life but despair, death, fear, and superficiality cast over an abyss of sorrow. [2]I see how peoples are set against one another, and in silence, unknowingly, foolishly, obediently, innocently slay one another. [3]I see that the keenest brains of the world invent weapons and words to make it yet more refined and enduring. [4]And all men of my age, here and over there, throughout the whole world see these things; all my generation is experiencing these things with me. [5]What would our fathers do if we suddenly stood up and came before them and proffered our account? [6]What do they expect of us if a time ever comes when the war is over? [7]Through the years our business has been killing. [8]Our knowledge of life is limited to death.

—Erich Maria Remarque, *All Quiet on the Western Front*

■ Why does the narrator put despair first in his list of the negative emotions of his life? Write your answer in a sentence. _____

_____

■ Underline the series of nouns and adverbs in the excerpt above. For two items, in each of these series, write a sentence showing why the writer feels it is wasting his youth. The first is an example: From the series that begins "despair death, fear . . .".

1. _____ *He has seen the death of other young men on the battlefield.* _____

2. _____

3. _____

4. _____

5. _____

■ Can you think of something your whole generation is concerned about? Write a sentence explaining what it is. _____

_____

LESSON 47a
More Commas to Separate
Items in a Series

As we saw earlier, the semicolon is used to separate the items in a list that has internal punctuation. For simpler lists, the comma is used. Usually, the last item will be followed by a comma before *and*. For example, *Apples, oranges, and lemons formed the centerpiece.*

The Gardens

[1]My mother adorned with flowers whatever shabby house we were forced to live in. [2]Before she left home for the fields, she watered her flowers, chopped up the grass, and laid out new beds. [3]When she returned from the fields she might divide clumps of bulbs, dig a cold pit, uproot and replant roses, or prune branches from her taller bushes or trees—until night came and it was too dark to see. [4]Because of her creativity with her flowers, even my memories of poverty are seen through a screen of blooms—sunflowers, petunias, roses, dahlias, forsythia, spirea, delphiniums, verbena. . .and on and on. [5]And I remember people coming to my mother's yard to be given cuttings from her flowers; I hear again the praise showered on her because whatever rocky soil she landed on, she turned into a garden.

—Alice Walker, *In Search of Our Mothers' Gardens*

■ Combine these sentences:

The family was poor. Mother always had a luxuriant garden. _____

_____

- There are two kinds of series in the excerpt above, one with verb phrases, the other with nouns. For the verb phrases, write the subject, verb, and direct object, if there is one, of each.

1. _____ *she watered her flowers* _____

2. _____

3. _____

4. _____

5. _____

6. _____

7. _____

- Now write the nouns that are separated by commas.

1. _____ *sunflowers* _____   5. _____

2. _____   6. _____

3. _____   7. _____

4. _____   8. _____

- Most people have some kind of hobby—collecting old comic books, fixing broken clocks, or watching romantic movie comedies. Write a sentence about a hobby you have enjoyed. _____

_____

LESSON 47b
Still More Series

Note that none of the series we have seen ended with *etc.* It is far better just to decide on the last item and end there. *The class was so boring that students found themselves looking out the window, drawing pictures in their notebooks, and taking naps.*

A Ship's Supplies Run Out

[1]The expedition had left Sanlúcar with 420 casks of wine. [2]All were drained. [3]One by one the other staples vanished—cheese, dried fish, salt pork, beans, peas, anchovies, cereals, onions, raisins, and lentils—until they were left with kegs of brackish, foul-smelling water and biscuits which, having first crumbled into a gray powder, were now slimy with rat droppings and alive with maggots. [4]These, mixed with sawdust, formed a vile muck men could get down only by holding their noses. [5]Rats, which could be roasted, were so prized that they sold for half a ducat each. [6]The capitán-general had warned them that they might have to eat leather, and it came to that.

—William Manchester, *A World Lit Only by Fire*

▪ Why do you think the food supplies ran out on this voyage? Write your answer in a sentence. _____

_____

▪ Write three lists in the spaces provided below, showing (1) foods that you might find being served for lunch in the cafeteria; (2) foods that you might have for dinner at home; and (3) foods that you might find in your favorite fast-food restaurant. The first is an example of what you might find in a vegetarian restaurant.

1. *stuffed peppers, asparagus, tomato and onion salad, and sliced kiwis*

2. _____

3. _____

4. _____

▪ Write a sentence describing what you like about your favorite food.

_____

LESSON 48
Commas That Set Off Subordinate Clauses

• • • • • • • •

When a subordinate clause begins a sentence or is part of a sentence with several clauses, it is separated from the independent clause by a comma. *Whenever Jake took time for lunch, he was late for class.*

War's Toll

[1]Just as we turn into animals when we go up to the line, because that is the only thing which brings us through safely, so we turn into wags and loafers when we are resting. [2]We can do nothing else; it is a sheer necessity. [3]We want to live at any price; so we cannot burden ourselves with feelings which, though they might be ornamental enough in peacetime, would be out of place here. [4]And this I know: all these things that now, while we are still in the war, sink down in us like a stone, after the war shall waken again, and then shall begin the disentanglement of life and death. [5]The days, the weeks, the years out here shall come back again, and our dead comrades shall then stand up again and march with us, our heads shall be clear, we shall have a purpose, and so we shall march, our dead comrades beside us, the years at the Front behind us—against whom, against whom?

—Erich Maria Remarque, *All Quiet on the Western Front*

■ Combine these sentences:

Wartime experiences mark the soldier. They will not be forgotten. _____

_____

■ Find four subordinate clauses in the excerpt above that are set off by commas and write them below, as shown in the example.

1. _____ *though they might be ornamental enough in peacetime.*

2. _____

3. _____

4. _____

■ Why do we sometimes get more accomplished when we work in a group? Write a sentence explaining your answer. _____

_____

LESSON 48a
Commas with Subordinate Clauses

A subordinate clause is separated from the independent clause by a comma, especially when it begins a sentence: *Although it was cold, Zelda did not wear a hat.*

Being a Star

[1]Although she had now achieved the success and adulation she had craved for so long, Madonna the individual struggled to cope with her new life as a modern icon. [2]At first she reveled in her celebrity status. [3]Ever since Madonna had first appeared in a fashion spread in the *Village Voice*, she had saved every press clipping about herself, carefully labeling and dating each one. [4]Each morning she read the New York tabloids and the *New York Times*, scouring them for stories about herself. [5]While publicly she feigned indifference when a critic wrote a withering review or when a reporter made up a negative story about her, she was frequently hurt by such coverage, often losing sleep if a particular remark hit home. [6]It would take several years before Madonna truly began to feel comfortable with her star status.

—Andrew Morton, *Madonna*

■ Why did Madonna save all the press clippings about herself? Write your answer in a sentence. _____

_____

■ Underline each of the subordinate clauses in the excerpt above that begin a sentence. Rewrite each of these sentences as two separate sentences, as shown in the example. *When she went to restaurants, other diners would talk about her or just stare.*

Subordinate Clause	Sentences
Publicly she feigned indifference. She was frequently hurt.	*While publicly she feigned indifference, she was frequently hurt.*

1. _____   _____

2. _____   _____

Subordinate Clause	Sentences
3. _____	_____
4. _____	_____

- Have you ever seen a crowd gather when a celebrity appears? Write a sentence explaining why you think this happens. _____

_____

LESSON 48b
More Subordinate Clauses

Remember that a subordinate clause is never a sentence by itself. It must always be joined to an independent clause. When it begins a sentence, it is followed by a comma. The sentence before this one is an example of that. Here is another one: *Because they were late, Gary and Bobby called a taxi.*

Ambushed by Dogs

[1]When I woke, the sun was low. [2]Looking down from where I lay, I saw a dog sitting on his haunches. [3]His tongue was hanging out of his mouth; he looked as if he were laughing. [4]He was a big dog, with a gray-brown coat, as big as a wolf. [5]I sprang up and shouted at him but he did not move—he just sat there as if he were laughing. [6]I looked about me—not far away there was a great, broken god-road [highway], leading north. [7]I went toward this god-road, keeping to the heights of the ruins, while the dog followed. [8]When I had reached the god-road, I saw that there were others behind him. [9]If I had slept later, they would have come upon me asleep and torn out my throat. [10]As it was, they were sure enough of me; they did not hurry.

—Stephen Vincent Benét, *By the Waters of Babylon*

- Combine these sentences:

The dogs were menacing. The man looked for a way to escape. _____

_____

■ Find the subordinate clauses that begin sentences in the excerpt above. Write a new sentence beginning with the same clause, as shown in the example.

1. _____ *When I woke, the alarm was ringing.* _____

2. _____

3. _____

4. _____

5. _____

■ Write a sentence about a time you were frightened by an animal. It might be when a bear appeared at your camp or when you heard that a shark was seen near the beach where you were swimming. _____

_____

LESSON 49
Commas That Set Off Connecting Words and Phrases

. . . .

When a connecting word or phrase begins a sentence, it is followed by a comma. If it occurs in the middle of a sentence, it is preceded and followed by a comma. For example, *At last, Greg got the car started. Manya, however, was not ready to go.*

Katczinsky

[1]We couldn't do without Katczinsky; he has a sixth sense. [2]Katczinsky is the smartest I know. [3]By trade he is a cobbler, I believe, but that hasn't anything to do with it; he understands all the trades. [4]It's a good thing to be friends with him, as Kropp and I are, and Westhus too, more or less. [5]For example, we land at night in some entirely unknown spot, a sorry hole, that has been eaten out to the very walls. [6]We are just dozing off when the door opens and Kat appears. [7]I think I must be dreaming; he has two loaves of bread under his arm and a blood-stained sandbag full of horse-flesh in his hand. [8]Kat gives no explanation. [9]He has the bread; the rest doesn't matter. [10]I'm sure that if he were planted down in the middle of the desert, in half an hour he would have gathered together a supper of roast meat, dates, and wine.

—Erich Maria Remarque, *All Quiet on the Western Front*

■ Write a sentence explaining why Katczinsky's friendship is so important to his fellow soldiers. _____

_____

■ Phrases that are set off by commas can sometimes act as adverbs—for example, *Help arrived quickly, in the nick of time.* Sometimes they are nouns, repeating in other words a noun in the sentence: *My wife, the novelist, has a new book out.* Occasionally, even a very short sentence may set off words with commas: *Larry, my best friend, was there.* These repetitions of a word in the sentence are called *appositives* or *parenthetical phrases* or *clauses.* In the excerpt above, find examples of each of these. Write them below, identifying whether they are acting as nouns, adverbs, or connecting phrases.

Word or Phrase	Purpose
1. _____ *I believe* _____	*connecting phrase*
2. _____	_____

227

Word or Phrase	**Purpose**
3. _____	_____
4. _____	_____

■ We all know someone who is exceptionally clever at making the best of a trying situation. Write your own sentence about such a person—it might even be you! _____

_____

LESSON 49a
More Connectors with Commas

· · · · · · · · · ·

Sometimes a phrase that is set off—or separated from the rest of the sentence—by commas signals that the words following will further clarify what has just been written. For example, *My newest friend, Allegra, loves peanut butter.*

The Spirit of the Kiowas

¹Houses are like sentinels in the plain, old keepers of the weather watch. ²There, in a very little while, wood takes on the appearance of great age. ³All colors wear soon away in the wind and rain; then the wood is burned gray and the grain appears and the nails turn red with rust. ⁴The windowpanes are black and opaque; you imagine there is nothing within, and indeed there are many ghosts, bones given up to the land. ⁵They stand here and there against the sky, and you approach them for a longer time than you expect. ⁶They belong in the distance; it is their domain. ⁷Once there was a lot of sound in my grandmother's house, a lot of coming and going, feasting and talk. ⁸Now there is a funeral silence in the rooms, the endless wake of some final word.

—N. Scott Momaday, *The Way to Rainy Mountain*

■ In what way are the plains houses evidence of the weather of that region? Explain your answer in a sentence. _____

_____

▪ In the excerpt above, there are several parenthetical repetitions of statements. Underline them, then write them below with the nouns they describe more fully. The example below shows what you might do.

1. _____ *many ghosts* _____   _____ *bones* _____

2. _____   _____

3. _____   _____

4. _____   _____

▪ Think of a house that holds memories for you. Now write a sentence explaining why those memories are important. _____

_____

LESSON 49b
More Parenthetical Phrases

Parenthetical phrases are very useful for providing more information about people—and things—that are part of your composition. They may tell someone's occupation, like *Mrs. Vega, a history teacher.* Or they may identify someone's hometown, *Rosalia, a native of Chicago.*

The Yacht Race

[1]I was assigned to the crew of the *Barbarian*, a yacht as appropriately named for the sport of ocean racing as any in the fleet. [2]There were eight of us in the crew. [3]There was a professional yachtsman from Australia named Bruce, who'd spent the last year transporting boats about the world and racing for anyone who could afford him. [4]There was Harris, an MIT graduate and a naval architect for Exxon; John, a mechanical engineer for the same company; Herb, an advertising executive; Riley, who has something to do with tax forms, but mainly races; and Donny, the skipper's son. [5]All were young, tan, and athletic.

—Giles Tippette, *Donkey Baseball and Other Sporting Delights*

■ Combine these sentences:

Ocean racing crews come from many occupations. They must be young and

athletic. _____

_____

■ Find five parenthetical expressions in the excerpt above that connect the
writer's ideas and write them below.

1. _____ *a yacht as appropriately named* _____

2. _____

3. _____

4. _____

5. _____

6. _____

■ Think of a trip you have made on water—anything from a cruise to a ride

on a ferryboat. Write a sentence about your experience. _____

_____

The Apostrophe

. . . .

The apostrophe, the upside down comma ', usually indicates that some-thing is missing. For example, in the contraction *hasn't* the apostrophe stands for the missing letter *o* of *has not*. In *o'clock*, the apostrophe replaces *of the*. The apostrophe in the possessive form of nouns—*Hector's* book, for in-stance—also stands for the letter *e* that was once part of the ending in Old English. (Remember this from Lesson 14?)

The Hospital Train

[1]Albert is feverish. [2]I don't feel too bad. [3]I hear from the sister [the nurse] that Albert is to be put off at the next station because of his fever. [4]On the sister's next round I hold my breath and press it up into my head. [5]My face swells and turns red. [6]She stops. [7]"Are you in pain?" [8]She gives me a ther-mometer and goes on. [9]I would not have been under Kat's tuition if I didn't know what to do now. [10]These army thermometers aren't made for old sol-diers. [11]All one has to do is to drive the quicksilver up and then it stays with-out falling again. [12]I stick the thermometer under my arm at a slant, and flip it steadily with my forefinger. [13]Then I give it a shake. [14]I send it up to 100.2°. [15]But that isn't enough. [16]A match held cautiously near to it brings it up to 101.6°. [17]Albert and I are put off together.

—Erich Maria Remarque, *All Quiet on the Western Front*

■ In one sentence explain the trick the narrator has played on the nursing sister.

_____

■ Find the words written with apostrophes in the excerpt above. List them in the appropriate column below.

Possessive	Contraction
1. _____*sister's*_____	_____*don't*_____
2. _____	_____
3. _____	_____

■ Did you ever avoid something you didn't want to do by playing a trick? Write a sentence about it. _____

_____

For more about punctuation, see Review Exercises 29, 40, 43, 44.

LESSON 50a
Apostrophes in Contractions

· · · · · · · · · · ·

Many of the words we contract are verbs with *not*—for example, *don't* and *wouldn't*. We also tend to turn *should have* to *should've* and *it is* to *it's*. We do this more often when we speak than when we write. It is important not to confuse the possessive pronoun *its* with the contraction *it's*.

Tears

[1]That night, for the last time in my life but one—for I was a big boy twelve years old—I cried. [2]I cried, in bed alone, and couldn't stop. [3]I buried my head under the quilts, but my aunt heard me. [4]She woke up and told my uncle I was crying because the Holy Ghost had come into my life, and because I had seen Jesus. [5]But I was really crying because I couldn't bear to tell her that I had lied, that I had deceived everybody in the church, that I hadn't seen Jesus, and that now I didn't believe there was a Jesus any more, since he didn't come to help me.

—Langston Hughes, *Salvation*

■ Combine these sentences:

The narrator pretended to be saved. The lie made him sad. _____

_____

■ For each of the contractions in this passage, write in full the verb phrase.

Contraction	Verb Phrase
1. _____ *couldn't* _____	_____ *could not* _____
2. _____	_____
3. _____	_____

■ Write a sentence about something you did as a child that made you sad because you believed it was wrong. _____

_____

LESSON 50b
Apostrophes to Show Possession

To show possession for a plural noun ending in *-s* put the apostrophe *after* the *-s* as in *the girls' team won easily.* An important thing to remember about apostrophes is that, when used with nouns, they indicate possession (remember Lesson 14), but they are not used with possessive pronouns.

Women's Sports

[1]The sport creed's slogans and myths taught me that we control our own fates. [2]If I found myself unable to teach women a sense of free agency, to pursue athletic excellence regardless of parents' or boyfriends' agendas and actions, then the fault must lie in me. [3]What I took away from coaching, besides this haunting sense of my own failure to effect what truly mattered, were only more questions. [4]How, specifically, does muscularity threaten a female's "femininity"? [5]Why would women's pursuit of sporting excellence jeopardize relationships with men? [6]And what, in any case, are issues of women's relationship to men and men's judgment of women's physical appearance doing in *women's* sport?

—Joli Sandoz, *Coming Home*

■ Combine these sentences:

Coaching raised questions for the writer. They had to do with relationships among women, men, and sports. _____

_____

_____

■ Find the possessive nouns in the excerpt above. Put the singular nouns in column 1 and the plural nouns in column 2.

Column 1	**Column 2**
1. _____*creed's*_____	1. _____*parents'*_____
2. _____	2. _____
	3. _____
	4. _____
	5. _____

■ Write a sentence about a team you have played on. Was it all men, all women, or both? _____

_____

L E S S O N   5 1
Quotation Marks

. . . .

We all know what quotation marks are: those comma-like marks go around anything that a person other than the writer has said or written. For example, *Lori said, "Is it time to go yet?"* As we see in the passage below, quotation marks are used even when the writer is quoting his own thoughts.

Return from Fear

[1]By afternoon I am calmer. [2]My fear was groundless. [3]The name troubles me no more. [4]The madness passes. [5]"Comrade," I say to the dead man, but I say it calmly, "today you, tomorrow me. [6]But if I come out of it, comrade, I will fight against this, that has struck us both down; from you, taken life—and from me—? Life also. [7]I promise you, comrade. [8]It shall never happen again." [9]The sun strikes low. [10]I am stupefied with exhaustion and hunger. [11]The twilight comes. [12]One hour more. [13]Now suddenly I begin to tremble; something might happen in the interval. [14]Suddenly it occurs to me that my own comrades may fire on me as I creep up; they do not know I am coming. [15]I will call out as soon as I can, so that they will recognize me. [16]I will stay lying in front of the trench until they answer me. The first star. [17]The front remains quiet. [18]I breathe deeply and talk to myself in my excitement: [19]"No foolishness now, Paul—Quiet, Paul, quiet—then you will be saved, Paul." [20]When I use my Christian name it works as though someone else spoke to me, it has more power.

—Erich Maria Remarque, *All Quiet on the Western Front*

- Combine these sentences:

Paul is alone on the battlefield. He tries to calm his fears. _____
_____

- Think of a conversation you had with a friend about an assignment. Write a short paragraph describing what each of you said. Be sure to put quotation marks in the appropriate places.

_____
_____
_____
_____
_____

235

LESSON 51a
Another Use for Quotation Marks

Quotation marks *must* enclose words that were spoken or written by someone other than the writer. But sometimes we will see these marks around a single word or a brief phrase, when a writer wants to show disagreement or irony. For example, *Jake thought that movie was "great."* We do *not* use quotation marks to emphasize or call attention to a word or phrase. We can do that by underlining or, better yet, by using italics.

A Man's World

¹When we say *men, man, manly, manhood,* and all the other masculine derivatives, we have in the background of our minds a huge vague crowded picture of the world and all its activities. ²To grow up and "be a man," to "act like a man"—the meaning and connotation is wide indeed. ³That vast background is full of marching columns of men, of changing lines of men, of long processions of men; of men steering their ships into new seas, exploring unknown mountains, breaking horses, herding cattle, ploughing and sowing and reaping, toiling at the forge and furnace, digging in the mine, building roads and bridges and high cathedrals, managing great businesses, teaching in all the colleges, preaching in all the churches; of men everywhere, doing everything—"the world." ⁴But when we say *women,* we think *female*—the sex.

—Charlotte Perkins Gilman, *Herland*

▪ Combine these sentences:

The men thought all accomplishments were done by men. The women here had

accomplished things themselves. _____

_____

▪ Write a short paragraph about the accomplishments of someone you admire—a friend, a member of your family, or a celebrity. Put quotation marks around any words that were written or spoken by someone else.

_____

_____

_____

_____

_____

_____

LESSON 51b
Quotations

• • • • • • • • •

In your writing for college courses, you will often be assigned work that requires quotations from books and other sources to prove the points you wish to make about your subject. You must identify these quotations clearly by putting quotation marks around any words that are not your own.

Swordfish

[1]New Englanders started catching swordfish in the early 1800s by harpooning them from small sailboats and hauling them on board. [2]Since swordfish don't school, the boats would go out with a man up the mast looking for single fins lolling about in the glassy inland waters. [3]If the wind sprang up, the fins were undetectable, and the boats went in. [4]When the lookout spotted a fish, he guided the captain over to it, and the harpooner made his throw. [5]The throw had to take into account the roll of the boat, the darting of the fish, and the refraction of light through water. [6]Giant bluefish tuna are still hunted this way, but fishermen use spotter planes to find their prey and electric harpoons to kill them.

—Sebastian Junger, *The Perfect Storm*

■ Write a paragraph about different kinds of fishing—from boats, in rivers or streams, or any other kind you can think of. Use at least one quotation from the passage on swordfish in your paragraph.

_____

_____

_____

_____

_____

_____

YOUR WRITING
Making a Point

Throughout the passages you have been reading from *All Quiet on the Western Front*, you have seen some of the psychological as well as physical effects of war on a young man. Now, for the composition you are about to write on the lines below, think of an experience you have lived through that produced lasting feelings and perhaps changed the way you look at the world. As you give details of the events or encounters that led to these feelings, remember all you have learned about producing a paper of three paragraphs that makes a point.

- Stay focused on your purpose: to provide information, *not* to express an opinion or tell a story.
- Begin with a thesis statement that makes clear to your reader what point you are making.
- Be sure *every* sentence that follows, but especially your topic sentences, provides further information about that point.
- Use specific details and examples to make your points clear.
- Combine sentences to show how ideas are related to one another.
- Use connective words and phrases so the reader can follow your thoughts easily.
- Write a concluding sentence that echoes your thesis without repeating it.

_____

_____

_____

_____

_____

_____

_____

_____

_____

_____

_____

_____

_____

_____

_____

_____

_____

Review Exercises

. . . .

Sentences

Remember that every sentence must have a subject, which is often, but not always, a noun or a pronoun: *Joan of Arc....*

Every sentence must also have a verb. Usually the verb is part of a group of words we call the *predicate:* Joan of Arc <u>led</u> the French army.

Led is the verb and *led the French army* is the predicate. Note that *led* is the past tense of *lead.* The verb in a sentence must have a tense. In the passages below underline the subject of each sentence once, and the verb twice.

1

Caution: Cellphone in Use

[1]In Japan, where the police have kept track of accidents caused by the use of cellphones, cellphone-related crashes plummeted by 75 percent after 1999 when the country banned the use of hand-held phones when driving. [2]Having a phone in a car is a good idea. [3]It can relieve anxiety in unavoidable delays and be lifesaving in an emergency. [4]But safety-conscious drivers would be wise to avoid using it for casual conversations and should always pull off the road when dialing, talking or answering it.

—Jane E. Brody, "Cellphone: A Convenience, a Hazard or Both?"

■ For each subject in the excerpt above, write a predicate of your own, following the example below.

Subject	Predicate
1. _____ *the police* _____	_____ *keep the city safe* _____
2. _____	_____
3. _____	_____
4. _____	_____
5. _____	_____
6. _____	_____

■ Write a sentence about a situation in which you think a cellphone is useful.

2

Covering the Palace

[1]Only after many hours of frantic reporting did I have a chance to take a breath and think about Diana's death. [2]I had covered her closely for nearly a year, reporting when she went public about an affair, an eating disorder, her suicide attempts, her unhappiness in her marriage. [3]Just about any woman who is plagued by low self-esteem, who worries about her weight, who has trouble with men, who tries to find herself at the gym or with psychic healers—any woman with everyday problems of the 1990s—found a spokeswoman of sorts in Diana.

—Siobhan Darrow, *Flirting with Danger*

■ Sentence 3 has four relative clauses. Remember, relative clauses cannot stand as sentences on their own but must be connected to an independent clause. Change each of the dependent relative clauses into an independent clause, as the example shows.

Relative Clause	**Independent Clause**
1. *Who is plagued by low self-esteem*	*The student with poor grades is plagued by low self-esteem.*
2. _____	_____
3. _____	_____
4. _____	_____

■ Write a sentence about someone who "has it all" but is still unhappy.

3

Promised Land

[1]The Mets entered the promised land on October 16, 1969, after seven years of wandering through the wilderness of baseball. [2]In a tumultuous game before a record crowd of 57,397 in Shea Stadium, they defeated the Baltimore Orioles, 5–3, for their fourth straight victory of the sixty-sixth World Series and captured the championship of a sport that had long ranked them as comical losers. [3]They did it with a full and final dose of the magic that had spiced their unthinkable climb from ninth place in the National League—100-to-1 shots who scraped and scrounged their way to the pinnacle as the waifs of the major leagues.

—Joseph Durso, "The Miracle Mets"

■ For each verb in the excerpt above, write your own sentence as shown in the example.

Verb	Sentence
1. _____ *entered* _____	*The class <u>entered</u> the auditorium.*
2. _____	_____
3. _____	_____
4. _____	_____
5. _____	_____
6. _____	_____

■ Write a sentence about a championship—anything from an athletic competition to a spelling bee or a chess match—that you attended or took part in.

_____

4

One Girl's Life

[1]Maureen Connolly at eighteen was the top woman tennis player in the world and the first in history to hold all four of the world's major crowns. [2]Connolly loved a good time as much as any teenage girl and tried to have as much fun as any player of the top flight. [3]Her hobbies were dancing and music of any and every kind. [4]She liked to eat hamburgers and drink Cokes, go to baseball games and parties. [5]On the court she was all business and had no thoughts for anything but beating her opponent into submission as quickly as she could. [6]But once she was finished, she became a different person, a bubbling eighteen-year-old full of gaiety and friendliness for everyone.

—Allison Danzig, *Little Girl, Big Racquet*

■ For two of the sentences in the excerpt above, change the subject to you or to someone you know and write a new predicate, as shown in the example.

Sentence 2: _____ *Jane loved going to the movies.* _____

1. _____

2. _____

■ Write a sentence explaining why your favorite leisure-time activity is what it is. _____

_____

5

Super

¹Bryan Bartlett "Bart" Starr, the quarterback for the Green Bay Packers, led his team to a 35–10 victory over the Kansas City Chiefs on January 15, 1967, in the first professional football game between the champions of the National and American Football Leagues. ²Doubt about the outcome disappeared in the third quarter when Starr's pretty passes made mere Indians out of the AFL Chiefs and Green Bay scored twice. ³The outcome served to settle the curiosity of the customers, who paid from five to twelve dollars for tickets. ⁴The final score was an honest one, meaning it correctly reflected what went on during the game. ⁵The great interest had led to naming the event the Super Bowl, but the contest was more ordinary than super.

—William N. Wallace, *The First Super Bowl*

■ Find the dependent clauses in the excerpt above and rewrite them to make them independent clauses. The first, from sentence 3, has been done as an example.

Dependent Clauses	**Independent Clauses**
1. *who paid from five to twelve dollars for tickets.*	*The customers paid from five to twelve dollars for tickets.*
2. _____	_____
3. _____	_____

■ Did you ever look forward to a big event that turned out to be unexciting? Write a sentence about it. _____

6

Escaping the War

¹The Crawfords had half an hour to pack before the last train left the city. ²Immediately after they had crossed the Seine, Emily heard a terrific explosion. ³Looking back, she saw that the railway bridge had been blown up. ⁴There were many other hazards on the journey, as Emily was to report for several English and American newspapers. ⁵After being detained for many days on the line, another train ran into theirs killing eighteen passengers. ⁶She and her husband were spared only because, minutes before the crash, they had moved to the rear of the train.

—Anne Sebba, *Battling for News*

■ Look at the subjects from the sentences in the excerpt above. Write the full predicate for each of them.

1. The Crawfords _____ *had half an hour to pack.* _____

2. The last train _____

3. They _____

4. Emily _____

5. She _____

6. The railway bridge _____

7. Other hazards _____

8. Emily _____

9. Another train _____

10. She and her husband _____

11. They _____

■ Write a sentence about a narrow escape you had from some danger. _____

_____

7

A New Life

[1]Rose found herself craving for sugar after the excitement of the day, and significantly enough, made no effort to combat the craving. [2]Freedom and responsibility and an open-air life and a foretaste of success were working wonders on her. [3]Those big breasts of hers, which had begun to sag when she had begun to lapse into spinsterhood, were firm and upstanding now again, and she could look down on them swelling out the bosom of her white drill frock without misgiving. [4]Even in these ten days her body had done much towards replacing fat where fat should be and eliminating it from those areas where it should not. [5]Her face had filled out, and though there were puckers round her eyes caused by the sun, they went well with her healthy tan, and lent piquancy to the ripe femininity of her body.

—C. S. Forester, *The African Queen*

■ You probably noticed that some of the verbs in the excerpt above were made of helpers with a past or present participle. Write both parts of those verbs below and identify the kind of participle that completes it.

Verb	Participle
1. _____ were working _____	_____ present participle _____
2. _____	_____
3. _____	_____
4. _____	_____

■ Write a sentence about an activity you took part in that made you more

physically fit. _____

_____

8

Lady on a Ship

[1]As he studied Regina Clausen, he decided that she could use a makeover. [2]She was one of those fortyish women who could have been quite attractive if she only knew how to dress, how to present herself. [3]She was wearing an expensive-looking ice-blue dinner suit that would have been stunning on a blonde, but it did nothing for her very pale complexion, making her look washed out and wan. [4]And her light brown hair, her natural and not unflattering color, was so stiffly set that even from across the wide room it seemed to age her, and even to date her, as though she were a suburban matron from the fifties.

—Mary Higgins Clark, *You Belong to Me*

■ Some of the sentences in the excerpt above have verbs with helpers. Write these verbs below, with a new subject of your own.

Verbs	Subjects
1. _____ could use _____	_____ Mona _____
2. _____	_____
3. _____	_____
4. _____	_____

■ Write a sentence about your favorite color for a special outfit. _____

_____

9
Varieties of English

[1]There are formal and informal dialects, as well as standard and nonstandard ones. [2]Furthermore, standard English is no less of a dialect than any other variety of the language. [3]It is no better and no worse, no more expressive or flexible or beautiful, than any other English dialect. [4]It simply is the variety of English that found itself in the right place at the right time, the dialect that happened to be used by "the right people," those who came to direct the political, economic, and literary affairs of England and eventually, the United States.

—Dennis Baron, *Declining Grammar and Other Essays on the English Vocabulary*

- Underline all of the subjects and verbs in the excerpt above, then decide which clauses are dependent and which are independent. Write the dependent clauses below, underlining the connecting word that identifies them as dependent, as shown in the example.

1. _____ *that found itself in the right place at the right time.*

2. _____

3. _____

- Do you speak the same in class as you do with your friends? Write a sentence explaining a difference between the two manners of speech. _____

10
The Final Victory

[1]The continent below them was slowly settling beneath the mile-high waves that were attacking its coasts. [2]The last that anyone was ever to see of Earth was a great plain, bathed with the silver light of the abnormally brilliant moon. [3]Across its face the waters were pouring in a glittering flood toward a distant range of mountains. [4]The sea had won its final victory, but its triumph would be short-lived for soon sea and land would be no more. [5]Even as the silent party in the control room watched the destruction below, the infinitely greater catastrophe to which this was only the prelude came swiftly upon them.

—Arthur C. Clarke, *Rescue Party*

- Helping verbs, or auxiliaries, are used with the present tense form of a verb and with the present and past participles. Find at least one of each of these in the excerpt above and write both helper and verb below, noting which form of the verb is used.

	Helper	Verb	Form
1.	*was*	*settling*	*present participle*
2.			
3.			
4.			
5.			

■ Have you read a story or seen a movie about a disaster? Write a sentence about it. _____

Prepositions

Most prepositions will be part of prepositional phrases, those groups of words that indicate direction (*under the bridge*) or time (*on the hour*) or means (*by hook or by crook*). Many of these words also form particles—two-word verbs such as *take off, look up,* and *find out.*

11
Finding the Answer

¹Sherlock Holmes preserved his calm professional manner until our visitor had left us, although it was easy for me, who knew him so well, to see that he was profoundly excited. ²The moment that Hilton Cubitt's broad back had disappeared through the door my comrade rushed to the table, laid out all the slips of paper containing dancing men in front of him, and threw himself into an intricate and elaborate calculation. ³For two hours I watched him as he covered sheet after sheet of paper with figures and letters, so completely absorbed in his task that he had evidently forgotten my presence. ⁴Finally he sprang from his chair with a cry of satisfaction, and walked up and down the room rubbing his hands together.

—Sir Arthur Conan Doyle, *The Adventure of the Dancing Men*

■ Underline the prepositional phrases in the excerpt above. For five of them, write another sentence using that phrase, following the example below.

Prepositional phrase	**Sentence**
1. _through the door_	_The teacher walked through the door as the bell rang._
2. _____	_____
3. _____	_____
4. _____	_____
5. _____	_____
6. _____	_____

■ Write a sentence about a time you discovered the answer to a difficult question._____

_____

12

Relearning Joy

[1]We came to meadows full of flowers. [2]We saw and realized that they were there, but we had no feelings about them. [3]The first spark of joy came when we saw a rooster with a tail of multicolored feathers. [4]But it remained only a spark; we did not yet belong to this world. [5]In the evening when we all met again in our hut, one said secretly to the other, "Tell me, were you pleased today?" [6]And the other replied, feeling ashamed as he did not know that we all felt similarly, "Truthfully, no!" [7]We had literally lost the ability to feel pleased and had to relearn it slowly.

—Victor Frankl, *Man's Search for Meaning*

■ Some of the sentences in the excerpt above contain more than one clause. Identify these clauses as dependent or independent and underline the word that connects them, as the example shows.

1. _We saw and realized [ind] that they were there [dep] <u>but</u> we had no feelings about them [ind]._

2. _____

3. _____

4. _____

5. _____

■ Write a sentence about an event that made you very happy. _____

_____

13

Making It

[1]A lot of movie stars are short. [2]I think it's because you have to have a lot of fight to make it big and short people learn how to fight from the get go, especially men. [3]Tall guys have got it made. [4]Natural selection has already favored them. [5] They're usually good at sports. [6]Other guys don't beat them up as often. [7]They don't have to try so hard to impress women. [8]They don't have to learn to do colorful things like acting in order to get noticed. [9]I am prepared to say that being short culturally prepares the male to develop the character traits that help him become a compelling actor, traits such as vulnerability, courage in the face of adversity and perseverance in the pursuit of goals.

—Marco Perella, *Adventures of a No Name Actor*

■ Some of the sentences in the excerpt above use *do* to form a negative. *Do* is often used to ask a question as well. Following the example, turn four of the sentences into questions using *do*.

1. _____*Do tall guys have it made?*_____

2. _____

3. _____

4. _____

5. _____

■ Is physical appearance important to a movie star? Write your answer in a

sentence. _____

_____

14

Stuck in the Ditch

[1]One morning I backed the car into a ditch while turning it around for my run home. [2]I spun the wheels for a while, then got out and looked things over. [3]I spun the wheels some more, until I was dug in good and deep. [4]Then I gave up and started the trek back to camp. [5]It was nearly three o'clock, and the walk home would take at least four hours. [6]They would find me missing before I got there, the car too. [7]I let off a string of swear words, but they seemed to be coming at me, not from me, and I soon stopped.

—Tobias Wolff, *This Boy's Life*

■ Underline the prepositional phrases in the excerpt above. Then, following the example, write five more sentences using these phrases.

1. _____ *The dog jumped into a ditch.* _____

2. _____

3. _____

4. _____

5. _____

6. _____

■ Write a sentence about a time when a car wouldn't start, or a bus broke down, or a train was an hour late. _____
_____

15

Football Fame

[1]Perhaps still the most famous football player ever, Harold (Red) Grange looked in wonderment at the joggers going past his home in Indian Lake, Florida. [2]"I think they're crazy," he said in an interview before Super Bowl XVI in 1982. [3]"If you have a car, why run?" [4]But once he ran like few others. [5]He was fast and strong and so elusive that he seemed to vanish from tacklers. [6]He was a star halfback in the 1920s for the University of Illinois—he once scored four long touchdowns in the first quarter against powerful Michigan— and then went on to play for the Chicago Bears. [7]Grange almost single-handedly popularized professional football.

—Ira Berkow, *A Conversation with the Ghost*

■ Underline the words in the excerpt above that use suffixes to form nouns or adjectives. Write them in the spaces provided, along with the new word that is formed, as shown in the example. For each indicate the part of speech.

	New Words	**Original Word**
1.	*player [noun]*	*play [verb]*
2.		
3.		

New Words	**Original Word**
4. _____	_____
5. _____	_____

■ Think of a name that you associate with football or with some other sport. Write a sentence about why this name means that sport for you. _____

_____

16

A Call from Movieland

[1]When Hollywood entered my life I was sitting in a tiny room in Fort Worth eating meatloaf. [2]The phone rang, and I was informed that some people I had never heard of had just bought the movie rights to my first novel. [3]Three nights later I was sitting in the best restaurant in Fort Worth, eating a steak so thick that in most parts of Texas it would have been called a roast and discussing title changes with a gentleman from Paramount. [4]At the time it never crossed my mind to wonder whether the movie would turn out to be better than the book; what I knew for a certainty was that the steak was better than the meatloaf.

—Larry McMurtry, *Film Flam*

■ Underline the verbs in the excerpt above that are formed with a helper and a past or present participle. Write them below, following the example.

1. _____ *was sitting [present participle]* _____
2. _____
3. _____
4. _____
5. _____

■ Think about a movie you have seen that was based on a book. Write a sentence about which version you preferred. _____

_____

17

A Profitable Plan

[1]Uncle Hal would go to Richmond and set up his company funded with her capital. [2]He would make her an officer of the company; her income from the investment would supplement her other earnings until the company

generated enough profit to let her quit working. [3]After the lumber business began to prosper—Easy Street. [4]To start his company Uncle Hal wanted her to put up $100 from her bank account. [5]She wasn't totally credulous about Uncle Hal's ability to put us on Easy Street. [6]If he was asking for $100, she reasoned, he could probably make do with $75. [7]That's what she gave him. [8]The Colonel instantly launched plans to proceed to Richmond and set up business. [9]Before leaving, he sat in the parlor at New Street and wrote her his receipt for $75, "same to be invested by me, Col. B. H. Robinson, in walnut timber, in the name of E. Baker & Co. of Belleville, N. J., which sum she is to receive. . ." [10]It went on and on, finally stating that if he died she was to receive "all proceeds" accruing to the company, "both gross and net."

—Russell Baker, *Growing Up*

- Give examples in the excerpt above of periods that mark the end of a declarative sentence or the abbreviation of a name, place, or business. Follow the example shown.

Period	Reason for Period
1. _____ *her capital.* _____	*end of a declarative sentence*
2. _____	_____
3. _____	_____
4. _____	_____
5. _____	_____

- Think of your first job, or the first time you earned money. Write a sentence about it. _____

_____

18

Hollywood's Bad Boy

[1]After a long acting drought, Sean Penn's career is undergoing an El Niño-like resurrection. [2]Penn, who makes no bones about how much he dislikes the job he does so well, says this flurry of activity was triggered by the chance to finally film *She's So Lovely*. [3]It's ironic that Penn's return comes in a movie about love, since much of his life has been filled with anger. [4]His temper, his paparazzi punching and his liquor-fueled self-destructiveness are legendary. [5]And for someone who hates the celebrity aspects of show business as passionately as he loves cinema's potential for great artistry, Penn's media-mauled first marriage to Madonna still seems like a willful act of career suicide.

—Bob Strauss, *Q and A with Sean Penn*

■ Underline the nouns and adjectives in the excerpt above that are formed by suffixes. Write them in the spaces provided along with the word from which they are formed. Underline the suffix.

New Word	Original Word
1. _resurrec<u>tion</u> [noun]_	_resurrect [verb]_
2.	
3.	
4.	
5.	
6.	

■ Are people more interested in celebrities who have a reputation for getting in trouble? Write a sentence explaining why or why not. _____

_____

19

Meeting the Star

[1]The next evening we show up at a room in the hotel and Kevin Costner meets us there. [2]We congratulate Kevin on his good fortune in bagging this role and he confides in us that not only does he have the lead in *this* picture, he has a glorious part in something called *The Big Chill*. [3]This work of art will come out soon and the studios are calling and he is, in general, slicing through the butter of life with a very hot knife. [4]Since we are obviously expected to be impressed, Diane and I make soft, reassuring cooing sounds and touch him reverently on his godlike shoulders.

—Marco Perella, *Adventures of a No Name Actor*

■ In the excerpt above, underline the homophones—words that have a different meaning when they are spelled differently. Write both forms of the word below.

1. _we_	_wee_
2.	
3.	

4. _____   _____

5. _____   _____

6. _____   _____

7. _____   _____

■ Would you enjoy meeting someone who is considered a celebrity? Write a sentence about your feelings. _____

_____

20

Trapped

[1]The bed was good, and the pajamas of the softest silk, and he was tired in every fiber of his being, but nevertheless Rainsford could not quiet his brain with the opiate of sleep. [2]He lay, eyes wide open. [3]Once he thought he heard stealthy steps in the corridor outside his room. [4] He sought to throw open the door; it would not open. [5]He went to the window and looked out. [6]His room was high up in one of the towers. [7]The lights of the chateau were out now, and it was dark and silent; but there was a fragment of sallow moon, and by its wan light he could see, dimly, the courtyard. [8]Rainsford went back to the bed and lay down. [9]He had achieved a doze when, just as morning began to come, he heard, far off in the jungle, the faint report of a pistol.

—Richard Connell, *The Most Dangerous Game*

■ Words ending in -*d* can be past tense verbs, helper verbs, or past participles, or they may simply be words spelled that way. Find two examples of each and write them below.

1. Spelling: _____ *bed, good* _____

2. Past tense verbs: _____

3. Helper verbs: _____

4. Past participles: _____

■ Rainsford is frightened because he is locked in his room. Write a sentence about something that frightens you. _____

_____

21

The Star Athlete

[1]Bobby had played football for Concrete High. [2]He'd been their quarterback, the smallest and best player on the team, so much better than the others that he seemed alone on the field. [3]His solitary excellence made him beautiful and tragic, because you knew that whatever prodigies he performed would be undone by the rest of the team. [4]He made sly, unseen handoffs to butter-fingered halfbacks, long bull's-eye passes to ends who couldn't catch them. [5]But his true wizardry was broken field running: sprinting and stopping dead, jumping sideways, pirouetting on his toes and wriggling his hips girlishly as he spun away from the furious hulks who pursued him, slipping between them like a trout shooting down a boulder-strewn creek.

—Tobias Wolff, *This Boy's Life*

▪ Underline the conjunctions and relative pronouns that connect clauses in the excerpt above. Identify the clauses as dependent or independent, as shown in the example.

	Independent Clause	Connector	Dependent Clause
1.	*He'd been their quarterback*	*that*	*he seemed alone on the field*
2.			
3.			
4.			
5.			

▪ Write a sentence about a person you know who has accomplished something extraordinary in a sport, on a musical instrument, or in a school subject. (It might be you!) _____

22

The New Russia

[1]Living in Moscow as a CNN correspondent in the 1990s was a completely different experience from life there as the impoverished young wife of a Soviet citizen in the 1980s. [2]I had a BMW so I never rode the metro. [3]I always shopped in the hard-currency stores, spending my dollars on meat imported from Finland instead of lining up for the shoe leather they called meat

in the domestic stores. [4]My clothes were bought mostly during vacations to Italy. [5]Instead of trudging through the snow to a laundromat that seemed to eat as many clothes as it cleaned, I had a maid. [6]Just like the natives, I learned to be a capitalist in the new Russia.

—Siobhan Darrow, *Flirting with Danger*

■ Capital letters are used in several different ways in the excerpt above. In addition to identifying the first word of a sentence, there are abbreviations of company names and names of cities and countries as well. Write the words below, indicating why they are capitalized.

Capitalized Word	Reason
1. _____CNN_____	_____company name_____
2. _____	_____
3. _____	_____
4. _____	_____
5. _____	_____
6. _____	_____
7. _____	_____

■ Have you ever lived in a different city or country, even if just for a short time? Write a sentence about the most striking difference you observed in the new area. _____

_____

23

A Lady's Skills

[1]Sir Marhalt's lady dazzled him with glowing hair and skin like a rose petal. [2]She moved with the slow dignity of music in her gown of blue and gold, and she wore a tall blue cone and a flowing wimple of sheer white satin. [3]And when she saw the golden prize her eyes shone so that Sir Marhalt said, "My lady, if fortune and my knighthood can equal my wish, you will wear the prize." [4]She smiled at him and blushed, and her hands, which could tighten a girth and cook a forest stew, fluttered like pale butterflies, so that Sir Marhalt was aware that being a good lady is as much a skill as being a good knight.

—John Steinbeck, *The Acts of King Arthur and His Noble Knights*

■ The -*s* at the end of some words can indicate a plural, a possessive, or the ending for the third person singular present tense. Sometimes the -*s* has no meaning; it is just the way the word is spelled. Find one word having each type of -*s* ending in the excerpt above and write it in the space provided, as the example shows.

	Word Ending in -*s*	**Meaning of -*s***
1.	*eyes*	*plural noun*
2.		
3.		
4.		
5.		

■ People can have a talent for doing more than one thing. Write a sentence about someone you know who can do two or more things well. _____

24

Knights at Play

¹When there were no wars or tournaments it was the custom of knights and fighting men to hunt in the great forests which covered so much of England. ²In the breakneck chase of deer through forest and swamp and over rutted and rock-strewn hills, they tempered their horsemanship, and meeting the savage charge of wild boars, they kept their courage high and their dexterity keen. ³And also their mild enterprise loaded the turning spits in the kitchens with succulent meat for the long tables of the great hall. ⁴On a day when King Arthur and many of his knights quartered the forest in search of quarry, they started a fine stag and gave chase. ⁵The proud, high-antlered stag drew them on, and with whip and spur they pushed their foaming horses through tangled undergrowth and treacherous bogs, leaped streams and fallen trees until they overdrove their mounts and the foundered horses fell heaving to the ground, with bloody bits and rowel stripes on their sides.

—John Steinbeck, *The Acts of King Arthur and His Noble Knights*

■ Underline the prepositional phrases in the excerpt above. In the spaces provided, write the phrase that best answers each of the questions, following the pattern shown in the example.

1.	*Where*	*in the great forests*
2.	*When*	

3. _____ *Whose* _____ _____

4. _____ *Why* _____ _____

5. _____ *How* _____ _____

■ Write a sentence about your favorite recreation after class or after work.

_____

25

The Other Babe

[1]Implausible is the adjective which best befits the Babe. [2]As far as sport is concerned, she had the golden touch of a Midas. [3]When she was only six-teen, she was named to the all-America women's basketball team. [4]She once hit thirteen home runs in a softball doubleheader. [5]Her top bowling score was 237. [6]In the 1932 Olympics she won two events, setting world records in each, and placed second in the third test, although again break-ing the world record. [7]At least part of Zaharias's success would be attributed to her powers of concentration and diligence. [8]When she decided to center her attention on golf, she tightened up her game by driving as many as 1,000 golf balls a day and playing until her hands were so sore they had to be taped. [9]She developed an aggressive, dramatic style, hitting down sharply and crisply on her iron shots like a man and averaging 240 yards off the tee with her woods.

—Arthur Daley, *Implausible Is Best*

■ Find four different uses of the -*s* ending in the excerpt above. Write them in the spaces provided, identifying the use, as shown in the example.

Word Ending in -*s*	**Reason**
1. _____ *Midas* _____	*the way the word is spelled*
2. _____	_____
3. _____	_____
4. _____	_____
5. _____	_____

■ Write a sentence about an athlete who excels in two or more sports. _____

_____

26

Crossing the Lake

¹The barge moved silently across the Lake. ²Even now, after years of know-ing that it was no magic, but intensive training in silencing the oars, Morgaine was still impressed by the mystical silence through which they moved. ³She turned to call the mists, and was conscious of the young man behind her. ⁴He stood, easily balanced beside his horse, one arm flung across the saddle blanket, shifting his weight easily without motion, so that he did not visibly sway or lose balance as the boat moved and turned. ⁵Morgaine did this herself from long training, but he managed it, it seemed, by his own natural grace.

—Marion Zimmer Bradley, *The Mists of Avalon*

■ A number of words in the excerpt above end in *-d*. This can indicate the past tense, a past participle, or a verb used with a helper or as an adjective, or it may be the way the word is spelled. Find examples of these uses and write them below.

1. _____*moved*_____   _____*past tense*_____

2. _____   ____*past participle as adjective*____

3. _____   ____*past participle with helper*____

4. _____   _____*spelling*_____

■ Think of a skill you have developed in sports or in some other activity and write a sentence about a physical or mental attribute it requires. _____

_____

27

Nim and Nature

¹Nim had just begun to feel comfortable running about by himself. ²During his summer in East Hampton, Nim the Chimpanzee discovered nature. ³While he wandered around outside the house, he often paused to smell and touch flowers. ⁴He also discovered birds. ⁵For many minutes at a time, Nim would gaze up into the branches of a tree as if trying to figure out what produced the bird songs he heard. ⁶If a bird moved away from the tree, Nim would try to catch it while hooting attack cries at the top of his lungs. ⁷He also tried—and failed—to catch rabbits. ⁸Such things occurred almost every time Nim went outside.

—Herbert S. Terrace, *Nim: A Chimpanzee Who Learned Sign Language*

■ Prepositional phrases can answer the questions *when, where, how, whose,* and *why.* Find examples of each in the excerpt above and write them in the spaces provided along with the questions they answer.

Question	Answering Phrase
1. _____ *where* _____	_____ *outside the house* _____
2. _____	_____
3. _____	_____
4. _____	_____
5. _____	_____

■ Most people have a favorite aspect of nature—flowers, the sea, birds. Write a sentence about that part of nature that you especially enjoy. _____

_____

28

Listen and Learn

¹Studies are showing that spoken language has an astonishing impact on an infant's brain development. ²In fact, some researchers say the number of words an infant hears each day is the single most important predictor of later intelligence, school success and social competence. ³There is one catch— the words have to come from an attentive, engaged human being. ⁴ As far as anyone has been able to determine, radio and television do not work. ⁵This relatively new view of infant brain development, supported by many scientists, has obvious political and social implications. ⁶It suggests that infants and babies develop most rapidly with caretakers who are not only loving, but also talkative and articulate, and that a more verbal family will increase an infant's chances for success.

—Sandra Blakeslee, *Talking with Infants Shapes Basis of Ability to Think*

■ Many words change their part of speech when a suffix is added: verbs and adjectives become nouns, verbs become adjectives, and adjectives become adverbs. Underline the words formed from such suffixes in the excerpt above and show for five of them the word from which the changed form was derived.

New Word	Original Word
1. _____ *attent-ive* [adjective]	_____ *from attend* [verb]
2. _____	_____

New Word	Original Word
3. _____	_____
4. _____	_____
5. _____	_____
6. _____	_____

■ Write a sentence about a word that you like or dislike because you associate it with something else. _____

29

Animal Talk

[1]The attempts to communicate with apes have been marked by controversy from the time of the first successful attempt to converse with another animal. [2]The problems are twofold. [3]First of all, the idea that language is what separates man from animal is enormously important to the way we view and act in the world, and is not the type of concept that can be cast aside blithely. [4]Secondly, it is one thing to seem to converse with another animal, but it is quite another to be able to prove that the animal's responses are not simple mimicry or trickery. [5]After all, stories about "talking cats" or "talking dogs" inevitably turn out to be whimsy. [6]Why should anyone take the notion of "talking apes" any more seriously?

—Francine Patterson and Eugene Linden, *The Education of Koko*

■ Several different marks of punctuation can be found in the excerpt above. Name them in the spaces provided, along with the reason for their use.

Punctuation Mark	Reason For Use
1. _____*period*_____	*end of a declarative sentence*
2. _____	_____
3. _____	_____
4. _____	_____
5. _____	_____

▪ Everyone who has a pet has seen that animal do something remarkable. Write a sentence about an animal whose action impressed you. _____

_____

30
Writing the Unwritten

[1]Jesus Salinas Pedraza, a rural schoolteacher in the Mexican state of Hidalgo, sat down to a word processor a few years back and produced a monumental book, a 250,000-word description of his own Indian culture written in the Nahnu language. [2]Nothing seems to be left out: folktales and traditional religious beliefs, the practical uses of plants and minerals and the daily flow of life in field and village. [3]But it is more than the content that makes the book a remarkable publishing event, for Mr. Salinas is neither a professional anthropologist nor a literary stylist. [4]He is, though, the first person to write a book in Nahnu, the native tongue of several hundred thousand Indians but a previously unwritten language. [5]Such a use of microcomputers and desktop publishing for languages with no literary tradition is now being encouraged by anthropologists for recording ethnographies from an insider's perspective. [6]They see this as a means of preserving cultural diversity and a wealth of human knowledge. [7]With even greater urgency, linguists are promoting the techniques as a way of saving some of the world's languages from imminent extinction.

—John Noble Wilford, *Books in "Unwritten" Languages*

▪ The present participle, the form of the verb that ends in *-ing*, can be used, with a helper, as a verb. While it can also be used as a noun or adjective, it should not be confused with words whose spelling ends in *-ing*. In the spaces provided, write each of the *-ing* words in the excerpt above identifying its use, as shown in the example.

Word Ending in -*ing*	**How Used**
1. _____*publishing*_____	_____*adjective*_____
2. _____	_____
3. _____	_____
4. _____	_____
5. _____	_____

■ What would you miss most if we had no written language? Write a sentence about it. _____

_____

31

The Predator

¹Its nose twitching, the small mouse makes its way along the narrow branch. ²The animal's quivering body speaks of caution, yet it remains oblivious to its impending doom. ³The owl is perched on a higher branch, his sharp eyes riveted on the prey. ⁴Silently, motionlessly, the bird calculates the best method of attack. ⁵Suddenly, he swoops down and, with scarcely a pause in his wingbeats, snatches the rodent in his talons. ⁶A few thrusts of his powerful wings and the deadly hunter is safely roosting in another tree, savoring his meal. ⁷Watching the northern spotted owl are three other sets of eyes, the eyes of men. ⁸Two biologists and I have walked to this patch of woods on the northern edge of Washington State's Olympic Peninsula, in pursuit of the most controversial bird in America.

—Keith Ervin, *A Life in Our Hands*

■ An -*s* at the end of a word can mean that the word is plural, that it signifies possession, or that it is a verb in the third person singular present tense. It can also signify nothing more than that is the way the word is spelled. Underline all of the -*s* words in the excerpt above, then write six of them in the spaces provided, identifying how they are used. Be sure to choose at least five different uses.

Word Ending in -*s*	**Reason**
1. *makes*	*third person singular present tense*
2. _____	_____
3. _____	_____
4. _____	_____
5. _____	_____
6. _____	_____
7. _____	_____

■ Write a sentence about an unusual bird you have seen. _____

_____

32

The Family Dog

¹It used to be that you could tell just about how poor a family was by how many dogs they had. ²If they had one, they were probably doing all right. ³It was only American to keep a dog to represent the family's interests in the intrigues of the back alley; not to have a dog at all would be like not acknowledging one's poor relations. ⁴Two dogs meant that the couple were dog lovers, with growing children, but still might be members of the middle class. ⁵But if a citizen kept three, you could begin to suspect he didn't own much else. ⁶Four or five irrefutably marked the household as poor folk, whose yard was also full of broken cars cannibalized for parts. ⁷The father worked not much, fancied himself a hunter; the mother's teeth were black.

—Edward Hoagland, *Dogs and the Tug of Life*

▪ Underline the punctuation marks in the excerpt above. Identify two uses for each of these marks, citing the sentence in which the use appears.

	Punctuation Mark	Sentence	Reason Used
1.	comma	Sentence 2	separate dependent from independent clause
2.	comma	Sentence 4	separate phrase in apposition
3.			
4.			
5.			
6.			

▪ Do you know, or have you heard about, someone who has a large number of pets? Write a sentence describing that person. _____

_____

33

The Cowboy Life

¹Seventy-five years ago, when travel was by buckboard or horseback, cowboys who were temporarily out of work rode the grub line—drifting from ranch to ranch, mending fences or milking cows, and receiving in exchange a bed and meals. ²Gossip and messages traveled this slow circuit with them, creating an intimacy between ranchers who were three and four weeks' ride apart. ³One old-time couple I know, whose turn-of-the-century

homestead was used by an outlaw gang as a relay station for stolen horses, recall that if you were traveling, desperado or not, any lighted ranch house was a welcome sign. [4]Even now, for someone who lives in a remote spot, arriving at a ranch or coming to town for supplies is cause for celebration. [5]To emerge from isolation can be disorienting. [6]Everything looks bright, new, vivid. [7]Because ranch work is a physical and, these days, economic strain, being "at home on the range" is a matter of vigor, self-reliance, and common sense.

—Gretel Ehrlich, *The Solace of Open Spaces*

■ Many words look and sound the same but have different meanings. Find five such words in the excerpt above and write them in the spaces provided with two of their meanings and their part of speech.

Word	Meaning 1	Meaning 2
1. _travel_	_[noun] a journey_	_[verb] to go on a trip_
2. _____	_____	_____
3. _____	_____	_____
4. _____	_____	_____
5. _____	_____	_____
6. _____	_____	_____

■ Do you prefer to be alone or with other people? Write a sentence explaining your choice._____

34

After the Storm

[1]One place where the eraser came down squarely was in the Cathedral Pines, a famous forest of old-growth white pine trees close to the center of town. [2]To enter Cathedral Pines on a hot summer day was like stepping out of the sun into a dim cathedral, the sunlight cooled and sweetened by the trillions of pine needles as it worked its way down to soft, sprung ground that had been unacquainted with blue sky for the better part of two centuries. [3]The storm came through at about five in the evening and it took only a few minutes of wind before pines more than one hundred fifty feet tall and as wide around as missiles lay jackstrawed on the ground like a fistful of pencils dropped from a great height. [4]The wind was so thunderous that people in

houses at the forest's edge did not know trees had fallen until they ventured outside after the storm had passed. ⁵The following morning, the sky now clear, was the first in more than a century to bring sunlight crashing down onto this particular patch of earth.

—Michael Pollan, *The Idea of a Garden*

■ Underline all of the connecting words in the excerpt above. Write them in the spaces provided, indicating whether each is a coordinating or a subordinating conjunction or a relative pronoun.

Sentence Number	Connecting Word	Kind of Connector
1. _____2_____	_____that_____	subordinating relative pronoun
2. _____3_____		
3. _____3_____		
4. _____4_____		
5. _____4_____		
6. _____5_____		

■ Some people like storms; others are frightened by them. Write a sentence explaining what your reaction might be to a fierce storm. _____

_____

35

Us Versus Nature

¹It does seem that we do best in nature when we imitate her—when we learn to think like running water, or a carrot, an aphid, a pine forest, or a compost pile. ²That's probably because nature, after almost four billion years of trial-and-error experience, has wide knowledge of what works in life. ³Surely we're better off learning how to draw on her experience than trying to repeat it, if only because we don't have that kind of time. ⁴Nature does not teach its creatures to control their appetites except by the harshest of lessons—epidemics, mass death, extinctions. ⁵Nothing would be more natural than for humankind to burden the environment to the extent that it was rendered unfit for human life. ⁶Nature in that event would not be the loser nor would it disturb her laws in the least—operating as it has always done, natural selection would unceremoniously do us in.

—Michael Pollan, *The Idea of a Garden*

- The verb *do* is sometimes used as a helper, especially, with *not*, in forming a negative. Sometimes it is added for emphasis. Underline all forms of *do* in the excerpt above and identify how each one is used.

Form of Do	Use of Do
1. *don't have*	*helper to make have negative*
2.	
3.	
4.	
5.	
6.	

- Write a sentence about something in nature that we cannot control. _____

_____

36

TV in Our World

[1]Television is the chief way that most of us partake of the larger world, of the information age, and so, though none of us owe our personalities and habits entirely to the tube and the world it shows, none of us completely escape its influence either. [2]Why do we do the things we do? [3]Because of the events of our childhood, and because of class and race and gender, and because of our political and economic system and because of "human nature"—but also because of what we've been told about the world, because of the information we've received. [4]One study after another, not to mention the experience of most of us, indicates that we do in fact often watch television because of our mood or out of habit, instead of tuning in to see something in particular. [5]Even so, we're not staring at test patterns. [6]We also often eat because we're bored or depressed, but the effects are different if we scarf carrot sticks or Doritos.

—Bill McKibben, *Daybreak*

- Underline each of the punctuation marks in the excerpt above. Give an example of each in the spaces provided, indicating why it is used as it is.

Punctuation Mark	Why Used
1. *period*	*end of declarative sentence*
2.	
3.	

Punctuation Mark	Why Used
4. _____	_____
5. _____	_____
6. _____	_____

■ Write a sentence about what you learn about the world from watching television. _____

_____

37

A Shopping Spree

[1]It was exciting to walk through the great markets of Londinium; dirty and smelly as the city was, it seemed like four or five harvest fairs all in one. [2]Yet it was a little frightening to walk through the enormous market square, with a hundred vendors crying their wares. [3]It seemed to her that everything she saw was new and beautiful, something she wished for, but she resolved to see all of the market before she made any purchases; and then she bought spices, and a length of fine woven wool from the islands, far finer than that of the Cornish sheep. [4]And so she also bought for herself small hanks of dyed silks; it would be pleasant to weave on such brilliant colors, restful and fine to her hands after the coarseness of wool and flax. [5]She would teach Morgause, too. [6]And it would be high time, next year, to teach Morgaine to spin. [7]Four years was certainly old enough to start learning to handle a spindle and twist the thread, even though the thread would not be good for much except tying up bundles of yarn for dyeing.

—Marion Zimmer Bradley, *The Mists of Avalon*

■ Find the irregular verbs in the excerpt above. Write the principal parts of each of them in the spaces provided.

	Present Tense	Past Tense	Present Participle	Past Participle
1.	see	saw	seeing	seen
2.	_____	_____	_____	_____
3.	_____	_____	_____	_____
4.	_____	_____	_____	_____
5.	_____	_____	_____	_____

■ Write a sentence about the best shopping trip you ever had. _____

_____

38

Tire Mountain

[1]The world's largest pile of scrap tires is not visible from Interstate 5, in Stanislaus County, California. [2]But it's close. [3]Below Stockton, in the region of Modesto and Merced, the highway follows the extreme western edge of the flat Great Central Valley, right next to the scarp where the Coast Ranges are territorially expanding as fresh unpopulated hills. [4]The hills conceal the tires from the traffic. If you were to abandon your car three miles from the San Joaquin County line and make your way on foot southwest one mile, you would climb into steeply creased terrain that in winter is jade green and in summer straw brown, and, any time at all, you would come upon a black vista. [5]In some cases they are piled six stories high, compressing themselves, densifying. [6]From the highest elevations of this thick and drifted black mantle, you can look east a hundred miles and see snow on the Sierra. [7]Even before the interstate was there, a tire jockey named Ed Filbin began collecting them.

—John McPhee, *Duty of Care*

■ Circle all of the words beginning with capital letters in the excerpt above. Write five of them below, noting the sentence it is in and indicating why each word is being capitalized. (*Note:* Do not use "first word in a sentence" more than once.)

	Capitalized Word	Reason for Capitalization
1.	*Sentence 1: The*	*first word in a sentence*
2.		
3.		
4.		
5.		
6.		

■ Think about the largest collection of scrap you have ever seen. Write a sentence about it. _____

_____

39

Bird Watching

[1]There was a stirring high up in the peepul tree, and a bubbling noise like pots boiling. [2]A flock of green pigeons were up there, eating the berries. [3]Flory gazed up into the great green dome of the tree, trying to distinguish the birds; they were invisible, they matched the leaves so perfectly, and yet the whole tree was alive with them, shimmering, as though the ghosts of birds were shaking it. [4]Flo rested herself against the roots and growled up at the invisible creatures. [5]Then a single green pigeon fluttered down and perched on a lower branch. [6]It did not know that it was being watched. [7]It was a tender thing, smaller than a tame dove, with jade-green back as smooth as velvet, and neck and breast of iridescent colors. [8]Its legs were like the pink wax that dentists use.

—George Orwell, *Burmese Days*

■ The present participle, the *-ing* form of a verb, needs a helper, as in *is laughing*. The present participle can also be an adjective or a noun; some words just end in *-ing*. Write the *-ing* words from the excerpt above in the spaces provided and identify them as verbs, nouns, adjectives, or spelling.

Present Participle	Reason for Use
1. *bubbling*	*adjective describing noise*
2. _____	_____
3. _____	_____
4. _____	_____
5. _____	_____
6. _____	_____
7. _____	_____
8. _____	_____

■ Write a sentence about a wild creature you have watched. _____
_____

40

Tornado

[1]As a boy in Ohio I knew a farm family, the Millers, who not only saw but suffered from three tornadoes. [2]The father, mother, and two sons were pulling into their driveway after church when the first tornado hoisted up their mobile

home, spun it around, and carried it off. [3]With the insurance money, they built a small frame house on the same spot. [4]Several years later, a second tornado peeled off the roof, splintered the garage, and rustled two cows. [5]The Millers rebuilt again, raising a new garage on the old foundation and adding another story to the house. [6]That upper floor was reduced to kindling by a third tornado, which also pulled out half the apple trees and slurped water from the stock pond. [7]Soon after that I left Ohio, snatched away by college as forcefully as by any cyclone. [8]Last thing I heard, the family was preparing to rebuild yet again.

—Scott Russell Sanders, *Settling Down*

■ Some verbs consist of two words, like *take off*, which has a meaning different from *take* alone. Underline the two-word verbs in the excerpt above and write them in the spaces provided with a subject of your choice.

Verb	Sentence
1. _____*Carried off*_____	*The pirates carried off the treasure.*
2. _____	_____
3. _____	_____
4. _____	_____
5. _____	_____
6. _____	_____

■ Write a sentence about damage from fierce weather that you have seen.

_____

41

The Topic of the Day

[1]And their talk was of war and rumors of wars. [2]They raged against World War II when it broke out in Europe, blaming it on the politicians. [3]"It's these politicians. [4]They're the ones always starting up all this lot of war. [5]But what they care? [6]It's the poor people got to suffer and mothers with their sons." [7]If it was *their* sons, they swore they would keep them out of the Army by giving them soap to eat each day to make their hearts sound defective. [8]Hitler? He was for them "the devil incarnate." [9]Then there was home. [10]They reminisced often and at length about home. The old country. [11]Barbados—or Bimshire, as they affectionately called it. [12]The little Caribbean island in the sun they loved but had to leave. [13]"Poor—poor but sweet" was the way they remembered it.

—Paule Marshall, *From the Poets in the Kitchen*

■ Circle the punctuation marks in the excerpt above. Identify one of each kind in the spaces provided, along with the reason for its use.

Sentence Number	Punctuation Mark	Reason for Use
1. _Sentence 7_	_comma_	_separate dependent and independent clauses_
2. _____	_____	_____
3. _____	_____	_____
4. _____	_____	_____
5. _____	_____	_____
6. _____	_____	_____

■ Think of someone you know or have read about who came from another place. Write a sentence about that person. _____

_____

42

This Thing Called Love

[1]Love is still something one hears a great deal about in pop lyrics, but the contemporary version is more hard-headed and down-to-earth than the cosmic, effulgent Love of the 60s. [2]Many of today's songwriters argue that romance isn't as important as material values or sex. [3]"What's love got to do with it?" Tina Turner asked in her recent heavy-breathing hit of the same title. [4]And Madonna, whose come-hither pout and undulating style have made her pop's hottest video star, serves notice in her hit "Material Girl" that she won't worry much about love as long as there's money in the bank. [5]Madonna's carefully calculated image has struck a chord among many of today's more affluent young listeners, though she is perhaps too one-dimensional to be Queen of the Yuppies. [6]And she will never be the darling of the feminists.

—Robert Palmer, *What Pop Lyrics Say to Us Today*

■ Circle the punctuation marks in excerpt above. Write five of them in the spaces provided, along with an explanation of how each one is used.

Sentence Number	Punctuation Mark	Reason for Use
1. _Sentence 1_	_comma_	_separates items in a series_
2. _____	_____	_____

	Sentence Number	Punctuation Mark	Reason for Use
3.	_____	_____	_____
4.	_____	_____	_____
5.	_____	_____	_____
6.	_____	_____	_____

■ Write a sentence explaining what attitude about love is expressed by a pop song you know. _____

43

Women in the Tribes

¹Through all the centuries of war and death and cultural and psychic destruction have endured the women who raise the children and tend the fires, who pass along the tales and the traditions, who weep and bury the dead, who are the dead, and who never forget. ²There are always the women, who make pots and weave baskets, who fashion clothes and cheer their children on at pow-wow, who make fry bread and piki bread, and corn soup and chili stew, who dance and sing and remember and hold within their hearts the dream of their ancient peoples—that one day the woman who thinks will speak to us again, and everywhere there will be peace. ³Meanwhile we tell the stories and write the books and trade tales of anger and woe and stories of fun and scandal and laugh over all manner of things that happen every day. ⁴We watch and we wait.

—Paula Gunn Allen, *Where I Come From Is Like This*

■ Underline the words in the excerpt above that can be used as more than one part of speech. Following the example, write five of these words in the spaces provided, indicating the part of speech used here and, in a new sentence, its use as another part of speech.

	Original Word	Sentence
1.	*pass [verb]*	*I have a pass [noun] to the new movie.*
2.	_____	_____
3.	_____	_____
4.	_____	_____
5.	_____	_____
6.	_____	_____

- Think of someone you know who does many things. Write a sentence about some of those things. _____

_____

44

A Woman's Lot

[1]I was slow to understand the deep grievances of women. [2]This was because, as a boy, I had envied them. [3]No doubt, had I looked harder at their lives, I would have envied them less. [4]It was not my fate to become a woman, so it was easier for me to see the graces. [5]Few of them held jobs outside the home, and those who did filled thankless roles as clerks and waitresses. [6]I didn't see, then, what a prison a house could be, since houses seemed to me brighter, handsomer places than any factory. [7]I did not realize—because such things were never spoken of—how often women suffered from men's bullying. [8]I did learn about the wretchedness of abandoned wives, single mothers, widows; but I also learned about the wretchedness of lone men. [9]Even then I could see how exhausting it was for a mother to cater all day to the needs of young children. [10]But if I had been asked, as a boy, to choose between tending a baby and tending a machine, I think I would have chosen the baby. [11](Having now tended both, I know I would choose the baby.)

—Scott Russell Sanders, *The Men We Carry in Our Minds*

- Underline all of the verbs in the excerpt above that have a helper. Write five of these verbs with helpers in the spaces provided with a short sentence of your own that uses the verb and helper.

	Verb and Helper	**Sentence**
1.	*had envied*	*The sisters had envied Cinderella.*
2.		
3.		
4.		
5.		
6.		

- What housekeeping job do you find most distasteful? Write a sentence about it. _____

_____

45

A Man's Place

[1]People in the men's movement believe there was once a golden age of masculinity, when strong men hugged, expressed their feelings, honored their elders and served as mentors to younger men. [2]This era is sometimes said to have existed during Arthurian times, when kings, warriors and wise magicians served as role models. [3]These ancient societies offered men clear road maps of how they ought to behave through myths, legends and poetry. [4]There were ceremonies to show respect, and rites to initiate adolescents into adulthood. [5]In modern times, rites and myths no longer exist to set men right, and thus many are deeply confused. [6]A major focus at men's retreats is to enact latter-day rituals to replace the old ones.

—Trip Gabriel, *Call of the Wildmen*

■ Underline the words in the excerpt above that change to another part of speech by adding a suffix. Write five of these in the spaces provided, indicating what the suffix is and what change it has made.

	Word	**Formed from**
1.	*gold-en [adjective]*	*gold [noun]*
2.		
3.		
4.		
5.		
6.		

■ Write a sentence about a ceremony that makes a person part of a group.

_____

46

A New Look at the Family

[1]All family sitcoms, of course, teach us that wisecracks and swift put-downs are the preferred modes of affectionate discourse. [2]But Roseanne takes the genre a step further. [3]It is Barr's narrow-eyed cynicism about the family, even more than her class consciousness, that gives *Roseanne* its special frisson. [4]Archie Bunker got our attention by telling us that we (blacks, Jews, "ethnics," WASPs, etc.) don't really like each other. [5]Barr's message is that even within the family we don't much like each other. [6]We love each other (who

else do we have?); but The Family, with its impacted emotions, its lopsided division of labor, and its ancient system of age-graded humiliations, just doesn't work. [7]Or rather, it doesn't work unless the contradictions are smoothed out with irony and the hostilities are periodically blown off as humor. [8]Coming from Mom, rather than from a jaded teenager or a bystander dad, this is scary news indeed.

—Barbara Ehrenrich, *The Wretched of the Hearth*

■ Underline the dependent clauses in the excerpt above, then write them in the spaces provided with a new independent clause of your own.

New Independent Clause	Dependent Clause
1. *I don't believe*	*that we don't really like each other.*
2.	
3.	
4.	
5.	

■ Write a sentence about a television show that depends for its humor on wisecracks and put-downs. _____

47

The Job Hunt

[1]Before 1965, the white corporate establishment didn't realize that African Americans even existed. [2]College-trained blacks and middle-class business-people were attached to the separate economy of the ghetto. [3]African Americans who applied for jobs at white-owned companies found that their resumes weren't accepted. [4]Blacks who were hired were placed in low-paying clerical or maintenance positions. [5]With the impact of the civil rights movement, the public demonstrations and boycotts against corporations which Jim Crowed blacks, businesses were forced to change their hiring policies. [6]However, most blacks were placed in minority neighborhoods, having little contact with whites in supervisory roles. [7]They were assigned to mediate black employees' grievances or to direct affirmative action policies, rather than being placed in charge of a major division of the company. [8]Their managerial experiences were limited, and therefore their prospects for upward mobility into senior executive positions were nonexistent.

—Manning Marable, *Racism and Corporate America*

▪ Underline the homophones in the excerpt above, then write them in the spaces provided along with a new sentence using the word that sounds the same but is spelled differently.

Sentence Number	Homophones	New Sentence
1. _____2_____	_____to_____	*The class meets at two o'clock.*
2. _____	_____	_____
3. _____	_____	_____
4. _____	_____	_____
5. _____	_____	_____
6. _____	_____	_____

▪ Write a sentence about an experience you had applying for a job. _____
_____

48

The Welcoming Room

¹He stopped walking. ²He moved a bit closer. ³Green curtains were hanging down on either side of the window. ⁴The chrysanthemums looked wonderful beside them. ⁵He went right up and peered through the glass into the room, and the first thing he saw was a bright fire burning on the hearth. ⁶On the carpet in front of the fire, a pretty little dachshund was curled up asleep, with its nose tucked into its belly. ⁷The room itself, as far as he could see in the half darkness, was filled with pleasant furniture. ⁸There was a baby-grand piano and a big sofa and several plump armchairs, and in one corner he spotted a large parrot in a cage. ⁹Animals were usually a good sign in a place like this, Billy told himself, and all in all, it looked as though it would be a pretty decent house to stay in. ¹⁰Certainly it would be more comfortable than the Bell and Dragon.

—Roald Dahl, *The Landlady*

▪ Underline the irregular verbs in the excerpt above. Write their principal parts. Then write the principal parts of two regular verbs from this passage.

		Present Tense	Past Tense	Present Participle	Past Participle
1.	Irregular	*is*	*was*	*being*	*been*
2.	Regular	*stop*	*stopped*	*stopping*	*stopped*

	Present Tense	Past Tense	Present Participle	Past Participle
3. Irregular	_____	_____	_____	_____
4. Irregular	_____	_____	_____	_____
5. Irregular	_____	_____	_____	_____
6. Regular	_____	_____	_____	_____
7. Regular	_____	_____	_____	_____

- Write a sentence about your favorite room. _____

_____

49

A Missionary's Life

[1]She was hardly ever free from illness and pain, and yet she seemed able to do things which would have been fatal to most Europeans. [2]She never used mosquito-netting, she never wore a hat, she went barefoot despite the prevalence of jiggers and snakes. [3]She never boiled the water, she ate native food, and she kept most irregular hours, for she was often ministering at night and her days were taken up with long 'palavers'. [4]When she died in 1915, in her rough-built hut in Calabar with her native family—Janie, Annie, Maggie, Alice and Whitie—about her, she left the spell of her unconventionality behind her, and the romance of her name drew many others into foreign missions.

—Maria Aitken, *Women Adventures: Travelers, Explorers, and Seekers*

- Underline the irregular verbs in the excerpt above. Write them in the spaces provided below under the appropriate heading, and add the other principal parts in the remaining columns.

	Present Tense	Past Tense	Present Participle	Past Participle
1.	*do*	*did*	*doing*	*done*
2.	_____	_____	_____	_____
3.	_____	_____	_____	_____
4.	_____	_____	_____	_____
5.	_____	_____	_____	_____
6.	_____	_____	_____	_____

Present Tense	Past Tense	Present Participle	Past Participle
7. _____	_____	_____	_____
8. _____	_____	_____	_____

■ Write a sentence about someone who endured hardships in order to do a job properly. _____

_____

50

At Peace with the Animals

[1]There is nothing more disgusting to me than the slaughter of animals for the sake of sport. [2]It is sometimes necessary to kill a gazelle or a zebra for meat. [3]It is occasionally necessary to kill a buffalo or an elephant or a leopard or a lion in order to escape being killed yourself. [4]But on the whole it is safer to live among wild animals than to live in New York. [5]With the exception of the big cats, which are a treacherous lot, few of them will attack unless they are frightened or molested. [6]And I want to live at peace with them.

—Martin Johnson, *Camera Trails in Africa*

■ Underline the words in the excerpt above that are changed in some way by the addition of a suffix. For example, the participle form of a verb can become an adjective, a verb can become a noun, or an adjective can become an adverb. For five of the words you have underlined, explain how they have been changed by a suffix.

Word	How Changed by Suffix
1. _____*frightened*_____	_*past participle/adjective*_
2. _____	_____
3. _____	_____
4. _____	_____
5. _____	_____
6. _____	_____

■ Write a sentence about a time when you made peace as a conflict was about to break out. _____

_____

Glossary

. . . .

Adjective: A word that describes a noun: *growing girl, purple cow*.

Adverb: A word that provides further information about a verb, an adjective, or another adverb: *talked rapidly, narrowly missed, almost home, very often*.

Apostrophe: See *Punctuation*.

Appositive: A word or phrase that clarifies meaning by naming or describing the same thing: *my car, a red Mustang*.

Article: The words *a, an,* and *the,* which are used to indicate a specific noun or any one of a larger number of things. Articles are classified as definite (the dog next door) or indefinite (***a*** *barking dog,* ***an*** *unhappy cat*).

Auxiliary: Another name for a *helping verb*, a form of *to be, to do, to have* or one of the modals used to form a compound tense. See *Helping Verbs*.

Clause: A subject and predicate connected to one or more additional subjects and predicates: *I never saw a purple cow, but I've heard of them*.

> **Dependent Clause:** A clause that must be connected by a conjunction or relative pronoun to form a sentence: *when I was young*. This is also called a *subordinate clause*.

> **Independent Clause:** A clause that functions as a sentence by itself: *I liked to play catch*. It can be joined to another independent clause by a *coordinating conjunction: and now I like to play tennis*.

> **Relative Clause:** A dependent clause joined to the independent clause by a relative pronoun (*who, whom, whose, which, that*). We watched the boy *who* won the game.

Comma: See *Punctuation*.

Conjunction: A word that connects clauses by showing the relationship between them: ***When*** *I was younger, I played tennis*.

Contraction: The deletion of a letter or letters for ease of pronunciation. The deletion is replaced by an apostrophe: *can't, don't, didn't*.

Declarative: See *Sentence*.

Helping Verbs: Also called *auxiliary verbs*. The parts of the verbs to be or to have used with past or present participles: *she* ***is*** *going, he* ***has*** *gone, they* ***were*** *singing*.

> **Modal Auxiliaries:** A helper without tense: *can, could, do, may, might, must, ought, will, would, shall, should. The class* ***may*** *go to the museum*. See *Auxiliary*.

Homophone: One of a pair of words that sound alike but have different spellings and meanings: *new/knew, ewe/you*.

Infinitive: A verb form with *to* that has no tense: *It is fun **to take** a trip.*

Interjection: A word or phrase that expresses surprise, shock, or emotion: *How sad! For crying out loud! Holy moley!*

Mechanics: Devices such as spelling, punctuation, capitalization that are used to make writing more understandable.

Negative: The reversal of a statement: *She has a job. She does not have a job.* Often formed with *do* as a helper and *not.* Sometimes other helpers are used: *can, might, should.*

Noun: A person, place, or thing. It may be the subject of a sentence or the object of a sentence or prepositional phrase.

> **Common Noun:** The name of a person, place, or thing that is one of many: *a cat, a city, a telephone, a teacher.*

> **Proper Noun:** The name of a particular person, place, or thing: *James, Washington, Amtrak, McDonald's*

Number: The form of a word that indicates how many things, including persons, are referred to.

Object: The word or phrase that completes a predicate or a prepositional phrase: *The bat hit **the ball**. He sat down by **the old mill stream**.*

Participle: One of the principal parts of a verb. It must be used with a helper. *Jeff is going to the game. Monica has seen that movie.*

> **Past Participle:** A verb form used as part of a verb phrase: *The bird has **flown**.* It can also function as an adjective: *a **finished** product.*

> **Present Participle:** A verb form used with the verb to be: *The children are **running** home.* It can also serve as a noun (*a **meeting***) or as an adjective (***shining** lights*).

Particle: A preposition that combines with a verb to form a two word verb phrase: *She could not make out the form in the dark.* See *Preposition.*

Person: The form in verbs, and pronouns that indicates a speaker (first person, *I or we*); the one being spoken to (second person, *you*); and the one spoken of (third person, *she, he, it*).

Phrase: A group of grammatically related words. A noun phrase may be the complete subject of a sentence. *The boy named Greg answered the question.* A prepositional phrase may act as an adverb, answering *when, where, why, whose, how.*

> **Parenthetical Phrase:** A phrase that repeats the meaning of one that goes before in different words: *Rick's new car, **his pride and joy**, got a flat tire.*

Possessive: A word or mark indicating that something or someone belongs to something or someone else: *the end of the road, the road's end.* Possessive personal pronouns—*his, hers, its*—have no apostrophe.

Predicate: The verb phrase that completes a sentence. *The teacher **put the assignment on the board**. Put* is the verb, but the entire phrase is the predicate.

Prefix: The syllable added to a word's beginning that changes the meaning of a word: **un**happy, **re**write.

Preposition: The part of speech that opens a phrase to answer *where, when, how, why,* or *whose*: **over** *the river and* **through** *the woods.*

Pronoun: A word that substitutes for another: *The assignment was hard.* **It** *took me three hours.*

    Personal Pronoun: A word that substitutes for a person or thing—*I, me, mine, you, your, she, her, he, him, it.*

    Relative Pronoun: *Who, which,* or *that.* Introduces a dependent clause identifying the object of the clause it follows: *I finished the assignment,* **which** *took me three hours.*

Punctuation: Devices used in writing to indicate sentence boundaries, to separate words and phrases (never clauses), and to show missing letters or possession.

    Apostrophe: An inverted comma that, with - *s,* shows possession or, between letters, as a contraction, indicates that something is missing: *The bird's nest wasn't empty.*

    Capital Letters: Also called *uppercase letters.* They are used to begin sentences or proper nouns: *Professor Jones, River City.*

    Comma: A mark that is used to separate—a series of items, a word or phrase in apposition, the year in a date: The necklace was made of *rubies, diamonds, and pearls. Jose Nuñez, my old friend,* came to visit. *June 1, 2000* marks the anniversary of our meeting.

    Exclamation Point: The mark that follows a word or sentence expressing astonishment: *Good grief!*

    Period: The mark that ends a declarative sentence. It is also used with abbreviations: *Jan., Dr., St. Louis.*

    Question Mark: The mark that follows a question: *What time is it?*

    Quotation Marks: The marks that enclose the words of another, including those in books or other written works. *Maria said, "Let's go to the movies."*

    Semicolon: The mark that separates a series of phrases that contain commas. *Green, leafy vegetables are nutritious; rich, dark chocolate is delicious; but a certain amount of protein is necessary to a balanced diet.* It can also be used between closely related independent clauses. *You serve the cookies; I'll make the coffee.*

Rhetorical Question: A question that does not require an answer because it is an observation or opinion. *Who knows what tomorrow will bring?*

Root: That part of a word that does not change when a prefix or a suffix is added: **move**ment, **going**, **discover**, in**definite**.

Sentence: A group of words in which a subject and a verb, with tense, make a statement, ask a question, or give a command. Often a sentence contains more than one clause.

> **Compound Sentence:** A sentence with two independent clauses. *I would go for a bike ride, but it is raining.*
>
> **Complex Sentence:** A sentence with an independent clause and one or more dependent clauses. *The teacher handed out the papers as the class began.*
>
> **Declarative Sentence:** A sentence that makes a statement: *The author wrote the book.*
>
> **Exclamatory Sentence:** A sentence that expresses surprise or emotion: *What a frightening experience that was!*
>
> **Imperative Sentence:** A sentence that gives a command: *Go to the front of the class.*
>
> **Interrogative Sentence:** A sentence that asks a question: *Did you finish the homework?*

Singular: A form indicating one of anything. Singular verbs have as their subjects *I, you, he, she, it,* or a word that can be substituted for one of these: *Richard goes to work on the bus.*

Subject: The part of a sentence that performs the action. It can be a noun, a pronoun, an infinitive, or a participial phrase. ***To forgive*** *is divine.* ***Taking a test*** *can be difficult.* ***Olga*** *won first prize.*

Suffix: A syllable added to the end of a word that changes its part of speech or the way it functions in a sentence. For example, *teach* [verb] becomes *teacher* [noun]; *look* [present tense verb] becomes *looked* [past tense verb].

Tense: The time of an action, taking place in the past, present, or future. It is seen in the form of the verb or of its helper. *I talk, you talked, she will talk.* Irregular verbs may change the forms of their tenses. *I go, you went, she will go.*

Verb: The word that indicates the action occurring in a sentence. It is often part of a phrase: *The squirrel climbed the tree.* Verbs have four principal parts: (1) present, (2) past (*-ed*), (3) present participle (*-ing*), and (4) past participle (*-ed*). The forms of these parts change in irregular verbs: *see, saw, seeing, seen.*

Bibliography

Allen, Paula Gunn. "Where I Come from Is Like This." *The Sacred Hoop*. New York: Beacon Press, 1986

Angell, Roger. *Late Innings: A Baseball Companion*. New York: Ballantine, 1982.

Bâ, Mariama. *So Long a Letter*. Trans. Modupé Bodé-Thomas. Oxford: Heinemann, 1989.

Baker, Russell. *Growing Up*. New York: Congdon and Weed, 1982.

Baron, Dennis. *Declining Grammar and Other Essays on the English Vocabulary*. Urbana, IL: National Council of Teachers of English, 1989.

Benét, Stephen Vincent. "By the Waters of Babylon." *Thirteen O'clock: Stories of Several Worlds*. Freeport, NY: Books for Libraries Press, 1971.

Brody, Jane E. "Cellphone: A Convenience, a Hazard or Both." *New York Times*, 1 October 2002: 24.

Brontë, Emily. *Wuthering Heights*. London: Zodiac Press, 1955.

Carroll, Lewis. *Alice in Wonderland and Through the Looking Glass*. New York: Macmillan, 1966.

Carson, Rachel. *The Sea Around Us*. New York: Oxford University Press, 1951.

Clark, Mary Higgins. *You Belong to Me*. New York: Simon & Schuster, 1999.

Clarke, Arthur C. "Rescue Party." *Great Tales of Action and Adventure*. Ed. George Bennett. New York: Dell, 1958.

Conan Doyle, Sir Arthur. "The Adventure of the Dancing Men." *Great Tales of Action and Adventure*. Ed. George Bennett. New York: Dell, 1958.

Connell, Richard. "The Most Dangerous Game." *Great Tales of Action and Adventure*. Ed. George Bennett. New York: Dell, 1958.

Conrad, Joseph. *The Secret Sharer*. New York: Bantam, 1981.

Dahl, Roald. "The Landlady." *Kiss Kiss*. New York: Alfred A. Knopf, 1959.

Danzig, Allison. "Little Girl, Big Racquet." *The New York Times Book of Sports Legends*. Ed. Joseph J. Vecchlione. New York: Random House, 1991.

Darrow, Siobhan. *Flirting with Danger: Confessions of a Reluctant War Reporter*. London: Virago Press, 2000.

Duggan Alfred. *Devil's Brood: The Angevin Family*. London: Arrow Books, 1960.

Dunne, John Gregory. *Monster: Living off the Big Screen*. New York: Random House, 1997.

Durso, Joseph. "The Miracle Mets." *The New York Times Book of Sports Legends*. Ed. Joseph J. Vecchlione. New York: Random House, 1991.

Ehrenreich, Barbara. "The Wretched of the Hearth." *New Republic,* 2 April 1990: 28–31.

Ehrlich, Gretel. *The Solace of Open Spaces*. New York: Viking Penguin, 1985.

Eiseley, Loren. "How Flowers Changed the World." *The Star Thrower*. New York: Harvest, 1978.

———. "One Night's Dying." *The Night Country*. New York: Scribner, 1971.

Eliot, George. *Middlemarch*. Stamford, CT: Longmeadow Press, 1994.

Ervin, Keith. "A Life in Our Hands." *Fragile Majesty: The Battle for North America's Latest Great Forest.* Seattle, WA: The Mountaineers, 1989.

Fast, Howard. *April Morning.* New York: Bantam, 1951.

Fischer, Louis. *Gandhi: His Life and Message for the World.* New York: New American Library, 1954.

Forester, C. S. *The African Queen.* New York: Bantam, 1964.

Frankl, Viktor E. *Man's Search for Meaning.* New York: Washington Square Press, 1984.

Fuller, Margaret. *"These Sad but Glorious Days": Dispatches from Europe 1846–1850.* Eds. Larry J. Reynolds and Susan Belasco Smith. New Haven: Yale University Press, 1991.

Gilman, Charlotte Perkins. *Herland.* New York: Pantheon Books, 1979.

Greene, Graham. *Journey Without Maps.* New York: Compass Books, 1961.

Hillerman, Tony. *The Fallen Man.* New York: Harper Collins, 1996.

Hilton, James. *Lost Horizon.* New York: Pocket Books, 1960.

Hoagland, Edward. "Dogs and the Tug of Life." *Red Wolves and Black Bears.* New York: Random House, 1976.

Hough, Richard. *The Last Voyage of Captain James Cook.* New York: William Morrow, 1979.

Howarth, David. *1066, The Year of the Conquest.* New York: Viking, 1977.

Hughes, Langston. "Salvation." *The Big Sea.* New York: Farrar, Straus and Giroux, 1940.

Jones, Constance. *1001 Things Everyone Should Know About Women's History.* New York: Doubleday, 1998.

Junger, Sebastian. *The Perfect Storm.* New York: Harper Paperbacks, 1997.

Lansing, Alfred. *Endurance: Shackleton's Incredible Voyage.* New York: McGraw-Hill, 1959.

Lawrence, D. H. "The Rocking Horse Winner." Mankato, MN: Creative Education, 1982.

Lindbergh, Charles A. *The Spirit of St. Louis.* New York: Scribner's, 1953.

Lopez, Barry. "The Country of the Mind." *Arctic Dreams.* New York: Vintage Books, 1986.

Lord, Walter. *A Night to Remember.* New York: Bantam, 1956.

Luciano, Ron, and David Fisher. *The Umpire Strikes Back.* New York: Bantam, 1983.

Madison, James. *The Federalist Papers.* Ed. Clinton Rossiter. New York: Mentor, 1961.

Manchester, William. *A World Lit Only by Fire.* New York: Little, Brown, 1993.

Mansfield, Katherine. "The Fly." *The Dove's Nest and Other Stories.* New York: Knopf, 1923.

Marable, Manning. "Racism and Corporate America." *The Crisis of Color and Democracy.* Monroe, ME: Common Courage Press, 1991.

Marshall, Paule. "From the Poets in the Kitchen." *Reena and Other Stories.* New York: Feminist Press, 1983.

McKibben, William. *The Age of Missing Information.* New York: Random House, 1992.

McMurtry, Larry. *Film Flam: Essays on Hollywood.* New York: Simon and Schuster, 1987.

Momaday, N. Scott. *The Way to Rainy Mountain*. Albuquerque: University of New Mexico Press, 1969.

Morris, Lloyd. *Postscript to Yesterday: American Life and Thought 1896–1946*. New York: Harper and Row, 1947.

Morrison, Toni. *The Bluest Eye*. New York: Penguin, 1994.

Morton, Andrew. *Madonna*. New York: St. Martin's Press, 2001.

Murphy, Austin. *The Sweet Season: A Sportswriter Rediscovers Football, Family and a Bit of Faith at Minnesota's St. John's University*. New York: HarperCollins, 2001.

Obst, Lynda. *Hello, He Lied and Other Truths from the Hollywood Trenches*. New York: Little, Brown, 1996.

Orwell, George. *Animal Farm*. New York: Harcourt Brace, 1946.

———. *Burmese Days*. New York: Time Inc., 1950.

———. "Marrakesh," "Shooting an Elephant." *The Orwell Reader*. New York: Harcourt Brace Jovanovich, 1956.

Overbye, Dennis. "The End of Everything." *New York Times*, 1 Jan. 2002: F1.

Patterson, Francine, and Eugene Linden. *The Education of Koko*. New York: Holt, Rinehart and Winston, 1981.

Perella, Marco. *Adventures of a No Name Actor*. New York: Bloomsbury, 2001.

Pollan, Michael. *Second Nature: A Gardener's Education*. Grove/Atlantic, 1991.

Prejean, Helen, C.S.J. *Dead Man Walking*. New York: Vintage Books, 1994.

Pym, Barbara. *Crampton Hodnet*. New York: New American Library, 1985.

Reid, Elwood. "My Body, My Weapon, My Shame." *The Best American Sports Writing of 1998*. Ed. Bill Littlefield. New York: Houghton Mifflin, 1998.

Remarque, Erich Maria. *All Quiet on the Western Front*. New York: Ballantine, 1958.

Roberts, Fletcher. "Explosive, Realistic, but Most of All Funny." *New York Times*, 3 Feb. 2002: 13.5.

Robertson, Linda. "On Planet Venus." *The Best American Sportswriting of 1998*. Ed. Bill Littlefield. New York: Houghton Mifflin, 1998.

Salamon, Julie. *The Devil's Candy: The Bonfire of the Vanities Goes to Hollywood*. Boston: Houghton Mifflin, 1991.

Sanders, Scott Russell. "Settling Down." *Staying Put: Making a Home in a Restless World*. Boston: Beacon Press, 1993.

———. "The Men We Carry in Our Minds." Minneapolis: *Milkweed Chronicle, 1984*.

Sandomir, Richard. "For Saturday, Buy the Chips and the Visine." *New York Times*, 4 June 2002: D5.

Sandoz, Joli. "Coming Home." *Whatever It Takes: Women on Women's Sport*. Eds. Joli Sandoz and Joby Winans. New York: Farrar, Straus and Giroux, 1999.

Seabrook, John. "Tackling the Competition." *The Best American Sportswriting of 1998*. Ed. Bill Littlefield. New York: Houghton Mifflin, 1998.

Sebba, Anne. *Battling for News: The Rise of the Woman Reporter*. London: Hodder and Stoughton, 1994.

Sheets, Dr. Bob, and Jack Williams. *Hurricane Watch: Forecasting the Deadliest Storms on Earth*. New York: Knopf, 2001.

Siddle, Sheila, with Doug Cress. *In My Family Tree: A Life with Chimpanzees*. New York: Grove Press, 2002.

Skinner, B. F. *Walden Two*. Englewood Cliffs, NJ: Prentice Hall, 1976.

Smith, Liz. *Natural Blonde*. New York: Hyperion, 2000.

Spark, Muriel. *The Mandelbaum Gate*. New York: Knopf, 1965.

Stark, Steven D. *Glued to the Set: The 60 Television Shows and Events That Made Us Who We Are Today*. New York: Free Press, 1997.

Steinbeck, John. *The Red Pony*. New York: Bantam, 1955.

Stewart, Mary. *The Crystal Cave*. New York: Morrow, 1970.

————. *The Hollow Hills*. New York: Morrow, 1973.

Stoker, Bram. *Dracula*. New York: Dell, 1965.

Strauss, Bob. "So Is Hollywood's Most Notorious Bad Boy Really a Lovely Guy at Heart?" *Eonline* 3 Mar. 2002 <**http://www.eonline.com/Celebs/Qa/Penn**>.

Taub, Eric A. "Cell Yell: Thanks for (Not) Sharing." *New York Times*, 22 Nov. 2001: G1.

Telander, Rick. "Asphalt Legends." *The Best American Sports Writing of 1998*. Ed. Bill Littlefield. New York: Houghton Mifflin, 1998.

Tippette, Giles. *Donkey Baseball and Other Sporting Delights*. Dallas, TX: Taylor Publishing, 1989.

Tuchman, Barbara. *A Distant Mirror*. New York: Knopf, 1978.

Twain, Mark. *Pudd'nhead Wilson*. New York: Bantam, 1959.

Vecchlione, Joseph J., ed. *The New York Times Book of Sports Legends*. New York: Random House, 1991.

Wade, Nicholas. "In Tiny Cells, Glimpses of Body's Master Plan." *New York Times*, 18 Dec. 2001: F1.

Wade, Nicholas, ed. *The Science Times Book of Language and Linguistics*. New York: Lyons Press, 2000.

Walker, Alice. *In Search of Our Mothers' Gardens*. New York: Harcourt Brace Jovanovich, 1983.

Wallace, William N. "The First Super Bowl." *The New York Times Book of Sports Legends*. Ed. Joseph J. Vecchlione. New York: Random House, 1991.

Weinman, Sam. "Kwan Goes It Alone." *Journal News*, 8 Feb. 2002: K1.

White, T. H. *The Once and Future King*. New York: Ace Books, 1987.

Wilford, John Noble. "The Man and the Aircraft Were One." *New York Times*, 21 May 2002: F1.

Wolff, Tobias. *This Boy's Life: A Memoir*. New York: Harper and Row, 1989.

Zinser, Lynn. "Mount Everest Is the Highest, But Not the Only One to Climb." *New York Times*, 5 May 2002: SP11.

Index

. . . .

A

Adjective, 4, 77, 85–88, 94, 100–104, 111, 118–125
  comparative, 122–125
  superlative, 122–125
Adverb, 4, 21, 33–34, 41, 96, 120, 154, 167, 227
Anecdote, 36, 108, 126–127
Apostrophe, 44, 49, 67–70, 139, 231–234
  in contractions, 44, 49, 231–232
  in possessives, 67–70, 231, 233
Appositive, 227
Article, 130, 147–149, 176
  definite article, 147
  indefinite article, 147
Auxiliary verb, 11, 24–26, 29–54, 81, 94, 96, 101, 203
  do as auxiliary, 51–54, 203
  for perfect tenses, 31–38
  modal auxiliaries, 43–46
  shall and *will,* 47–50

C

Capitalization, 211–214
Clause, 4, 15–22, 71, 153–154, 156–159, 160–166, 200, 215, 223–227
  dependent clause, 4, 19–21, 154, 160–163, 224
  independent clause, 4, 16, 19, 20–21, 154, 156–158 160
  relative clause, 22, 71, 154, 163–166
  subordinate clause, 17, 159, 223–226
Comma, 219–229
  with connecting words and phrases, 227–229
  with items in a series, 220
  with subordinate clauses, 223–226
Conjunction, 15, 16, 154–155, 159
  coordinating conjunctions, 15, 16, 155
  subordinating conjunctions, 15, 17, 159
Connectives, 27–29, 151, 153–154, 167–170

Contractions, 44, 49, 231–234
–*d* endings, 77–90

D

Declarative. *See* Sentence
Details, 75, 76, 92, 93, 126–127, 151
Determiner, 147–148, 98, 130

E

Exclamation point, 207–209

F

Figure of speech, 181

H

Helping verb. *See* Auxiliary verb
Homophone, 174, 183–186

I

Idiom, 129–130
Infinitive, 4, 23–26, 45, 116, 175–176
–*ing* ending, 94–107
Interjection, 207–208

L

Look–alike words, 173–182

M

Mechanics, 197
Morpheme, 57

N

Negative, 51–54
Noun, 59–62, 94, 98, 99, 102, 110–117, 176–182, 192–195, 211–214
  common noun, 211
  noun endings, 110–117
  plural nouns, 59–62, 192–195
  proper nouns, 211–214
Number, 59

O

Object, 2, 57, 99, 129

P

Paragraph, 75, 92, 108, 127, 151, 171, 196, 238
Participle, 4, 23–25, 33, 36, 39, 40–41, 81–84, 85–88, 91, 94–104, 187–188
   past participle, 4, 33, 36, 81–83, 85–87, 91
   present participle, 4, 40–41, 94–104
Particle, 143. *See also* Preposition
Period, 199, 201–202
   with abbreviations, 201–202
Person, 63–64
Phrase, 129–142, 145, 167–170, 209, 228–230
   parenthetical phrase, 227–230
   prepositional phrase, 129–142, 145
Plural, 13, 59–62, 67, 97, 192–195
Possessive, 57, 67–70, 139–142, 231–234
Predicate, 8
Prefix, 57
Preposition, 129–142, 145
   prepositions for *when*, 131, 133–134
   prepositions for *where*, 131
   prepositions for *how* and *why*, 136–138
Pronoun, 2, 63, 67, 69, 144, 163
   personal. 2, 63–64, 69
   relative, 17, 21, 154, 163–165
Punctuation, 6, 156, 197–210, 215–237
   apostrophe, 231–233
   capital letters, 211–214
   comma, 197, 219–227
   exclamation point, 199, 207–210
   period, 199–202
   question mark, 203–206
   quotation marks, 235–237
   semicolon, 156, 215–222

Q

Question, 53, 203–206
   rhetorical question, 204–205

R

Root, 4, 89

S

–*s* ending, 59–74
   for plural nouns, 59–62
   for verbs, 63–66
   for possessives, 67–70
Sentence, 1, 2, 3, 5–15, 27–28, 55, 92, 151, 153, 160, 171–172, 198, 203
   complex sentence, 15, 160
   compound sentence, 15, 151
   declarative sentence, 28, 198
   exclamation, 198
   imperative sentence, 198
   interrogative sentence, 198, 203
   thesis sentence, 27
   topic sentence, 55, 92, 151
Shall and *will*, 47–50
Singular, 63, 65
Subject, 3, 5, 7, 12, 13, 57, 99, 129, 153
Suffix, 57, 110–117, 118–125

T

Tense, 2, 3, 6, 23, 24, 31–33, 35, 47–50, 63–65, 77–80, 90–91, 95–97, 190
   future tense, 47–50
   past perfect tense, 31, 32, 35
   past tense, 31, 35, 77–80, 90–91, 190
   present perfect tense, 31–33
   present progressive tense, 95–97
   third person singular present tense, 63–65
Thesis, 27, 55, 56, 75, 92–93, 108, 172
Transitions, 154, 167–170

V

Verb, 2, 3, 5–7, 12, 13, 25, 29, 31–33, 36–39, 43, 46–47, 63–65, 77–80, 82, 96, 111, 114–116, 130, 143–146, 153, 174–182, 187–191
   compound verb, 29, 31–33, 36–38, 82, 96
   helping verbs, 11, 24–26, 29–54, 81–82, 94, 96, 101
   irregular verbs, 25, 39, 78–80, 174, 187–191
   principal parts, 187
   to be, 25, 39
   to have, 25, 31, 36–38
   two word verbs, 130, 143–146
   verb endings, 29, 63–65, 77–80